THE CONSTITUTION OF POLAND

Pictorial Narrative

The perpetual echo of Red and White: *The Constitution of Poland*

The composition includes a quartet of geometrically conceived architectural edifices. Bottom left is the Supreme Court with 1997 signifying Poland's contemporary Constitution of that year and it has the towering Palace of Culture and Science behind, to serve as a reminder of the Communist era. The fan-shaped dome of Parliament is flanked on the top left by gold stars springing from its dome, demonstrating Poland's accession to the EU. Lastly, the imposing entrance portal of the Constitutional Court is portrayed in shades of red in the lower central foreground.

Reading the composition from the bottom right, a portrait of Mieszko I, the leader of Poland's (Polanie) tribe, refers to a much earlier but significant phase in the nation's history, namely the conversion to Christianity, often referred to as the 'Baptism of Poland'. A field of red poppies, Poland's national flower, frames the right edges. Red denotes the struggles for freedom over the centuries. 'Rzeczpospolita' etched on a stone plaque stands for a republican system, and it is also the official name of the country. In the centre, above the plaque of independence achieved in 1989, the statue from Warsaw of the world-famous composer Chopin celebrates Poland's cultural heritage. On his left, a white eagle spreads its wings representing the nation's Coat of Arms, while towards the top right there is a dove with an olive branch, standing for Poland's quest for peace.

Putachad
Artist

Constitutional Systems of the World
General Editors: Benjamin L Berger, Rosalind Dixon, Andrew Harding, Heinz Klug, and Peter Leyland

In the era of globalisation, issues of constitutional law and good governance are being seen increasingly as vital issues in all types of society. Since the end of the Cold War, there have been dramatic developments in democratic and legal reform, and post-conflict societies are also in the throes of reconstructing their governance systems. Even societies already firmly based on constitutional governance and the rule of law have undergone constitutional change and experimentation with new forms of governance; and their constitutional systems are increasingly subjected to comparative analysis and transplantation. Constitutional texts for practically every country in the world are now easily available on the internet. However, texts which enable one to understand the true context, purposes, interpretation and incidents of a constitutional system are much harder to locate, and are often extremely detailed and descriptive. This series seeks to provide scholars and students with accessible introductions to the constitutional systems of the world, supplying both a road map for the novice and, at the same time, a deeper understanding of the key historical, political and legal events which have shaped the constitutional landscape of each country. Each book in this series deals with a single country, or a group of countries with a common constitutional history, and each author is an expert in their field.

Published volumes

The Constitution of the United Kingdom; The Constitution of the United States; The Constitution of Vietnam; The Constitution of South Africa; The Constitution of Japan; The Constitution of Germany; The Constitution of Finland; The Constitution of Australia; The Constitution of the Republic of Austria; The Constitution of the Russian Federation; The Constitutional System of Thailand; The Constitution of Malaysia; The Constitution of China; The Constitution of Indonesia; The Constitution of France; The Constitution of Spain; The Constitution of Mexico; The Constitution of Israel; The Constitutional Systems of the Commonwealth Caribbean; The Constitution of Canada; The Constitution of Singapore; The Constitution of Belgium; The Constitution of Taiwan; The Constitution of Romania; The Constitutional Systems of the Independent Central Asian States; The Constitution of India; The Constitution of Pakistan; The Constitution of Ireland; The Constitution of Brazil; The Constitution of Myanmar; The Constitution of Poland

Link to series website

www.bloomsburyprofessional.com/uk/series/constitutional-systems-of-the-world

The Constitution of Poland

A Contextual Analysis

Mirosław Granat
and
Katarzyna Granat

•HART•
OXFORD • LONDON • NEW YORK • NEW DELHI • SYDNEY

HART PUBLISHING

Bloomsbury Publishing Plc

Kemp House, Chawley Park, Cumnor Hill, Oxford, OX2 9PH, UK

First published in Great Britain 2019

A catalogue record for this book is available from the British Library.

A catalogue record for this book is available from the Library of Congress.

ISBN: HB: 978-1-50991-394-7
ePDF: 978-1-50991-396-1
ePub: 978-1-50991-395-4

Typeset by Compuscript Ltd, Shannon
Printed and bound in Great Britain by CPI Group (UK) Ltd, Croydon CR0 4YY

MIX
Paper from responsible sources
FSC® C013604

In memory of Zofia Granat (1928–2012)

Acknowledgements

WE WOULD LIKE to thank the editors of the series for giving us the opportunity to explain the Constitution of Poland and its historical, political and social context to a new audience. The book greatly benefited from their insights and expertise.

Our thanks are also due to colleagues at our home universities – Uniwersytet Kardynała Stefana Wyszyńskiego and Durham University – which provided a supportive environment to work on the manuscript. In addition, we would like to thank Ciarán Burke, Piotr Chybalski, Ewelina Gierach, Andrzej Granat, Katarzyna Królikowska, Jan-Peter Siedlarek, Aleksandra Syryt, Wioleta Wasil and Mirosław Wróblewski for their support, comments and suggestions.

Katarzyna would also like to acknowledge the Marie Curie Fellowship at Durham Law School under EU grant agreement No 267209 that enabled her to work on the manuscript.

Mirosław Granat
Katarzyna Granat
July 2019

Table of Contents

Table of Cases

Poland

Germany

Ireland

United States

EUROPE

Court of Justice of the European Union

European Court of Human Rights

Table of Legislation

INTERNATIONAL

1

Polish Constitutional History and Tradition

Monarchy – Republic – Nobles' Democracy – First European Constitution – 'Solidarity Movement' – Independence – Freedom

I. INTRODUCTION

THE REPUBLIC OF Poland (*Rzeczpospolita Polska*) is a Central European country encompassing a territory of 322,575 sq km, with a population of around 38 million.[1] It has a more than 1,000-year tradition as an independent state, formed from a collection of Slavic tribes around the ninth century. For centuries, Poland was an independent monarchy, first hereditary, then elective. It then lost its independence between 1795 and 1918 and was reborn as a republic following the First World War. Due to its geographical position in the centre of Europe, between Germany and Russia, its territories experienced both world wars, suffering six million casualties in the Second World War alone. The country also endured enormous material damage and losses to its territory when its borders were moved westward after the war. This in turn caused a wave of resettlement of citizens and migration. After the Second World War, Poland came under the influence of the Soviet Union, becoming a Communist state. It took until 1980 for real resistance against the Communist government to emerge, most visibly in the form of the social movement 'Solidarity', led by Lech Wałęsa. Because of its repeated suffering over the centuries, Poland has been, not without reason, labelled 'God's playground'.[2] Nowadays, having regained its

[1] Główny Urząd Statystyczny, *Rocznik Statystyczny Rzeczypospolitej Polskiej* (Warsaw, 2017) 82 and 205.

[2] See N Davies, *Boże igrzysko. Historia Polski* (Kraków, Wydawnictwo Znak, 2010).

independence for the most recent time in 1989, Poland benefits from its central position in Europe in the areas of trade, economic cooperation, services and new technologies. Poland today is a member of the North Atlantic Treaty Organization (NATO) (since 1999) and the European Union (EU) (since 2004).

This chapter highlights a number of key aspects characteristic of Polish constitutionalism: the thirst for independence; attachment to freedom, both as a nation and in its citizens; and peaceful conflict resolution. It also traces the development of freedoms and rights, and the formation of independent constitutional review.

Poland and its citizens are characterised by a strong desire for freedom and the perception of the state as *Rzeczpospolita*, referring not only to the Republic of Poland and thereby denoting the name of the state, but also its republican system and, at a more abstract level, its community of citizens. Poland's tradition of freedom and independence goes back to the late Middle Ages and these traditions remain meaningful for today's constitutionalism. In particular, Poland adopted a system called a 'nobles' democracy' (from the fifteenth to the eighteenth centuries) with a number of concepts that were original at the time, such as sovereignty of law and religious tolerance, but also some that led to the eventual failure of the state, for instance, *liberum veto*, a form of unanimity voting that disabled the functioning of the parliament.

Contemporary Polish constitutionalism is represented by the Constitution of 1997, which was adopted by the National Assembly on 2 April 1997. The Constitution was then approved by the nation in the referendum of 25 May 1997. It was supported by 53.45 per cent of the eligible voters, with a turnout of 42.86 per cent.[3] It entered into force on 17 October 1997.[4] It is a comprehensive tract, consisting of 243 articles. It contains, inter alia, a catalogue of fundamental rights and freedoms, provisions on the bicameral parliament (the Chamber of Deputies and the Senate), the executive (the President and the government), the judiciary, local self-government, public finances and the procedure for constitutional amendment. The Constitution of 1997 has been a symbol

[3] Announcement of the National Electoral Committee of 26 May 1997 on the outcome of vote and outcome of the constitutional referendum of 25 May 1997, JL 1997 No 54 Pos 353.

[4] *Konstytucja Rzeczypospolitej Polskiej z dnia 2 kwietnia 1997 r* (Constitution of the Republic of Poland of 2 April 1997), JL 1997 No 78 Pos 483, JL 2001 No 28 Pos 319, JL 2006 No 200 Pos 1471, JL 2009 No 114 Pos 946. This book relies on the English translation of the Constitution available on the website of the Polish parliament: https://www.sejm.gov.pl/prawo/konst/angielski/kon1.htm.

of a free Poland, based on the values of human dignity and the rule of law, and guaranteeing both the state's independence and the freedom of its citizens.

For over 20 years, under the 1997 Constitution, various government majorities held power. In 2015, the Law and Justice party (*Prawo i Sprawiedliwość*) won the parliamentary elections and began to make radical changes to the state system. These changes were effected in the form of statutes rather than formal constitutional amendments.[5] The Law and Justice government, despite retaining relatively broad support from the electorate, does not have a sufficient majority in the parliament to amend the Constitution. The negative changes that have taken place in Poland since 2015 concern the judiciary to the largest extent and as a consequence pose a threat to constitutional freedoms and rights.[6]

II. INDEPENDENCE AND REPUBLICANISM

A. Independence

Poland's statehood, in the form of an independent kingdom, took shape over the tenth and eleventh centuries. In 966, Mieszko I, the leader of the Polans (*Polanie*) tribe that inhabited the territories of what would eventually become Poland, converted to Christianity and was baptised, an event that has been called the 'Baptism of Poland'. The baptism greatly strengthened the country and Christianity quickly became the state religion. In 1025, the first king, Bolesław Chrobry, was crowned, which further stabilised the state and its authority. In the fifteenth and sixteenth centuries, the Polish court was one of the strongest in Europe, reflecting the political and economic status of the country at the time. In 1569, Poland joined into a union with the Grand Duchy of Lithuania, creating the Polish-Lithuanian Commonwealth (*Rzeczpospolita Obojga Narodów*). The Commonwealth spread over a vast territory of 1,000,000 sq km, governed by a monarch who was both the King of Poland and the Grand Duke of Lithuania. Until its fall in 1795, the Commonwealth remained a dualist state consisting of the Kingdom of Poland and the Grand Duchy of Lithuania. This was the only period during which Poland was a federation.

[5] Article 235 of the Constitution.
[6] See chs 5, 6 and 8.

In the eighteenth century, due to frequent wars, the reign of nobles who were landowners of vast terrains and a lack of reforms of state institutions, the country's importance diminished. It gradually lost its territories as a result of wars or on the basis of threats from foreign courts. Poland, in the form of an independent kingdom, existed until the end of the eighteenth century.

In 1795, Poland lost its independence and its territory was partitioned between the Russian Empire, the Kingdom of Prussia and Habsburg Austria. One of the reasons for the fall of the state was the anarchy caused by the nobility, who perceived themselves as being beyond the law, which undermined the state institutions, for example, making it impossible to conduct the necessary military reforms that would have strengthened the country. Attempts at reforms that followed the ideas of the Enlightenment were not sufficient to save Poland, which as a result disappeared from the maps.[7]

Poland regained its independence in 1918 thanks to the favourable political situation following the defeat of Austria and Germany in the First World War and the revolution in Russia. For over 120 years, the Catholic Church, the faith, and education played an important role in maintaining the spirit of independence. Great uprisings – in November 1830 and January 1863 – were bloodily suppressed by the invaders. The Little Treaty of Versailles specifically concerning Poland (1919), signed the same day as the main Treaty of Versailles, 'restored to the Polish nation the independence of which it had been unjustly deprived'.[8]

Poland resurfaced as a republic instead of a monarchy, a unitary instead of a federal state. The Constitution of 1921 ('the March Constitution') proclaimed that 'the Polish state is *Rzeczpospolita*'.[9] *Rzeczpospolita*[10] (Republic of Poland) was the formal name of the country, relating to the tradition that existed before 1795, and thereby underlining the continuity of Polish statehood. The notion of *Rzeczpospolita*, in Latin *res publica* (common good, common wealth), is still used in Poland as a synonym for a republican system and in the official name of the country.

Poland in 1918 was not a newly established state, but rather one that was reborn after a period of suppression and partition. It was the same

[7] See J Bardach, B Leśnodorski and M Pietrzak, *Historia ustroju i praw polskiego* (Warsaw, LexisNexis, 2016).

[8] Minorities Treaty between the Principal Allied and Associated Powers and Poland, signed at Versailles (28 June 1919).

[9] Constitution of 17 March 1921, JL 1921 No 44 Pos 267.

[10] Pronounced 'ʐɛt͡ʂpɔsˈpɔlʲita'.

nation that existed at the end of the eighteenth century. This idea was incontestable in terms of public perception. The March Constitution in its preamble confirmed the continuity of the nation and state, referring to, amongst other things, the historic Constitution of 3 May 1791 discussed below. The period between 1918 and 1939 was prosperous: it was possible to merge the territories that were previously under partition, to operate public institutions and to rebuild the economy.

In 1939, Nazi Germany and the Soviet Union, breaching all of their international obligations, invaded Poland. The invaders divided Polish territories between themselves according to the border delineated in the secret Ribbentrop-Molotov Pact of 23 August 1939. The occupiers introduced a system of terror, extermination and deportation of the citizens. The Nazis funded and operated concentration and extermination camps. The largest of the Nazi camps was Auschwitz-Birkenau, where 1.1 million people were killed.[11] The Soviet Union was responsible for a series of crimes, amongst them the infamous Katyń massacre (1940), a mass execution of Polish army officers and a mass deportation of Poles to Siberia. The Second World War was the cruellest experience for the nation and the state.

The peace treaties of Yalta and Potsdam (1945) that ended the Second World War pushed Poland into the Russian sphere of influence. Between 1945 and 1989, Poland functioned as a totalitarian Communist state. The Communists were violently suppressing demonstrations – such as 'the Poznań 1956 protests' or 'December 1970 protests' – directed against their government. The apogee of the Communist oppression was the introduction of martial law in 1981. The Soviet system of government implied that all power was in the hands of the Polish United Workers' Party (*Polska Zjednoczona Partia Robotnicza*, PZPR). This party was dependent upon and supported by the Soviet state security apparatus and its military. This situation created a 'protective umbrella' over the state authority at the time, which eliminated its enemies and paralysed any social resistance. However, the Catholic Church offered some resistance and fostered the development of social opposition by appealing to the Communist powers for respect towards fundamental human rights and supporting democratic opposition in various forms. At that time, the Catholic Church provided, among other things, an open meeting and discussion space for the opposition.[12] The eventual fall of the Communist system took place in a peaceful manner, manifested in the idea of

[11] See www.auschwitz.org.

[12] W Roszkowski, *Historia Polski 1914–2015* (Warsaw, PWN, 2017) 380–408.

the 'Round Table' talks (February–April 1989), with discussions between the Communist government and the opposition, and was finalised in the Round Table Agreement of 5 April 1989.

Taking its history into consideration, it is understandable that the Polish Constitution of 1997 underlines the importance of an independent country and the security thereof. The Preamble expresses gratitude to Polish ancestors for 'their struggle for independence achieved at great sacrifice' and 'our culture rooted in the Christian heritage of the Nation and in universal human values'. The Constitution recalls that in 1989, the nation 'recovered the possibility of a democratic determination of its fate' after the Communist dictatorship of 1944–89.

According to the Constitution, the first task of the Republic of Poland is to safeguard the independence and integrity of its territory.[13] The Constitution assigns the fulfilment of this task to the Armed Forces, which also ensure the security and inviolability of state borders.[14] At the same time, the Armed Forces remain politically neutral and subject to civil control. The Constitution also involves other state organs in this function. The President is designated as the guardian of sovereignty and security of the state, as well as of the inviolability and integrity of its territory.[15] The government ensures the external security of the state.[16] These provisions prove how important the nation's independence was for the drafters of the Constitution.

B. *Rzeczpospolita*

As discussed above, the notion of *Rzeczpospolita* has a rich and specific content. It functions as the name of the Polish state (*Rzeczpospolita Polska*) and features in the full name of the Constitution. In this sense, it can be translated into 'the Republic of Poland'. However, limiting this notion to this translation would be insufficient. *Rzeczpospolita* functions in a number of other contexts and each of them is meaningful.

First, *Rzeczpospolita* is the name of the Polish state, differentiating it from other countries. The Constitution's preamble distinguishes between the first, second and third Republics of Poland. The First Republic concerns the early period of the state's existence until 1795,

[13] Article 5 of the Constitution.
[14] ibid art 26.
[15] ibid art 126.
[16] ibid art 146(4) point 8.

while the Second Republic denotes the interwar period of 1918–45. The Third Republic of Poland is the form of state adopted in the Constitution of 1997. It is the continuation of the 'best traditions of the First and Second Republics'. However, in the common perception, the notion of the Third Republic of Poland is much broader than that implied by the Constitution. It is understood as the form of the state that had its beginnings in 1989.

The second meaning of the term *Rzeczpospolita* is even more peculiar. It denotes a community of citizens that functions within the state framework that is a common good. According to Article 1 of the Constitution, the Republic of Poland is 'a common good of all its citizens'. This understanding of the term derives from the country's history: in the past, Poland existed as a monarchy and the closest translation of this concept is the English *commonwealth*: state as a community or community for a common good.

In its third meaning, *Rzeczpospolita* is a synonym of the republican form of government. Within this meaning, *Rzeczpospolita* is understood as a republic, a political term that is common in many states. *Rzeczpospolita* as a government or republican authority is a constitutional principle. Its positive meaning describes a form of exercise of power that is in the hands of the majority of the citizens (*res publica* as a people's good or public affair), while its negative meaning excludes hereditary or lifetime power. In contemporary states, the republic takes the form of a state ruled by law, while in the Constitution of 1997 in addition to the rule of law,[17] the republic is also the common good of all its citizens.[18]

III. DEMOCRATIC TRADITION

A. The Nobles' Democracy

The nobles' democracy was a system of government that functioned in Poland from the sixteenth century until 1795.[19] The formal beginning of the nobles' democracy is traced back to 1505, when the parliament adopted the *Nihil Novi* resolution. This act prevented the king from issuing laws without the agreement of the parliament. In addition, the king could not amend the rights and privileges of this class. The main aspects

[17] ibid art 2.
[18] See further in ch 2.
[19] See J Tazbir, *Kultura szlachecka w Polsce* (Warsaw, Wiedza Powszechna, 1979).

of nobles' democracy that were decisive for the position of the nobility and, as a consequence, for the functioning of the state concerned the decision-making process in parliament under *liberum veto* (the free veto) and the election system of the king. The question of *liberum veto* and the free election were also among the causes of the fall of the First Republic at the end of the eighteenth century. In Polish constitutionalism, these institutions are therefore often used to make the point that unlimited nobles' democracy led to the dysfunctionality of the state.

The parliament (*Sejm*) has existed since the end of the fifteenth century. It consisted of three 'deliberating estates': the king, the Chamber of Deputies, and the Senate. The main function of the parliament was to decide on state laws. The Chamber of Deputies consisted of the representatives of the nobility elected in the provincial parliaments (*sejmiki ziemskie*) and bound by the instructions from these bodies.[20] After the end of the session of the parliament, the representatives would report to their provincial parliaments on the issues discussed and decided in the parliament. This represented a means for the nobility to gain influence on state affairs. The Senate consisted of the members of the former Royal Council, including the Roman Catholic archbishops and bishops, and the highest state officials. The king as the third 'deliberating estate' called the sessions of the parliament. In principle, the parliament met every two years for a six-week ordinary session or for a shorter, extraordinary session. The parliament adopted laws – at the time called constitutions – which concerned the income and expenses of the state, its taxes and the military.

The crucial issue for the functioning of the nobles' democracy was that the parliament would take decisions via unanimity. Forcing any decision by the majority against the minority was seen as violating the principle of equality of rights of provincial parliaments. As a consequence, by invoking the *liberum veto*, any member could force an immediate end to the session of the parliament and nullify any piece of legislation approved at the session. In practice, the *liberum veto* meant more than just an objection against an unwanted bill. It was a principle of the state system that protected the nobility from absolute monarchy. It also expressed the core of the freedoms of the nobility: the members of parliament were not obliged to justify the *liberum veto*. In consequence, the *liberum veto* paralysed the decision-making process. None of the attempts to limit the *liberum veto* and introduce majoritarian decision-making succeeded.

[20] See M Borucki, *Sejmy i sejmiki szlacheckie* (Warsaw, Książka i Wiedza, 1972).

In the noble's democracy, the king was chosen in the so-called free election, again granting influence to the noble class alone. The noblemen voted for a candidate from among themselves so that, in practice, anyone from within the class could become king. During the election process, the noblemen would agree with the candidate, in writing, a set of conditions that the future king had to fulfil (*pacta conventa*). These reflected the political and economic programme that the king undertook to implement.[21]

B. The Constitution of 3 May 1791

The system of nobles' democracy was unsustainable and threatened the independence of the state. In response, a group of patriots gathered around the last King of Poland, Stanisław August Poniatowski, and proposed a reform of the state in the form of the Constitution of 3 May 1791. This act introduced some of the modern principles of a political system of the Enlightenment period, such as the sovereignty of the nation and the separation of powers. In this respect, it followed the French Declaration of the Rights of Man and the Citizen (1789) in that: 'The principle of any sovereignty resides essentially in the Nation.'[22] The Constitution of 3 May 1791, adopted four months earlier than the constitution of revolutionary France of September 1791, made Poland the first country in Europe to enact a formal constitution.

What is the meaning of the Constitution of 3 May 1791 for Poland today? Why do the Poles refer to it whenever a new constitution is drafted? The Constitution of 3 May 1791 – labelled the testament for future generations of Poles – replaced the elective, feudal monarchy with a constitutional one.[23] Even during the period of the Enlightenment, it was seen as the 'real artwork of the nation'.[24] It expressed the idea that the fate of Poland and its citizens depended upon themselves. It was not imposed on the people in the way that happened later in 1807 by Napoleon I for the Duchy of Warsaw or in 1815 by Emperor Alexander I for

[21] See Bardach, Leśnodorski and Pietrzak (n 7).

[22] Article V of the Constitution of 3 May 1791.

[23] W Uruszczak, 'Konstytucja 3 Maja 1791 r. Testament polityczny I Rzeczypospolitej' (2011) 103 *Przegląd Sejmowy* 9.

[24] Z Szcząska, 'Ustawa Rządowa z 1791 r.' in M Kallas (ed), *Konstytucje Polski. Studia monograficzne z dziejów polskiego konstytucjonalizmu: praca zbiorowa* (Warsaw, PWN, 1990) 76.

the Kingdom of Poland. Moreover, the Constitution of 3 May 1791 signified the willingness of the Polish people to reform the political system and to save the country from collapsing. Although the Constitution of 3 May 1791 was in force for less than a year, it is seen in Poland as the foundation of its current constitutional system. The date of 3 May remains a national holiday to this day. Against this background, the discussion of selected principles of the state system under the Constitution of 3 May 1791 seems necessary.

The Constitution of 3 May 1791 designed the legislative branch as a Chamber of Deputies (*Sejm*) and a Senate. The crucial change was that the parliament approved laws by majority vote and no longer by unanimity. Majoritarian decision-making allowed the parliament to fulfil the legislative function more effectively than on the basis of unanimity. The members of the Chamber of Deputies became free in their vote (free mandate) and representative of the entire nation instead of the noble class alone. The Senate, presided over by the king, lost its position at the expense of the Chamber of Deputies.[25] The Senate could only either approve or suspend a bill, without the possibility of exercising a veto.

Within the executive branch, the Constitution of 3 May 1791 abolished the election of the king by the nobles.[26] Instead, the throne was to be passed on by the right of succession, thereby re-establishing a hereditary monarchy. The king became the commander in chief of the army during wartime. The executive power was vested in the king and the ministers nominated by the king to the Royal Council ('Guardians of the Laws'). Every resolution of the king needed to be signed by one of the ministers of the Royal Council, which in practice took away much of the executive power from the king. The parliament could hold the ministers of the Royal Council politically accountable, as well as constitutionally accountable before the Chamber of Deputies' court. Overall, these relatively modern approaches enabled the creation of an effective executive around the king, without granting the latter absolute power.

The judicial power was anchored in the civil and criminal courts.[27] The Constitution highlighted that neither the legislature nor the executive could exercise judicial power. Despite this formal introduction of the principle of the separation of powers, certain judicial activities were reserved to Chamber of Deputies' committees as well as to the Chamber's court dealing with constitutional accountability.

[25] Article VI of the Constitution of 3 May 1791.
[26] ibid art VII.
[27] ibid art VIII.

It is worth highlighting that the neighbouring absolutist European powers of the time – the Russian Empire, the Kingdom of Prussia and Habsburg Austria – perceived the Constitution of 3 May 1791 as a product of the French Revolution and thus as a threat. The resulting military attack destroyed the Polish state. In 1795, Poland was divided up between the neighbouring powers in the third partition of Poland and lost its independence for the next 123 years.

C. Peaceful Conflict Resolution

The Constitution of 3 May 1791 positioned itself against extreme solutions. Its drafters chose to take an inclusive path that would gain the greatest support at the time. The Constitution aimed at political and social change through peaceful reforms rather than a revolution that would end in bloodshed. Later on, Poland again relied on the heritage of the Constitution of 3 May 1791 in a crucial moment of its history: the fall of Communism and the adoption of a new constitution for the democratic state.

After 1945, Poland did not become an independent country, but instead came under Soviet influence. The imposed Communist state was politically and economically dependent upon the Soviet Union. These conditions also found an expression in the constitutional law of the time. The Constitution of the Polish People's Republic (which was the name of the state at the time) adopted in 1952 mirrored the Constitution of the Soviet Union of 1936.[28] The main idea of the 1952 Constitution, as well as the whole concept of constitutionalism of real socialism, was to express the notion of a 'constitution of results'. The constitution was understood predominantly as a political act, aimed at registering achievements in the process of the building of socialism rather than having any significance as a legal act.

After 1956, the political environment became somewhat freer. Yet, when 'Solidarity', a widely supported trade union and social movement, was created in 1980, the Communists did not hesitate to introduce martial law in 1981 with the aim of suppressing the aspirations of freedom of the nation. During that period, the Communist government tightened the screw on society by conducting a curfew, 'pacifications' of workplaces, disappearances and politically motivated murders. Despite

[28] Constitution of the Polish People's Republic of 22 July 1952, JL 1952 No 33 Pos 232.

this, 'Solidarity' decided to force the overthrow of the system through an evolutionary, rather than revolutionary, process. This led to talks between the democratic opposition and the Communist government, and the Round Table Agreement of 5 April 1989. The Communist Party, the power of which was diminishing, sought some form of co-governance, in order to share with the opposition the responsibility for the disastrous social and economic situation in Poland that was becoming evident. The first, partially free elections on 4 June 1989 played a key role in the peaceful removal of the Communist government. The elections for the reinstated Senate were fully free, while the Communist Party was guaranteed 65 per cent of seats in the Chamber of Deputies. The change in the system was not sudden; it did not immediately destroy the socialist order, but allowed for a gradual accession to power by the opposition.

The changes that took place in Poland concerning the peaceful transition from the Communist system to a democratic regime can be seen as a 'revolution without a revolution'.[29] Communist parties collapsed first in Poland in 1989 and subsequently in other Eastern European states during the so-called Autumn of Nations. Democratic and parliamentary institutions replaced legal concepts of Soviet origin. In Poland, this development manifested itself in the amendment of the old Constitution of 1952 on 29 December 1989, reinstating the traditional name of the state, the Republic of Poland, and the introduction of the principle of democratic state ruled by law. This principle, expressed in Article 1 of the amended Constitution of 1952, symbolically replaced the provision stating that Poland was a socialist state.

The 1989 political transition necessitated the adoption of a new constitution. Work on this document began in 1989. It continued in 1989–91, 1992–93 and then again during 1993–97. Between 1992 and 1997, the so-called Small Constitution was in force.[30] From the outset, it had a temporary character. The ongoing work on a 'big' constitution was lagging because of, among other things, the lack of clarity about the procedure for the drafting and adoption of the constitution. In the end, the Chamber of Deputies adopted the Act of 23 April 1992 establishing a procedural framework for the drafting and adoption of the new constitution by the National Assembly and its approval by the nation

[29] See A Dudek, *Reglamentowana Rewolucja: rozkład dyktatury komunistycznej w Polsce 1988–1990* (Kraków, Wydawnictwo Znak Horyzont, 2014).

[30] Constitutional Statute of 17 October 1992 on mutual relations between the legislative and executive power in the Republic of Poland and on the local self-government ('Small Constitution'), JL 1992 No 84 Pos 426, JL 1995 No 38 Pos 184 and 150, Pos 729, JL 1996 No 106 Pos 488.

in a referendum.[31] As a reflection of the period and the conditions of its drafting, the adopted Constitution of 1997 has an extremely consensual character.

IV. FREEDOM IN POLISH CONSTITUTIONALISM

The political effort to safeguard Poland's freedom – understood as independence from outside interference – represented a long struggle for the Polish nation throughout its history. Initial attempts to prevent the government from overstepping the rule of law took many years to manifest themselves in the constitution. Progress in the struggle for freedom was intertwined with periods of failure. The above-mentioned insurrections of 1831 and 1863 were examples of this struggle. Despite early success, both uprisings failed, worsening the situation of the people as a result. Later, during the Second World War, a major operation of the Polish resistance, the Warsaw Uprising of 1944, presented an attempt, albeit ultimately a failed one, to liberate Poland's capital from Nazi Germany. Even earlier, the 1943 uprising in the Warsaw ghetto was an armed resistance of Jewish underground organisations, opposing the liquidation of the ghetto by Nazi Germany.[32] In the period after 1945, despite the strength of Communist power, there were open forms of civic resistance, such as manifestations and violent street fights, for example, in Poznań (1956) and Gdańsk (1970). Despite the casualties incurred, seen in retrospect, these events aided the movement for freedom. Specifically, the workers' manifestations of 1970 enabled the creation of free trade unions, and in 1980, after another wave of strikes, the 'Solidarity' movement was born. Between August 1980 and December 1981, 'Solidarity' developed from a trade union into a massive social independence movement, demanding respect for human dignity, free speech and the social rights for workers. It grew into a movement of 10 million people in 1981 and became one of the pillars of Poland's independence.

The freedom regained presents a characteristic element of Polish constitutionalism in the sense that it finds explicit reflection in the constitutional text. When Poland became an independent state in 1918, the euphoria of freedom was transferred into the March Constitution, which described the state as an organisation protecting the individual

[31] Constitutional Statute of 23 April 1992 on the preparation and adoption of the Constitution of Poland, JL 1992 No 67 Pos 336.

[32] N Davies, *Boże Igrzysko* (Kraków, Znak, 2010) 927.

interests of its citizens as well as the freedom of the whole state. The March Constitution granted the individual a wide freedom for political, economic, social and cultural activity, reflected in a catalogue of rights and freedoms, protected by the principle of non-discrimination. In addition, the March Constitution introduced voting rights for women. It already contained almost all of the elements, known at the time, that were necessary for the functioning of the state and for maintaining the freedoms of its citizens. The only missing element known to and supported by legal scholars at that time was constitutional review.[33] Another issue was the lack of legislators' capability to combine 'the traditional, Polish attention to freedom' with the need for a strong government to keep the Polish territories unified after years of partition.[34] In 1926, the executive power was strengthened in the so-called August reform of the March Constitution by increasing the powers of the executive at the expense of the legislature.

Today's 1997 Constitution also expresses the elements of freedom. First, its origin is rooted in a deep political and social consensus. The drafters aimed at implementing the demands of different political powers. Sometimes the fact that the Constitution reflects different compromises is seen as a weakness or a drawback. Specifically, it is, wrongly, argued that the Constitution has a number of loopholes or that the Round Table was to some extent the 'patron' of the Constitution. Second, the Constitution of 1997 treats freedom as the natural state of the citizens. The Constitution does not define freedom; instead, its text implies that freedom enjoys primacy vis-a-vis the law and the law only endorses it. The law protects rather than guarantees freedoms that are already in the individual's possession. Freedom stands before the law and before the Constitution. The protection of human dignity contained in the Constitution of 1997 further strengthens this understanding of freedom. Both of these principles are discussed in Chapter 8, but it can already be highlighted at this point that the Constitution's approach to freedom has a positive influence on human rights and the social system of the state. Third, the Constitution created strong fundaments for the judicial power, discussed in Chapters 5 and 6. However, the separation

[33] See M Granat, 'Problem kontroli konstytucyjności prawa Polsce międzywojennej' in P Sarnecki (ed), *Prawo konstytucyjne II Rzeczypospolitej Polskiej. Nauka i konstytucja* (Kraków, Wydawnictwo Uniwersytetu Jagiellońskiego, 2006) 101. See section VI in this chapter.

[34] See W Komarnicki, *Ustrój państwowy Rzeczypospolitej Polskiej* (Warsaw, nakł Księg F Hoesicka, 1934) 24.

and independence of the judiciary have been threatened, as shown by the constitutional crisis that began in 2015.[35]

V. THE EVOLUTION OF HUMAN RIGHTS IN POLAND

The Communist Constitution of the Polish People's Republic – discussed earlier – degraded human rights. Most of all, in what was a one-party state, while in power the ruling Communist Party often violated human rights in a brutal fashion. The Constitution and legal doctrine of the time did not employ the notion of 'human rights' or 'freedoms and rights of the person'. Instead, the term 'citizens' rights' was applied, implying that the rights were collective rights which stemmed from the government in power at the time rather than being based on the protection of individual human rights set out in the constitution. Specifically, it was characteristic for a Soviet-type constitution to declare citizens' rights such as the right to work – implying that employment for everyone would be ensured – but not to grant that right the character of a subjective right.[36] Moreover, these types of constitutions encompassed elaborate programmes and previews of citizens' rights.[37] Yet, in fact, these were only political declarations; they did not have any legal meaning as justiciable constitutional provisions. For example, on the one hand, the 1952 Constitution declared that the state authorities cared about and supported the development of art and literature,[38] while on the other hand, censorship was strongly present in the Polish People's Republic, and many artists were forced to emigrate. As a consequence, the process of developing human rights in Poland post-1989 had to begin with the rejection of the Communist doctrine.

Thus, it is quite unsurprising that resistance to the Communist authorities in Poland developed against the background of a general proposal that people be treated subjectively as individuals. This idea was expressed in the establishment of the first organisations committed to the fight for human rights, including labour rights. In particular, this trend was evident with the emergence of illegal organisations such as the Movement for the Defence of Human and Civic Rights (*Ruch Obrony Praw Człowieka i Obywatela*, ROPCiO), and the Worker's Defence

[35] See further in chs 5 and 6.
[36] Article 58(1) of the Constitution of 1952.
[37] See, eg, ibid arts 62 and 63.
[38] ibid art 64.

Committee (*Komitet Obrony Robotników*, KOR), which were fought by the government.[39] Of particular significance was the establishment of 'Solidarity', which put forward economic and human rights proposals. Moreover, the Helsinki Final Act of the Conference on Security and Co-operation in Europe (1975) offered an important contribution, especially its third 'basket', which focused on human rights. Similarly crucial was the 1977 ratification of the International Covenant on Civil and Political Rights and of the International Covenant on Economic, Social and Cultural Rights. The fight for human rights was one of the main aspects of the opposition movement that led to the fall of the Communist system at the end of the 1980s. During that time, similar changes took place in other post-Communist states.[40]

In the 1990s, the recognition of human rights began to flourish in Poland. The case law of the Constitutional Court played an important role in this regard. The Constitutional Court began to invoke the European Convention on Human Rights (ECHR), ratified by Poland in 1993, in its judgments. Before 1997, some of the key legal principles crucial in human rights adjudication, such as the proportionality principle, were as yet unknown in Poland, and rights like the right to privacy had their source in the ECHR.[41] Moreover, at that time, the legal scholarship dealing with human rights was very active.[42] The impact of the ECHR and other international human rights instruments was crucial for the shaping of the concept of human rights in a free Poland. The Constitution of 1997 'consumed' those concepts to a large extent, with a major emphasis on the avenues for claiming individual rights.

The decisive step towards better protection of human rights was the regulation of freedoms and rights in the new Constitution of 1997. The Constitution delivered a completely new set of general principles of human rights (human dignity, freedom of the person and equality) and

[39] See A Paczkowski, *Pól wieku dziejów Polski 1939–1989* (Warsaw, Wydawnictwo Naukowe PWN, 2005); G Waligóra, *ROPCiO. Ruch Obrony Praw Człowieka i Obywatela 1977–1981* (Warsaw, Instytut Pamięci Narodowej, 2006).

[40] M Granat, *Likwidacja monopolistycznej pozycji partii komunistycznych* (Lublin, Centrum Samorządu i Administracji, 1992) 41.

[41] Constitutional Court, judgment of 24 June 1997, K 21/96, OTK ZU 2/1997, poz 23. On the early case law concerning the application of the right to privacy, see M Safjan, 'Prawo do ochrony życia prywatnego' in L Wiśniewski (ed), *Podstawowe prawa jednostki i ich sądowa ochrona* (Warsaw, Wydawnictwo Sejmowe, 1997).

[42] B Banszak, *Prawa jednostki i systemy ich ochrony* (Wrocław, Kolonia, 1995); P Hofmański, *Ochrona praw człowieka* (Białystok, Temida 2, 1994); M Piechowiak, 'Pojęcie praw człowieka' in L Wiśniewski (ed), *Podstawowe prawa jednostki i ich sądowa ochrona* (Warsaw, Wydawnictwo Sejmowe, 1997).

provided a catalogue of rights, following in this regard a scheme typical of United Nations (UN) human rights acts. The broad catalogue therein incorporates three clusters: (1) personal; (2) political; and (3) economic, social and cultural freedoms and rights. In addition, the catalogue of rights was supported by specific institutions dedicated to safeguarding human rights: the right of access to the court; the right to appeal a judgment; and the right to constitutional complaint. A crucial achievement was the establishment of the Ombudsman as early as 1987, at the end of the Communist period.[43] This office was then introduced in the Constitution of the Polish People's Republic in 1989.

The new approach to freedoms and rights embodied in the Constitution of 1997 and the contrast to the pre-1989 citizens' rights model is evident in many areas. The Constitution uses the notion of 'freedoms and rights' in that particular order. The sequence of those words is not accidental. First, it presents a reaction to the application of the notion of citizens' rights present in the Soviet-type constitutions, which de-emphasised the freedoms of those citizens. Second, this particular sequence – freedoms before rights – highlights that the human condition is more fundamental than that of the citizen, thereby also stressing the natural character of human rights. In addition, the Constitution set aside the notion that any exercise of rights is conditional upon fulfilling obligations towards the state, which was characteristic of the approach under Communism.

VI. THE DEVELOPMENT – AND CRISIS – OF CONSTITUTIONAL REVIEW

One of the most fascinating events in Polish constitutional law has been the establishment of constitutional review, a process that started even before the fall of Communism. The Constitutional Court was established in 1985. The 'Polish way' towards constitutional review took a trial-and-error approach to the adoption of the Kelsenian model of constitutional review. In this respect, it differed from other Central and Eastern European states, which introduced constitutional review later and based on ready-made concepts from Austria and Germany. In addition, already in the inter-war period (1918–39), both the March Constitution

[43] Law of 15 July 1987 on the Ombudsman, JL 2018 Pos 2179. See ch 8.

of 1921 and the April Constitution of 1935 prescribed that no statute could be contrary to the Constitution. However, neither a constitutional court nor a specific procedure for review of unconstitutional statutes was foreseen, although the scholarship of various legal traditions and political backgrounds underlined the value of a constitutional court.[44]

During the Polish People's Republic (1944–89), constitutional review was obviously not foreseen as part of the undemocratic Communist state. Formally, the Constitutional Court was introduced in 1982 by an amendment to the Constitution of the Polish People's Republic. Subsequently, in 1985, the Law on the Constitutional Tribunal offered a basis for the Court's functioning, and it began operating in January 1986 and pronounced its first judgment within the few first months. The creation of the Constitutional Court was a controlled concession of the Communist Party, which would have far-reaching consequences. The Communist authority formally accepted that laws had to comply with the Constitution. However, there was a safeguard, as judgments of the Constitutional Court declaring laws as unconstitutional were not final. Until 1997, the Chamber of Deputies, as the highest organ of state power, could, by a two-thirds majority, vote to reject such judgments of the Constitutional Court. As such, the establishment of the Constitutional Court was an achievement of the period of political liberalisation in late 1980s. Nonetheless, it remained a defective institution – a Kelsenian idea built in an undemocratic system of government. Despite this major flaw, the Constitutional Court even before 1989 represented the core idea of constitutionalism: the primacy of the Constitution and the importance of human rights protection.

The Constitution of 1997 finally introduced a fully independent Constitutional Court and a centralised model of constitutional review. The Constitution includes the Constitutional Court among the organs of the judicial power.[45] Its name (*Trybunał*), its members (described as judges), their independence and the judgments that follow hearings are all typical of an organ of the judiciary. Calling the Constitutional Court a 'court' is therefore uncontroversial. The Constitutional Court often labels itself as a 'court of law' (*sąd nad prawem*). In this sense, it does not deal with the facts of the case, with the sole exception of controlling the compliance of political parties' activities with the Constitution.

[44] See especially the writings of Władysław L Jaworski, Stefan Starzyński and Wacław Komarnicki.

[45] Article 10(2) of the Constitution.

The Constitution of 1997 rendered the judgments of the Constitutional Court final and universally binding. Thanks to the new competences enshrined in the Constitution of 1997 and through the development of its own case law, the Constitutional Court achieved an important position in the constitutional system of Poland. It was the sole and unquestioned instance of constitutional review. Its role and judgments were not called into question or rejected. The Constitutional Court, exercising constitutional review, decided on key issues for the young state's institutional system such as Poland's membership in the EU, as well as issues concerning day-to-day aspects of life, such as the retirement and pension system or the character of penalties for illegal tree cutting.[46] The existence of the Constitutional Court itself was a safeguard against the enactment of unconstitutional laws. As such, the value of constitutional review might obscure its possible disadvantages, failures in its functioning or other allegations, such as judicial activism. Over the years, the Constitutional Court maintained the rigour of rationality in its jurisprudence, something that is evident from its meticulously justified judgments and public hearings of cases. Although the Court attempted to maintain judicial self-restraint, this did not shield it from political attacks.

In 2015, the governing majority of the Law and Justice party began questioning the fundamental role of the Constitutional Court for maintaining the supreme position of the Constitution, underlining instead the role of the Chamber of Deputies and of the nation as the sovereign. This was illustrated by some politicians with the slogan: 'It is the nation that stands above the law, not the law above the nation.' Accordingly, the parliament in November and December 2015 adopted a series of laws that aimed at disrupting and blocking the issuing of judgments by the Constitutional Court. The governing majority labelled these statutes 'remedy laws', while in fact they had the effect of slowing down or even paralysing the work of the Court. The 'remedy laws', rather than being an incidental action of the legislature, aimed at extorting a constitutional change on the basis of a statute. Attempting to paralyse the work of the Constitutional Court, the 'remedy laws' moved the position of the Constitutional Court towards the legislative power. However, the governing majority repealed these 'remedy laws' at the end of 2016, with the entry into force of three new statutes that regulate the status of the

[46] Constitutional Court, judgment of 24 November 2010, K 32/09, OTK ZU 9A/2010, poz 108; judgment of 19 December 2012, K 9/12, OTK ZU 11A/2012, poz 136; judgment of 1 July 2014, SK 6/12, OTK ZU 7A/2014, poz 68, respectively.

Constitutional Court.[47] These laws do not end the conflict around the Constitution Court, the position of which, as a consequence, has been marginalised. The situation of the Constitutional Court after 2015 is discussed further in Chapter 6.

VII. CONCLUSION

Poland has its own constitutional heritage, with the Constitution of 3 May 1791 as its foundation. This heritage had practical meaning after the Second World War, when Poland was incorporated into the group of Communist states, and in spite of this process people did not succumb to the Communist system. The society maintained its culture, tradition and awareness of being connected to *Rzeczpospolita*. This was evident in the respect shown towards the cultural and legal achievements of the state referred to as *Rzeczpospolita*. For over 40 years – until 1989 – the Communist government in power did not succeed in eradicating this heritage. Following this, the 'Solidarity' movement and the efforts of civil society, as well as attachment to freedom, played a crucial role in the shaping of a fully independent state post-1989. Without any doubt, thanks to the constitutional heritage, the transition from a Communist system to a parliamentary democracy took a relatively smooth and non-conflictual form compared to other states in the Communist Bloc. As a result of these efforts and circumstances, Poland again became part of a free Europe, further expressed in its membership of the EU.

Nowadays, it is hard to imagine Poland as a system of government other than a republic and a democratic state ruled by law. Even the weakening of the rule of law after 2015 – which is discussed in the following chapters – did not annihilate these fundamental principles of the state system. Polish constitutionalism experienced – and continues to experience – defeats and periods of regression. Ignoring the more distant times of the First Republic, such retrogression notably took place during the Second Republic, especially evident in the May Coup (1926), and in the circumstances of adoption of the April Constitution of 1935

[47] Law of 13 December 2016 on Introductory Provisions on the Law on Organisation and Procedure before the Constitutional Court, JL 2016 Pos 2074, JL 2018 Pos 849; Law of 30 November 2016 on the Status of the Judges of Constitutional Court, JL 2018 Pos 1142; Law of 30 November 2016 on the Organisation and Procedure before the Constitutional Court, JL 2016 Pos 2072.

in which some principles were undemocratic in character. In addition, the Communist period as a whole represented a negation of democratic constitutionalism. So-called socialist constitutionalism was simply a doctrine of the exercise of power by the Communist Party and should not be called constitutionalism at all.

Finally, the attack of the governing majority on the judicial power after 2015 presents another period of retrogression that is best described as constitutional violence.

FURTHER READING

Davis, N, *God's Playground: A History of Poland. Vol. 1: The Origins to 1795; Vol. 2: 1795 to the Present* (Oxford, Oxford University Press, 1981).

——. *Rising '44: The Battle for Warsaw* (London, Pan Books, 2004).

Dudek, A, *Historia polityczna polski 1989–2015* (Kraków, Znak, 2016).

Grzeskowiak-Krwawicz, A, *Regina Libertas. Wolność w polskiej myśli politycznej w XVIII wieku* (Gdańsk, Wydawnictwo słowo/Obraz terytoria, 2006).

Michalski, J (ed), *Historia Sejmu Polskiego* (Warsaw, PWN, 1984).

2

The Fundamental Principles of the Polish Constitution

Common Good – Democracy – Rule of Law – Sovereignty – Separation of Powers – Parliamentary Government – Civil Society – European Integration – Sources of Law – Constitutional Amendment

I. INTRODUCTION

THE CONSTITUTION OF every state can be well characterised by a careful study of its underlying principles, which determine the core of the constitution and reflect the values upon which the constitution is based. This chapter provides an overview of the principles that are central to the Constitution of 1997 and, as a consequence, form the basis for the constitutional system of Poland. Moreover, this chapter shows that the Constitution is based upon the same principles that underlie other traditional European constitutional systems, while at the same time incorporating modifications necessary to adjust these principles to the needs of the Polish constitutional system. For example, the Constitution did not adopt a classic parliamentary system, but rather an adjusted form of rationalised parliamentarism. Some of the principles discussed in this chapter reflect the idiosyncratic historic trajectory of Poland and are thus unique to the Polish system, such as the principle of civil society.

Formally, the Constitution does not offer a closed catalogue of constitutional principles. The significance of those principles, as well as of other constitutional provisions, stems from the jurisprudence of the Polish Constitutional Court (*Trybunał Konstytucyjny*). The Constitutional Court, established in 1985, is the judicial organ of constitutional review, based on Kelsen's model, practised in Austria and Germany, rather than on the US tradition of constitutional control.[1] In its judgments, the Constitutional Court often deals with constitutional conflicts trying to reconcile conflicting principles. A number of provisions of the 1997 Constitution possess the character of constitutional principles. This chapter limits its analysis to the most important examples. According to the Polish legal doctrine, the most important principles include the common good, the principle of a democratic state ruled by law and implementing the principles of social justice, as well as the principles of sovereignty of the nation, the separation and balance of powers, a parliamentary system of government, the principle of civil society and that of openness towards international cooperation.[2]

In addition, the chapter presents the sources of law prescribed in the Constitution, arguing that the closed catalogue of sources has managed to bring some order to the Polish legal system following periods characterised by relatively few constraints. Finally, it maintains that whilst the Constitution of 1997 has proved remarkably stable in its form, its principles have evolved over time. One example of this evolution was the Constitutional Court's interpretation of the principles of the 1997 Constitution, which enabled Poland's accession to the EU in 2004.

II. KEY PRINCIPLES OF THE POLISH CONSTITUTION

A. The Common Good

Article 1 of the Constitution proclaims that: 'The Republic of Poland shall be the common good of all its citizens.' The Polish doctrine does not offer a formal definition of the common good.[3] The difficulty in defining 'common good' and, as a consequence, its indeterminate meaning does not undermine the metaphoric importance of Article 1 of the Constitution. This provision is usually understood as characterising Poland as a country where the citizens determine their aims and the state creates conditions for the optimal achievement thereof.[4] Thus, 'common good' is not understood as the majority interest, or the interests of a specific

[1] See ch 6.

[2] L Garlicki, *Polskie Prawo Konstytucyjne. Zarys wykład* (Warsaw, Wolters Kluwers, 2017) 67–99.

[3] See M Piechowiak, 'Prawne a pozaprawne pojęcia dobra wspólnego' in W Arndt, F Longchamps de Bérier and K Szczucki (eds), *Dobro wspólne. Teoria i praktyka* (Warsaw, Wydawnictwo Sejmowe, 2013) 44–45.

[4] M Piechowiak, *Dobro wspólne jako fundament polskiego porządku konstytucyjnego* (Warsaw, Biuro Trybunału Konstytucyjego, 2012) 288.

group, or as the interests of the state or its organs. Various provisions of the Constitution, such as the freedoms and rights of citizens, are expressions of the path towards achieving the common good.

The Constitutional Court has not applied this principle very frequently; in fact, it is quite rare for the Court to refer to the common good in its argumentation at all. The Court treats it differently from other principles, instead perceiving it as a primary value and not as one that is to be confronted with and balanced against other values. Instead, the Court usually assigns the common good the role of final arbiter in conflicts between colliding values. Hence, the common good plays a role similar to that of human dignity.[5] Both principles present a point of reference for the other principles and constitutional values.

An example of this approach is visible in the judgment of the Constitutional Court concerning the reform of the election law for local self-government bodies.[6] This reform, introduced shortly before the elections of 2006, concerned the possibility of grouping electoral lists, consequently allowing for the bypassing of electoral thresholds by those parties in the group that did not receive sufficient support. The Constitutional Court criticised this law and was ready to declare it unconstitutional. However, in this situation the elections – the date of which fell just days before the delivery of the judgment – would have not taken place. In the view of the Court, the value of the common good – understood as the holding of elections on the scheduled day – prevailed over the shortcomings of the law in question. The Court's reasoning proved somewhat controversial, which was evident in the dissenting opinions.

B. A Democratic State Ruled by Law and Implementing the Principles of Social Justice

The principle of a democratic state ruled by law and implementing the principles of social justice has been present since the 1989 revision of the Constitution of the Polish People's Republic of 1952. Its introduction was a symbol of the democratic reforms of the time and of the break with the Communist system. The 1952 Constitution specified that Poland was 'a State of People's Democracy' ('państwo demokracji ludowej').[7] In 1976,

[5] See ch 8.

[6] Constitutional Court, judgment of 3 November 2006, K 31/06, OTK ZU 10A/2006, poz 147.

[7] Article 1(1) of the Constitution of the Polish People's Republic of 22 July 1952, JL 1952 No 33 Pos 232.

this provision was amended and it was declared that Poland was a socialist state. Only with the 1989 revision of the Constitution of 1952 were these Soviet notions relating to the character of the state removed. For these reasons, Article 1 of the current 1997 Constitution characterises the state as a common good. In turn, the principle of being a democratic state ruled by law is enshrined in Article 2 of the Constitution.

The principle of a democratic state ruled by law has both a formal and a material meaning. In the formal sense, it offers a label for a number of more detailed legal principles. According to the Constitutional Court, the principle of a democratic state ruled by law consists of three parts.[8] First, it encompasses principles concerning human rights (eg, *nullum crimen sine lege*, the right to a fair trial, the right to life, the right to privacy, the rule of law and others).[9] Second, it incorporates principles concerning the law-making process (*lex retro non agit*, *vacatio legis*, the protection of acquired rights). Third, it includes principles concerning the organisation of the state (eg, a balanced state budget). The structure of a democratic state ruled by law changed after 1997. With the entry into force of the new Constitution, some of these principles – which were implicit to Article 2 – became independent constitutional provisions. This is the case, for example, for *nullum crimen sine lege*, independently expressed in Article 42 of the Constitution. This is why the Constitution of 1997 has to some extent diminished the formal meaning of the 'democratic state ruled by law' principle.

In the material sense, the principle means that the state should aim to provide certain values – for example, implementing human rights. Within this meaning, the principle of a democratic state ruled by law refers to some ideal type of state that would represent the model for legal relations without defining precisely what this model is. For instance, it is unclear whether it is a *Rechtsstaat* model (with the emphasis on the formal aspects of law), or the rule of law model (with the emphasis on the content of the law), or, indeed, some third solution.

In sum, the democratic state ruled by law fulfils obligations such as the respect for human dignity and the protection of the individual rights and freedoms of its citizens; it pays attention to the quality of law and its history (eg, it respects the *lex retro non agit* principle and observes *vacatio legis*). A democratic state ruled by law may limit the rights of its

[8] W Sokolewicz, 'Kometarz do artykułu 1 Konstytucji RP' in L Garlicki et al (eds), *Konstytucja Rzeczypospolitej Polskiej. Komentarz* (Warsaw, Wydawnictwo Sejmowe, 2007) vol V, 10. See also ch 5.

[9] For example, on right to life, see Constitutional Court, judgment of 28 May 1997, K 26/96, OTK ZU 2/1997, poz 19.

citizens by demanding respect for the rights of fellow citizens, but, above all, it limits its own public authority.

C. Sovereignty of the Nation

Article 4 of the Constitution expresses the principle of sovereignty of the nation in a manner that is typical of liberal constitutionalism: 'Supreme power in the Republic of Poland shall be vested in the Nation. The Nation shall exercise such power directly or through their representatives.' Although the Constitution places this principle at the forefront, the contemporary meaning of the sovereignty principle has undergone certain challenges.

In contrast, the principle of sovereignty was easier to explain in the past, in the constitutional doctrine of the nineteenth century or even at the beginning of the twentieth century, meaning that the nation, a community of all the citizens, exercises supreme power. Sovereignty was explained based on the notions coined by Jean-Jacques Rousseau. This traditional meaning of sovereignty has been changed in the process of European integration and globalisation. As seen by some academic commentators, 'EU law shifted understandings of sovereignty by presenting it as something to be justified'.[10] Moreover, even in the classic understanding of sovereignty, not the nation, but rather its representatives, executed the state power.

The principle of the sovereignty of the nation in Poland has changed under the influence of international processes, especially European integration. If this principle is not exposed to the process of European integration, the sovereignty of the nation becomes merely a noble notion rather than a living constitutional principle. The Constitution prescribes the conditions under which limitations of the principle of sovereignty may be undertaken during the process of European integration. Specifically, Poland may 'by virtue of international agreements, confer upon an international organization or international institution the competence of organs of state authority in relation to certain matters'.[11] So far, two EU treaties qualify sovereignty and confer competence over organs of state authority upon the EU: first, the Accession Treaty of 2003, which was the basis for the accession of Poland and nine other states to the

[10] D Chalmers, 'European Restatements of Sovereignty' in R Rawlings, P Leyland and AL Young (eds), *Sovereignty and the Law* (Oxford, Oxford University Press, 2013) 187.
[11] Article 90(1) of the Constitution.

EU on 1 May 2004; and, second, the Lisbon Treaty of 2007, which introduced major changes to EU primary law.[12] The consent for the ratification of such agreements may be granted in a nationwide referendum or in a statute supported by a two-thirds majority of each parliamentary chamber.[13] The Chamber of Deputies chose a referendum as the appropriate procedure for granting consent to the ratification of the Accession Treaty. The nation agreed by an overwhelming majority of votes to the ratification of the Accession Treaty, and thereby to EU accession, during the referendum held on 7–8 June 2003.[14] This process exemplifies that the Constitution enables a limited and conditional conferral of power to state organs, in fact resulting in a limitation of national sovereignty.

The Constitutional Court in its judgments concerning the compliance of EU treaties with the Constitution has further developed the understanding of sovereignty in the EU integration process. The Court sees Poland's membership of the EU as an expression of Poland's capability to decide its own fate and in fact as a confirmation of the sovereignty of the state.[15] In other words, EU membership constitutes an expression of Poland's sovereignty. However, the Court sees the conferral of competences to the EU as an exception to the principle of sovereignty, meaning that the competences conferred upon the EU cannot be interpreted in a way that broadens their scope. In this respect, in its jurisprudence, the Court underlined some safeguards that would block an excessive and unnecessary conferral of competence. First, the procedure for the Chamber of Deputies and the Senate to grant consent to EU treaties under Article 90 of the Constitution demands the high majority thresholds mentioned earlier. Second, the Court sees itself as competent to review EU law for its compliance with the Constitution. Both EU treaties (as ratified international agreements), as well as EU regulations, the latter only if contested in a constitutional complaint under certain circumstances, fall under such a review.[16] The Court has underlined that 'on fundamental matters concerning systemic issues it remains the final arbiter with

[12] Accession Treaty [2003] OJ L236, 23 September, Lisbon Treaty [2012] OJ C326, 26 October, 13–390.

[13] Article 90(3) of the Constitution.

[14] The voter turnout was 58.85 per cent of eligible voters, of whom 77.45 per cent voted in favour of EU accession. On the background of the referendum, see A Szczerbak, 'History Trumps Government Unpopularity: The June 2003 Polish EU Accession Referendum' (2004) 27 *West European Politics* 671.

[15] Constitutional Court, judgment of 24 November 2010, K 32/09, OTK ZU 9A/2010, poz 108, para III 2.5.

[16] Constitutional Court, judgment of 16 November 2011, SK 45/09, OTK ZU 9A/2011, poz 97, para III 2.5. See K Granat, 'Kontrolle des EU-Sekundärrechts durch den polnischen

regard to the Polish Constitution'.[17] Third, following other European constitutional courts (most prominently the German Constitutional Court), the Polish Constitutional Court indicated that there are certain competences of state organs which are decisive for the constitutional identity of Poland that cannot be transferred to the EU.[18] Constitutional identity, in the view of the Court, is expressed by the Constitution as a whole, its preamble and by specific constitutional principles, such as democracy and the fundamental rights and freedoms of the citizens.[19]

D. Separation and Balance of Powers

It is not easy to faithfully transfer the principle of separation of powers shaped by the classical liberalism of Montesquieu and John Locke to contemporary constitutions. This is why this principle takes different institutional forms. In the Constitution of 1997, the separation and balance of power is enshrined in Article 10. This principle can be characterised by the following elements: first, political authority is divided between the legislative, executive and judicial powers; second, each of these powers has its own state organs; and, third, there is a system of checks and balances of these powers, which forms the core of the separation of powers.

The principle of the separation and balance of powers entered Polish constitutional law system in two steps. First, the Constitutional Court derived this principle from the principle of a democratic state ruled by law.[20] Second, the Small Constitution of 1992 and then the Constitution of 1997 formally introduced the principle of the separation and balance of powers as a constitutional principle. It thus originated from the jurisprudence, but then received formal content typical of other European constitutions.[21]

The 1997 Constitution explicitly states that the Polish system of government is based upon the separation of and balance between the legislative, executive and judicial powers. This underlines the fundamental

Verfassungsgerichtshof – Anmerkung zum Beschluss des polnischen Verfassungsgerichtshofs vom 16. November 2011, SK 45/09' (2013) 2 *Zeitschrift Europarecht* 205. See also ch 5.

[17] Constitutional Court, SK 45/09, para III 2.4.

[18] Constitutional Court, K 32/09, para III 2.1.

[19] See section IV below and also ch 8.

[20] Constitutional Court, judgment of 19 June 1992, U 6/92, OTK ZU 1992, poz 13.

[21] G Kuca, *Zasada podziału władzy w Konstytucji RP z 1997 r* (Warsaw, Wydawnictwo Sejmowe, 2014) 321.

character of this principle. Furthermore, the Constitution assigns the legislative power to the Chamber of Deputies and the Senate, and the executive power to the President and the Council of Ministers. In contrast, the Constitution assigns the judicial power to courts as such (without distinguishing their types) and tribunals (according to the Constitution, these are the Constitutional Court and Tribunal of State). All the courts and tribunals together constitute the judicial power.

Moreover, the Constitutional Court established two further characteristics of the principle of separation and balance of powers.[22] First, each of the powers must be provided with 'material competences that correspond with the core of that power'. This means that each of the powers maintains some 'minimum of exclusive competences'. Specifically, the core of the legislative power is the exclusivity of making laws without any limitation as to their subject matter. The core of the executive power is the execution of these laws. In the case of the judicial branch, the minimum of exclusive competence is the administration of justice to enable the right to a fair trial. The notion of the 'core' of power can also be explained negatively. For example, no other power can replace the Chamber of Deputies in terms of making laws or courts in pronouncing judgments. Both in parliamentary and presidential systems, the competences of the executive and legislative branches cut across one another and overlap, sometimes reaching the core of the competence. For example, the state budget effectively amounts to an agenda of governmental tasks, although it is formally an act of parliament.[23]

Against the background of such a relationship between the legislative and executive powers, the judicial power stands out. In contrast to the legislative and executive powers, its independence is built in a bottom-up manner. The point is that independent judges and independent courts lead to a separation of the judiciary as a whole from the other powers.[24] There are no exceptions to this principle, in contrast to the case of the legislative and executive powers. None of the other powers can interfere with the structure, composition or actions of the judiciary, unless the Constitution provides for an exception. Despite the separation of powers, the judiciary cooperates with the other powers as demanded by the principle of the balance of powers. For example, the courts operate on the basis of laws established by the parliament, while judges are appointed by the President on the motion of the National Council of

[22] Constitutional Court, judgment of 21 November 1994, K 6/94, OTK ZU 1994, poz 39.
[23] See ch 3.
[24] Articles 178 and 173 of the Constitution. See ch 5.

the Judiciary. However, those functional relations between the branches cannot interfere with the separation of the judiciary or influence their jurisprudence.

The Constitutional Court perceives the principle of separation of powers as a dynamic system in which the elements can change and balance each other out. The essence of this principle in the view of the Court is not the separation, but rather the balance of powers. The branches of government interact with and complement each other by cooperating with and controlling one another. This guarantees the respect for the competences of each of the powers and builds the basis for a democratic state.

The balancing of powers demonstrates the internal dependence of the branches of government and enhances the cooperation between the powers. This cooperation, also referred to in the preamble to the Constitution, in turn supports the balance of powers. However, the balance of powers is not synonymous with putting a brake on another branch. Although the Constitutional Court plays a distinguished role by deciding on the compliance of laws with the Constitution, it is not the final arbiter of the balance of powers and remains an organ of the judiciary that itself is in balance with other powers. This balance of power is dynamic in character. For instance, in a 1992 case, the Constitutional Court intervened in the autonomy of the parliament. The Chamber of Deputies decided to carry out – on the basis of its own resolution (instead of a statute) – a wide-ranging lustration process unmasking high-ranked state officials who collaborated with the Communist secret police.[25] It was unclear whether a resolution constituted a sufficient legal basis for such a process. The Constitutional Court, invoking largely fundamental rights standards, found the resolution unconstitutional and suspended it. In turn, in a 2016 case, the Constitutional Court declared itself not competent to assess the resolutions of the Chamber of Deputies of November and December 2015 concerning the election of new judges of the Constitutional Court for the seats that had already been occupied.[26] Its case law indicates that on balance, the Constitutional Court does not interfere in the position of the parliament. The autonomy of the Chamber of Deputies is particularly appreciated in a system of parliamentary government and protected by the Constitutional Court accordingly. Nonetheless, recognising a forceful interference with citizens' human rights, the Constitutional Court declared the lustration

[25] Constitutional Court, judgment of 19 June 1992, U 6/92, OTK ZU 1992, poz 13.
[26] Constitutional Court, decision of 7 January 2016, U 8/15, OTK ZU A/2016, poz 1.

resolution of 1992 unconstitutional. Overall, the Constitutional Court remains within the organs of judicial power and balances itself with the parliament. These examples highlight that the separated branches of government represent one joint construction with the aim of providing a reliable and efficient functioning of the state. Even powers that are separated – although in competition with each other – must cooperate with one another.[27]

The constitutional principle of the separation and balance of powers remains the fundamental basis of the state system. However, the state power should also be exercised according to other principles. One such example is the subsidiarity principle, which strengthens the powers of citizens and their communities, as expressed in the preamble to the Constitution.[28]

After 2015, the governing majority started to put into question the independence of the judiciary, which in turn weakens the principle of separation and balance of power. Chapter 5 discusses the circumstances and forms of this attack on the courts.

E. Parliamentary Government

In the Constitution of 1997, the principle of parliamentary government directs the relationship between the President, parliament and the Council of Ministers (cabinet). The politically neutral President appoints and dismisses the Council of Ministers, which in its composition and functioning remains under the control of the Chamber of Deputies. The principle of parliamentary government was already in force in Poland prior to the Second World War, under the March Constitution of 1921 inspired by the French Constitutional Laws of 1875.[29] However, the system of parliamentary government was rejected in the subsequent April Constitution of 1935, which elevated and strengthened the role of the indirectly elected President.[30] In a completely different period – after the Second World War – the Communists rejected a parliamentary system in any form. The Constitution of 1952 introduced a system of unitary

[27] For similar cases, see Constitutional Court, judgment of 15 January 2009, K 45/07, OTK ZU 1A/2009, poz 3; judgment of 9 November 2005, Kp 2/05, OTK ZU 10A/2005, poz 114.

[28] See ch 7.

[29] W Komarnicki, *Polskie prawo polityczne. Geneza i system* (Warsaw, Wydawnictwo Sejmowe, 2008 [1922]) 4–5.

[30] Constitution of 23 April 1935, JL 1935 No 30 Pos 227.

state power. This system – which in its essence was undemocratic – was the opposite of a parliamentary system of government.

After the democratic transition of 1989, the Small Constitution of 1992 introduced another, quite original presidential-parliamentary system. This system was adjusted to the political and leadership style of Lech Wałęsa, the first president elected by the nation in December 1990.[31] It was characterised by a strengthened position for the directly elected President. For example, the President had a decisive voice in the process of the nomination of the key ministries (internal, foreign and defence). The President could also dissolve the parliament on quite numerous grounds. A well-known example concerned the dissolution of the Chamber of Deputies on 31 May 1993. Paradoxically, President Wałęsa dissolved the Chamber of Deputies of the first term, which was the first parliament freely elected in 1991. Moreover, the loss of exclusive law-making competence on the part of the parliament was characteristic of the system of government under the Small Constitution. The government was competent to issue decrees – regulations that had the same legal force as parliamentary acts – though this prerogative was never used. In sum, the Small Constitution offered an interesting regulation of the state system that was applied in the first years of democratic transition.

The Constitution of 1997 reverted to a parliamentary system, not in its classic form, but rather as 'rationalised parliamentarism'. After the Second World War, this system expressed the idea that the influence of the government on the parliament should follow some aim, such as an effective law-making process. In the case of the Constitution of 1997, the rationalised parliamentarism strengthened the position of the Council of Ministers and of the Prime Minister in the system of government. Their position, and in particular that of the Prime Minister, is based upon three key elements of the German 'chancellor' system. First, in the constructive vote of no confidence, the government can be held politically responsible only if the parliament has gathered enough support for a prospective successor in the same vote. Although this procedure existed under the Small Constitution of 1992, it became obligatory under the 1997 Constitution. It represents the only means to change the government. Second, the Prime Minister can be dismissed only together with the cabinet as a whole during the constructive vote of no confidence. Third, the position of the Prime Minister vis-a-vis the ministers has been strengthened. For these reasons, the mechanisms for the functioning of

[31] See ch 4.

the government established by the Constitution of 1997 are often referred to as a 'half-chancellor' system.[32]

Finally, the Polish parliamentary system under the Constitution of 1997 is bicameral, with the Chamber of Deputies and the Senate. The characteristic feature of this system is that only the Chamber of Deputies forms an active part of the principle of parliamentary government. For instance, only the Chamber of Deputies adopts statutes and controls the government. The Senate plays only a secondary role in Polish bicameralism.[33]

In practice, the system of rationalised parliamentarism has proven to be an effective way to maintain the stability of public authority in Poland. Changes to the Council of Ministers or the Prime Minister take place regularly, but effectively mainly as a consequence of parliamentary elections.[34] However, the system of rationalised parliamentarism also has some weaknesses. One of them is that it protects weak cabinets that function despite relatively limited political support in the parliament. For instance, this was the case for the cabinets of Donald Tusk and of Ewa Kopacz during the Chamber of Deputies of the seventh term (2011–15).

The political basis of the parliamentary system lies in the political parties. Their significant function is reflected in the fact that their position and role are regulated in the Constitution itself. The Constitution guarantees the freedom of the creation and functioning of the political parties, as well as their equality.[35] The only constitutional limitation is the prohibition of some types of political parties depending on their political programme. The Constitution rules out parties which in their programme refer to totalitarianism, Nazism, Fascism and Communism, racial or national hatred, or violence for the purpose of obtaining power or to influence state policy.[36] In addition, parties cannot maintain a secret structure or membership.

Prior to 1989, it was not possible to create a political party. The Constitution of 1952 established the monopoly of the Communist Party, and those who attempted to form other political parties were jailed. Only after the fall of Communism could political parties be freely created.

[32] See ch 4.

[33] See P Sarnecki, 'Funkcje i struktura parlamentu według nowej Konstytucji' (1997) 11–12 *Państwo i Prawo* 35–37; L Garlicki, 'Komentarz do Art. 121 Konstytucji' in L Garlicki (ed), *Konstytucja Rzeczypospolitej Polskiej. Komentarz* (Warsaw, Wydawnictwo Sejmowe, 2001) 3.

[34] See ch 4.

[35] Article 11 of the Constitution.

[36] ibid art 13.

In order for a party to gain legal personality, it was sufficient to sign up on a court-administered list. The idea behind the relatively lax regulation of the functioning of political parties at the time was to rebuild political pluralism. This aim was achieved as by the 1990s, there were more than 100 political parties. However, many of these were only 'quasi-parties'. For instance, the Polish Beer-Lovers' Party existed between 1990 and 1993 with the aim of promoting beer drinking instead of vodka drinking, and hence combating alcoholism. In the 1991 elections, this party won 16 seats in the Chamber of Deputies. The existence of such parties diminished the seriousness of political life.

Following the brief period of the relatively free establishment of political parties (1990–97), the legislature decided to rationalise the system and primarily support parties that contribute to state politics. Parties can still be freely created without prior permission or registration, but the Law on Political Parties of 1997 introduced stricter requirements for parties to acquire legal personality.[37] The main reform was a de facto obligation to register a new party with at least 1,000 members (compared to 15 members under the previous regime) at the District Court in Warsaw and a new supervision procedure. Only the Warsaw District Court monitors the process of registration and, in case of doubt, the Constitutional Court reviews whether the programme of the party complies with the Constitution. Another supervision procedure concerns already active political parties. In such a case, the Constitutional Court can control both the aims and the activities of the party.[38]

Since the reform of 2001, registered political parties are eligible for financing from the state budget. First, they can receive funding as compensation for expenses incurred during elections in a manner that is proportional to the number of seats won in parliament. Second, political parties obtain funds from the state budget to finance their functioning. This type of funding depends on their electoral performance and in order to claim the funds, parties need to win at least three per cent of valid votes in the relevant election (six per cent in the case of party coalitions). At the same time, parties are banned from running their own businesses. Overall, these provisions increase the transparency of party funding.

The regulation of political parties brought some order to political affairs and they became more professional. The number of political parties has been limited to those that represent mainstream political life. For example, there are liberal, conservative and socialist parties.

[37] Act of 27 June 1997 on Political Parties, JL 2018 Pos 580.

[38] See ch 6.

However, a drawback of these regulations is that the pluralism of political life, especially its spontaneity, has diminished. Still, at the end of 2016, there were 86 registered political parties and 72 of them were politically active in public debate, while only a few had members in the parliament or local self-government.[39]

F. Civil Society

The principle of civil society derives from a number of other constitutional principles. The first is the freedom of creation and functioning of different organisations and institutions that allow for the association of citizens. The Constitution gives as examples trade unions, socio-occupational organisations of farmers, societies, citizens' movements, other voluntary associations and foundations.[40] The freedom of association implies that people are free to associate and that the public authorities cannot limit this activity.

This freedom is of great importance to Poland, in particular because of the role played by the trade unions, especially 'Solidarity', during the 1980s and 1990s. During the Communist era, 'Solidarity' was deeply involved in the political life of the country and contributed significantly to its democratic transformation. Nowadays, the Constitution distinguishes between the functioning of trade unions[41] and political parties.[42] Trade unions have a right to bargain, especially to resolve collective disputes, conclude collective labour agreements as well as organize workers' strikes. Political parties, which can be financed from the state budget depending on their performance in the elections, at the beginning of this century, enabled the development of a party system with a domination of two forces: a liberal and a conservative one. Beyond trade unions and political parties, thousands of organisations that do not have a political character function on the basis of the Constitution.[43] These organisations distinguish Poland as a country of social pluralism.

The second constitutional principle contributing to civil society is the social market economy.[44] The Constitution defines a social market

[39] See http://stat.gov.pl/obszary-tematyczne/gospodarka-spoleczna-wolontariat/gospodarka-spoleczna-trzeci-sektor/partie-polityczne-w-2016-r-,7,3.html.

[40] Article 12 of the Constitution.

[41] ibid art 59.

[42] ibid art 11.

[43] ibid art 12.

[44] ibid art 20.

economy as an economic system based on the freedom of economic activity, private ownership and solidarity, as well as dialogue and cooperation between the social partners. The Constitution thus connects the economic system based upon private ownership with cooperation between employers and workers. The crucial meaning of 'social market economy' is that it precludes a return to the economic system of real socialism that operated in Poland during the Communist period from the end of the 1940s until 1989. Real socialism was characterised by economic planning and state property, resulting in long periods of a lack of basic goods and low standards of living. In contrast, the social market economy is based upon market mechanisms and the activity and entrepreneurship of the citizens. Thanks in part to this economic system, Poland's economy has been developing since the 1990s and the gap in living standards between Poland and Western Europe has been shrinking.

The third element necessary for the functioning of civil society is local self-government.[45] It is organised in a three-tier structure consisting of communes (*gmina*), counties (*powiat*) and regions called voivodeships (*województwo*).[46] In practice, local self-government enjoys real political support from the local population, is directly elected and exercises a major impact on local affairs. For example, the government of a voivodeship can decide whether to build an airport, while the commune government may resolve to build cycle lanes. The introduction of local self-government was one of the most successful reforms since 1989, enabling citizens to have an impact upon local matters, thereby strengthening civil society.

Furthermore, churches and other religious organisations play a vital role in the development of civil society. The Constitution introduced certain principles that govern their functioning.[47] First, all churches and religious organisations have equal rights. Second, the state remains impartial (neutral) with regard to one's religious or philosophical convictions, or worldview. Third, the relationship between the state and churches or religious organisations is anchored in the respect for their autonomy, independence from each other and cooperation for individual and the common good. Finally, agreements between the state and the representatives of churches and religious organisations – for instance,

[45] ibid art 16. See also ch 7.
[46] See ch 7.
[47] Article 25 of the Constitution.

the agreement of 1993 between the Holy See and Poland (concordat) – regulate their mutual relationship.[48]

The constitutional dimension of the relationship between the state and churches is that they cooperate for the common good.[49] The Constitution introduced a 'friendly separation' of state and church.[50] On the one hand, the Constitution thus delineates the relationship between the state and churches as separation, while on the other hand – in another provision – it establishes freedom of conscience and religion.[51] Although these two issues are separated in the Constitution, they are perceived as being complementary.[52] Such an approach makes it possible to establish private schools, including denominational schools,[53] and ritual slaughter (despite the prohibition of inflicting suffering on animals).[54] Another example of this approach is the possibility of supplementing the oath of office by an MP, president or member of the government with the phrase 'So help me God', complementing the freedom to express religious views in the public sphere.[55] Moreover, the Constitutional Court declared the presence of a cross in school classrooms constitutional,[56] and its presence in the Chamber of Deputies was declared admissible by the ordinary courts.[57]

In Polish society, the Catholic Church plays a particularly significant role since 92.8 per cent of Poles profess themselves to be Roman Catholic.[58] The Catholic Church is active both in the spiritual and moral aspects of people's lives, as well as in the communities through charity and education. Indirectly, it also has an impact on the political life of Poland. For example, it played an important part in the overthrow of Communism, acting as an intermediary in the talks between the opposition and the Communist government, encouraging compromise and a peaceful transition to democracy.

[48] Concordat between the Holy See and the Republic of Poland, signed 28 July 1993, JL 1998 No 51 Pos 318.

[49] Article 1 of the Constitution. See section II.A above.

[50] See L Garlicki, 'Komentarz do art. 25' in L Garlicki and M Zubik (eds) *Konstytucja Rzeczypospolitej Polskiej. Komentarz. Tom I* (Warsaw, Wydawnictwo Sejmowe, 2016) 594–630.

[51] Article 53 of the Constitution.

[52] See Garlicki (n 50).

[53] Article 70(3) of the Constitution.

[54] ibid art 53(5). See Constitutional Court, judgment of 10 December 2014, K 52/13, OTK ZU 11A/2014, poz 118.

[55] Articles 104(2), 130 and 151 of the Constitution.

[56] Constitutional Court, judgment of 20 April 1993, U 12/92, OTK ZU 1993, poz 9.

[57] Warsaw Court of Appeal, judgment of 9 December 2013, I Aca 608/13.

[58] Data for 2015 available at: http://stat.gov.pl/obszary-tematyczne/inne-opracowania/wyznania-religijne/zycie-religijne-w-polsce,3,1.html.

G. Openness to International Cooperation

One of the key novelties introduced by the Constitution of 1997 is the clarification of the position of international law and EU law within the system of the sources of law. The Constitution declares that Poland 'shall respect international law binding upon it'.[59] Following Poland's accession to the EU, the system of sources of law became more complex or, as labelled by the Constitutional Court, 'multicentric': legal acts issued by the Polish parliament co-exist with the *acquis communautaire* and acts issued by EU institutions.[60] Despite this compound legal structure, the Constitution still occupies the pivotal position. Specifically, it declares itself 'the supreme law of the Republic of Poland'.[61]

The Constitution divides international treaties into those requiring and those not requiring ratification. Those demanding ratification can be further divided into two groups, commonly referred to as requiring 'big' or 'small' ratification. The international treaties that fall under the 'big ratification' category necessitate the agreement of the Chamber of Deputies and the Senate before their ratification by the President. To this extent, the parliament adopts a statute that empowers the President to ratify the treaty at hand. As regards the subject of such treaties, the Constitution lists alliances and peace, political or military treaties, as well as treaties concerning Poland's membership in an international organisation, treaties imposing considerable financial responsibilities on the state and treaties concerning the freedoms, rights or obligations of citizens specified in the Constitution.[62] Nonetheless, the most important type of international treaty adopted by the 'big ratification' procedure, and regulated by Article 90 of the Constitution, is one that delegates to an international organisation or international institution the competence of organs of state authority in relation to certain matters.[63] This provision is the legal basis for Poland's membership in the EU. Accordingly, the Chamber of Deputies requested the consent of the nation for the ratification of the EU Accession Treaty via a national referendum, and following its positive outcome, the President ratified the treaty.[64] Such a procedure of ratification of the EU Accession Treaty, in which the Chamber of Deputies appealed to the will of the nation, can

[59] Article 9 of the Constitution.
[60] Constitutional Court, K 32/09, para III 2.3.
[61] Article 8 of the Constitution.
[62] ibid art 89.
[63] See section II.C above.
[64] See section IV below.

be seen as a 'particularly big ratification'. So far, it has been applied only once, for the Accession Treaty in 2003. This ratification procedure is also particular in a different sense: its formal requirements are more demanding in comparison to a constitutional amendment.[65] Other examples of treaties adopted in the 'big ratification' procedure – concerning which the parliament expressed its consent for ratification, although a referendum was not held – include the North Atlantic Treaty, the Lisbon Treaty and the Council of Europe Convention on preventing and combating violence against women and domestic violence. In turn, treaties covered by 'small ratification' have relatively less meaning for state affairs. These treaties are also ratified by the President, but they do not require the consent of the parliament prior to their ratification. In contrast, the President ratifies such treaties and informs the parliament about their ratification. Finally, constitutional law distinguishes international agreements that do not demand ratification at all. They are approved by the Council of Ministers in the form of a resolution and become part of internally binding law. An example of an inter-governmental treaty is an agreement between Poland and Germany regarding the construction of a bridge over a border river.

Ratified international treaties must comply with the Constitution. To this end, prior to the ratification of an international treaty, the President may request the Constitutional Court to review the compliance of such a treaty with the Constitution ('preventive control').[66] If the act is declared unconstitutional, the President will deny ratification of such a treaty. Upon ratification by the President, international treaties subject to 'big ratification' have the same legal effect as a statute and in the event of a conflict between the two, ratified international treaties enjoy primacy. In contrast, in the event of a conflict between international treaties subject to 'small ratification' and statutes, the latter have priority of application. Thus, the position of the ratified international treaties in the Polish legal system – in relations to statutes – is dynamic. It depends on the applied ratification procedure and, consequently, the subject matter of the treaty.

The status of EU primary law (the treaties) is governed by Article 91 of the Constitution. After its ratification by the President and publication in the *Journal of Laws*, an EU treaty becomes part of the national legal order. In the event of a conflict, the application of EU treaties enjoys primacy over statutes if the treaty cannot be reconciled with the provisions of such an act. In Poland, as in all the EU Member States,

[65] ibid.

[66] Article 133(2) of the Constitution. See ch 6.

EU regulations are directly applicable and enjoy primacy over national statutes in case of collision.[67] In turn, EU directives are implemented at the national level in a form of a statute (so-called implementing statutes).[68]

Therefore, what is the position of the Constitution in the Polish legal system since Poland's accession to the EU? In the view of the Constitutional Court, the Constitution remains 'the supreme law of the Republic of Poland' as guaranteed in its Article 8.[69] However, in cases of conflict between EU law and the Constitution, the former may take precedence in application. Such precedence does not contradict the supreme legal force of the Constitution; on the contrary, it takes place with constitutional consent. According to the Constitutional Court, in the event of an ultimate, unresolvable conflict between EU law and the Constitution, the legislature should decide on the best way to resolve the situation.[70] The Polish legislature can decide to either amend the Constitution or can exercise its influence to engineer changes to the conflicting provision at the EU level. As a final step, the nation or its representatives can decide on withdrawal from the EU.

III. SOURCES OF LAW

One of the aims of the Constitution of 1997 was to bring some sense of order to the system of sources of law. This system, stemming from the times of the Polish People's Republic, was unclear, and allowed the government and the government administration to issue legal acts arbitrarily. In addition, the pre-1997 system of sources of law had loopholes, such as the lack of a specific position for international agreements. The 1997 Constitution brought about two major changes: first, it introduced a closed catalogue of sources of law; and, second, it included in that catalogue international (and EU) law discussed above.

Chapter III of the Constitution contains the catalogue of sources of law. It divides them into those that are universally binding and those that are internally binding. In other words, the Constitution adopted a dualist approach, meaning that each legal act must be subordinated either to

[67] Article 288 of the Treaty on the Functioning of the European Union (TFEU); art 91(3) of the Constitution.

[68] For practice, see ch 3.

[69] Constitutional Court, judgment of 11 May 2005, K 18/04, OTK ZU 5A/2005, poz 49, para III 2.1; K 32/09, para III 2.5; SK 45/09, para III 2.2.

[70] K 18/04, para III 6.4.

universally or to internally binding law. Universally binding law includes acts that are addressed to all legal subjects (citizens, legal persons etc) and that determine their rights and obligations.[71] The Constitution incorporates the catalogue and hierarchy of those acts: the Constitution, statutes (*ustawy*), ratified international agreements, laws established by an international organisation if foreseen by an international agreement ratified by Poland in accordance with Article 91(1), regulations (*rozporządzenia*) and local law.[72] Local law is universally binding, but only within the territorial scope of the organ of local self-government that adopted the act at stake. In addition to the catalogue of sources of law, during a period of martial law, the President may issue regulations having the force of statutes.[73]

The closed system of universally binding acts, despite its drawbacks, stands in stark contrast to the open system of sources of law under the Constitution of 1952 and the Small Constitution of 1992. The open system led to some arbitrariness in the law-making process, as well as failing to provide for clear collision rules between different sources of law. Nevertheless, the closed system is not as hermetic in practice as one would expect from the text of the Constitution. In principle, the catalogue of universally binding acts indicated in the Constitution is enumerative.[74] However, to some extent, normative facts such as customary law or precedent may also flow into this system, since the Constitution leaves this aspect open. Another issue is that the Constitution indicates the subjects that can issue universally binding acts. Thus, only those subjects that have a specific constitutional competence to issue a specific act can adopt it. The Constitutional Court quite strictly decided in this respect that state organs that are not explicitly listed in the Constitution, despite their significant economic and social role, cannot issue such acts. For instance, the Court denied the National Bank of Poland competence to issue universally binding acts.[75]

As already mentioned, the Constitution also includes a category of internally binding laws. The categorisation of these acts is not exhaustive. The Constitution includes in this category resolutions of the Council of Ministers and orders of the Prime Minister and other ministers.[76] These acts, which are indicated only as an example, are binding for the organ

[71] Constitutional Court, judgment of 28 June 2000, K 25/99, OTK ZU 5/2000, poz 141.
[72] Article 87(1) of the Constitution.
[73] ibid art 234.
[74] ibid arts 87 and 234.
[75] K 25/99.
[76] Article 93 of the Constitution.

that has adopted them and for the organisational units that are subordinate to that organ. Such acts cannot regulate the freedoms and rights of citizens.

IV. THE FUNCTIONING OF THE CONSTITUTION WITHOUT A FORMAL AMENDMENT

Overall, the Constitution of 1997 has proven remarkably stable. From its entry into force on 17 October 1997 until 2019, the Constitution has been amended only twice, in 2006 and 2009; however, these amendments can be classed as insignificant.[77] The first amendment introduced an exception to the prohibition of extradition of a Polish citizen in order to accommodate the European Arrest Warrant.[78] The second excluded persons sentenced to imprisonment by a final judgment for an intentional indictable offence from being eligible candidates for the parliamentary elections.[79] Aside from these two amendments, the Constitution has not formally been changed.

In part, this is a reflection of the high hurdles for formal constitutional amendment that are in place. In this respect, the Constitution establishes a number of safeguards.[80] One concerns the initiators of the amendment procedure, namely at least 90 Members of Parliament, the Senate and the President. Next, two-thirds of the Members of Parliament and an absolute majority of the senators, in the presence of at least half of the statutory number of members in each of the chambers, need to approve the statute amending the Constitution. Finally, a national referendum might take place if the amendment concerns the provisions of Chapter I, II or XII of the Constitution on constitutional principles, fundamental rights and the constitutional amendment procedure, respectively.

It is quite striking that despite the absence of a formal amendment, the Constitution of 1997 did change fundamentally when seen from the perspective of its principles. The most prominent example concerns precisely Poland's EU membership. Specifically, the Constitution was not amended as a consequence of the Accession Treaty or the Lisbon Treaty. Still they were approved via extraordinary procedures that required even greater political support than a regular constitutional amendment.

[77] Garlicki (n 2) 47.
[78] Article 55 of the Constitution.
[79] ibid art 99(3).
[80] ibid art 235.

The ratification procedure of those EU treaties followed Article 90 of the Constitution, which demands a two-thirds majority in each of the parliamentary chambers, with the possibility of holding a national referendum. Thus, the conditions for the ratification of EU treaties are more stringent than those of the constitutional amendment foreseen in Article 235 of the Constitution. Such a ratification procedure introduces amendments to the content of the Constitution and its crucial provisions, such as the principle of sovereignty and the system of sources of law.

The EU treaties influenced the understanding of key constitutional principles and the relationship between them. As this chapter has argued, the understanding of the principle of sovereignty of the nation, as well as that of the supremacy of the Constitution, was changed by the EU accession. The Constitutional Court in its recent judgments has relied on constitutional identity in shaping the principle of sovereignty of the nation within the EU, in particular in situations where the competences of state organs are conferred upon EU institutions.[81] Constitutional identity can reconcile conferral of competences with sovereignty so that neither the nation nor the state loses its sovereignty. From this perspective, membership of the EU is understood not as a loss of sovereignty, as in the classic understanding of that principle, but as an expression of Poland's ability to decide for itself. It enables Poland to influence certain policy areas from which it was completely absent pre-accession.

The interpretation of key constitutional principles changed without formal amendment of the text of the Constitution. This indicates the immense role of the Constitutional Court in the interpretation of the Constitution and in adjusting it to the changing times.[82]

V. CONCLUSION

The Constitution of 1997 has had to respond to two main challenges, one historic and one contemporary. First, during its creation, the Constitution had to take on board the difficult past of the Polish state, which, although it possessed a rich constitutional history, had been severely damaged by the period of Communism from 1946 to 1989. In response, the Constitution, instead of starting with carte blanche, took an evolutionary approach to the past, trying to accommodate different and often conflicting values.

[81] K 32/09, para III 2.1.

[82] See also ch 6.

As a result, many of the principles adopted by the Constitution of 1997, mainly those in its first chapter, are common to constitutional systems of democratic states. This is the case with regard to the principle of parliamentary government (in its rationalised form) or the principle of separation of powers, which takes into account the balance between those powers. These principles were already known in Poland in the inter-war period (1921–35) and, in 1997, were introduced as one of the achievements of European constitutionalism.

In contrast, other principles, such as that of a social market economy, are less common elsewhere and characteristic of the specific period of transformation in Poland (from real socialism to democracy) during which the drafting of the Constitution of 1997 took place. Some of the constitutional principles express the idea of the Round Table during the spring of 1989. The Communists, who were already in the process of giving up power, and the widely supported 'Solidarity' movement agreed that the transformation of the political system should have an evolutionary and not a revolutionary character. This approach was made possible by the approval and adoption of the rule of law principle. Political, economic and social change during the period of transformation took place on the basis of and within the limits of the law.

Second, Poland's membership of the EU strengthened the international position of the country and added impetus to its economic growth. In the post-2004 legal system, the Constitution remains the supreme law of the state. In cases of conflict between the Constitution and EU law, the Constitutional Court acts as a conciliator between the two legal systems, leaving EU withdrawal as the ultimate option. Nonetheless, as all chapters in this book demonstrate, the positions of all important constitutional bodies have experienced a profound impact as a consequence of EU integration.

In retrospect, the set of constitutional principles discussed in this chapter successfully fulfilled its role over the past 20 years. During this time, Poland has transformed into a democratic European state and integrated into international structures, joining both NATO and the EU. This return to the Western world was possible thanks partly to the openness of the Constitution to international cooperation and its credibility as a democratic state ruled by law. Parliamentary and presidential elections have already taken place a few times, changing the political spectrum, yet always within the framework of a democratic system. The Constitution, through its principles, has contributed to the stabilisation of democracy in Poland.

FURTHER READING

Ekiert G and Kubik, J, 'Myths and Realities of Civil Society' (2014) 25 *Journal of Democracy* 46–58.

Granat, M, 'Konstytucja RP na tle rozwoju i osiągnięć konstytucjonalizmu polskiego' (2007) 81 *Przegląd Sejmowy* 11–32.

——. *Prawo konstytucyjne. Pytania, odpowiedzi* (Warsaw, Wolters Kluwer, 2018).

Komarnicki, W, *Polskie prawo polityczne. Geneza i system* (Warsaw, Wydawnictwo Sejmowe, 2008 [1922]).

Kordela, M, *Zasady prawa. Studium teoretycznoprawne* (Poznań, Wydawnictwo UAM, 2013).

Łazowski, A, 'Accession Treaty: Polish Constitutional Tribunal – Conformity of the Accession Treaty with the Polish Constitution. Decision of 11 May 2005' (2007) *European Constitutional Law Review* 148–62.

Sarnecki, P, (ed), *Konstytucjonalizacja zasad i instytucji ustrojowych* (Warsaw, Wydawnictwo Sejmowe, 1997).

3

Parliament

Chamber of Deputies – Senate – Bicameralism – Electoral System – Political Parties – Legislative Process – Government Oversight – European Integration

I. INTRODUCTION

THE POLISH PARLIAMENT is structured along bicameral lines, with two chambers: the Chamber of Deputies (*Sejm*) and the Senate (*Senat*). The Constitution grants the legislative power to both the Chamber of Deputies and the Senate within a system of separation and balance of powers.[1] Beyond the legislative task, the Chamber of Deputies also fulfils an oversight function over the government: it holds the government politically accountable. In addition to its interactions with the executive, the Chamber of Deputies has a certain, albeit limited, degree of impact upon the judiciary via the appointment of some justices.

The position of the Senate – despite the wording of the Constitution – is very limited.[2] The Senate, as the second chamber of the parliament, has played a rather restricted role. The Senate existed in the interbellum period, but after the Second World War, it was abolished by the Communist government as an undemocratic chamber (a 'chamber of resistance' vis-a-vis the progressive Chamber of Deputies). Thus, until 1989, Poland had a unicameral parliament. The Senate was reinstated as a consequence of the Round Table talks in April 1989.[3] Nonetheless, during the work on the 1997 Constitution, the decision to maintain a bicameral structure was passed by a very narrow majority of three votes.[4]

[1] Article 10 of the Constitution.

[2] ibid. See A Bisztyga and P Zientarski (eds), *Kierunki zmian pozycji ustrojowej i funkcji Senatu RP* (Warsaw, Kancelaria Senatu, 2014).

[3] See M Dobrowolski, 'Ustrój państwa w porozumieniach Okrągłego Stołu' (2009) 92 *Przegląd Sejmowy* 77.

[4] Constitutional Committee of the National Assembly, Biuletyn XII (Warsaw, 1996) 62.

In theory, this constitutional framework for parliament is constructed in an exemplary, balanced way. The Constitution provides for an efficient legislative process and enables the Chamber of Deputies to scrutinise the government. However, recent political practice has raised a number of issues. First, the electoral system has tended to create coalitional governments that have limited the degree to which the legislative and control activities of the parliament reflect the intended checks and balances. Since the entry into force of the Constitution of 1997, a number of coalitions were formed. The first was the centre-right coalition of the Solidarity Electoral Action and Freedom Union parties (1997–2001). The second was the coalition of social democrats and the agrarian Polish People's Party (2001–05). Next followed the coalition of conservative parties (2005–07) controlled by the Law and Justice party. The coalition of centrist parties (2007–11 and 2011–15) led by the Civic Platform remained in power for the longest period under the 1997 Constitution so far. The situation changed after the 2015 elections, when the Law and Justice party gained a majority, with slight support from other conservative parties. The governments formed under the 1997 Constitution were able to adopt almost any legislative act without needing to negotiate with the opposition. Since 2015, this is especially characteristic of the governing style of the Law and Justice party. When a strong parliamentary majority forms a cabinet, control over the government may weaken. The opposition may become discouraged by the lack of any realistic possibility of succeeding in eliminating the government by a vote of no confidence. In this sense, there appears to be a divergence between constitutional theory and the practice of governing.

A second feature of the constitutional system that has transpired to have an important impact is the weak bicameral structure of the parliament. The tradition of parliamentarism sees many benefits in a bicameral structure. For instance, it is an additional political forum within the parliament that consults different social groups and can therefore support the overall authority of the government. The second chamber can improve the quality of decision-making by offering another source of advice, especially in cases where the second chamber has more experience or some other specific distinction.[5] A different justification of bicameralism stems from federalist theory, developed and employed first in the United States and then in Europe (Germany and Switzerland). There, the second chamber embodies the representation

[5] D Shell, 'The History of Bicameralism' (2001) 7 *Journal of Legislative Studies* 5, 6.

of the federated states.[6] Other benefits of having a strong second chamber include 'a more independent view' because of a less party-dominated environment; the moderating influence of 'veto players' in the policy-making process; and an ability to complement the work of the lower chamber.[7]

However, in its experience with the Constitution of 1997, Poland has been unable to take advantage of these benefits and its system qualifies as relatively weak bicameralism with asymmetrical and congruent chambers.[8] There are two main reasons for this. First, both chambers of the Polish parliament tend to have a very similar composition, which may be a consequence of the electoral system. Second, Poland is a unitary state and, as such, the Senate does not provide for any type of regional representation. After 1989, within the group of Central and Eastern European states, only Poland and the Czech Republic adopted a bicameral parliament, despite the absence of a federal structure in either jurisdiction.

Against this background, this chapter evaluates in greater detail how well the parliament fulfils the functions endowed upon it by the Constitution, highlighting the areas of controversy around parliamentary majorities and the weak position of the Senate. This demands an analysis of the electoral system (especially of voting methods and election thresholds), the role of the political parties, and the specific powers of the chambers within the legislative and control procedures. Finally, this chapter shows that Poland's EU membership has increased the incentives for a more profound control of the government by the Chamber of Deputies and has boosted the role of the Senate at the national level. This discussion concludes with an assessment of the future of the Polish bicameral system.

II. THE ELECTORAL SYSTEM AND THE COMPOSITION OF PARLIAMENT

The two chambers of the Polish parliament, the Chamber of Deputies (consisting of 460 Members of Parliament (MPs)) and the Senate (consisting of 100 senators), are each elected for a four-year term of office.[9] Elections to both the Chamber of Deputies and the Senate are universal,

[6] ibid 12.

[7] M Russell, 'What are Second Chambers for?' (2001) 54 *Parliamentary Affairs* 442, 443.

[8] See A Lijphart, *Patterns of Democracy: Government Forms & Performance in Thirty-Six Countries*, 2nd edn (New Haven, Yale University Press, 2012) 192 ff.

[9] Articles 96–97 of the Constitution.

direct and secret. However, they differ with regard to the voting mechanisms utilised. The Constitution prescribes that the members of the Chamber of Deputies be elected via an equal and proportional system. However, the Constitution remains silent regarding the voting mechanism for the Senate. This allowed the legislature to make changes to that mechanism. The latest reform, in 2011, introduced single-member constituencies and a majority voting rule for the Senate.[10]

A. Voting Rights

Every Polish citizen who has reached 18 years of age has the active right to vote in elections for both chambers of parliament (as well as in all other type of elections).[11] However, under some specific conditions, a citizen can lose this active voting right.[12] First, a final court judgment can deprive a person of his or her public rights, including the right to vote. This punishment can be applied for crimes that belie a motivation that deserves particular condemnation with a sentence of at least three years of imprisonment. The second premise concerns certain state officials that can be held responsible before the Tribunal of State.[13] It can deprive a person of the right to vote, for example, if the President violates the Constitution. Finally, a person loses the right to vote if he or she is rendered legally incapacitated by a final court judgment.

The passive right to vote – that is, the right to be elected – is afforded to all citizens who possess active voting rights and fulfil the additional, more restrictive age requirements: a minimum age of 21 for the Chamber of Deputies and 30 for the Senate.[14] The Constitution immediately strips any person sentenced to imprisonment by a final judgment for an intentional, indictable offence of the right to be elected.[15] This exclusion from running for elections also extends to so-called 'lustration liars', that is, persons who were found by a court to have withheld details of their cooperation with the secret services during the Communist period (1946–89).[16]

[10] M Jarentowski, 'Zmiana systemu wyborczego do Senatu RP z 2011 r' (2011) 104 *Przegląd Sejmowy* 33.

[11] Article 62(1) of the Constitution.

[12] Article 10 §2 of the Law of 5 January 2011, Electoral Code, JL 2018 Pos 112, 1000, 1349.

[13] See ch 6.

[14] Article 99(1)–(2) of the Constitution.

[15] ibid art 99(3).

[16] Article 11 §2(2) of the Electoral Code.

The electoral system does not include any type of additional criteria, such as wealth, education or residence. However, candidates for the European Parliament elections are obliged to reside for at least five years in Poland or another EU Member State.[17]

B. Principles of the Electoral System

The principle of universal elections is safeguarded by the constitutional requirement that elections for the Chamber of Deputies and the Senate must take place on a 'non-working day', which is traditionally a Sunday.[18] In 2011, the Electoral Code introduced the possibility that some of the elections could take place on two days: Saturday and Sunday.[19] However, the Constitutional Court decided that only Sunday was a 'non-working day'.[20] Thus, the attempt to conduct the elections over two days failed. Beyond the day of the elections, the Electoral Code of 2011 contains additional requirements guaranteeing the universality of elections. For instance, the electoral census and the list of voters are prepared *ex officio* and even a change of residence by a voter does not limit his or her active voting right.

The directness aspect of elections in Poland is understood as a 'one-step' vote, whereby the voter directly elects a candidate to the Chamber of Deputies or the Senate without intermediate electors who would vote for the candidate in the name of the voter. The Electoral Code of 2011 introduced two new provisions concerning the directness of elections: voting by proxy, which was previously unheard of in Poland, and postal voting for all. The Constitutional Court confirmed both measures as compatible with the principle of direct elections.[21] However, in 2018 the Law and Justice government limited postal voting – it is available only to disabled persons – arguing that this form of voting increases the possibility of fraud. In practice, no evidence of fraud has been discovered to date.

The secrecy of elections concerns the casting of a vote. Only the voter knows the content of his or her vote. This principle demands that the

[17] ibid art 11 §2(5).
[18] Article 98(2) of the Constitution.
[19] On this and other reforms introduced by the Electoral Code, see A Rakowska and K Skotnicki, 'Zmiany w prawie wyborczym wprowadzone przez Kodeks wyborczy' (2011) 105 *Przegląd Sejmowy* 9.
[20] Constitutional Court, judgment of 20 July 2011, K 9/11, OTK ZU 6A/2011, poz 61.
[21] ibid.

voting process should take place in conditions enabling secrecy of the vote, for example, by providing cabins and a ballot box at the polling station.

In addition, the Constitution requires elections to the Chamber of Deputies to be equal and proportional. The principle of equal elections has a formal and a material aspect in Polish electoral law. Formally, it means 'one person, one vote'. Materially, it is understood as 'one vote, one value', meaning that each vote is of the same value. In practice, this material aspect is reflected in electoral districts that are designed such that the ratio of the population to the available number of seats is approximately the same across Poland. In this regard, minimum electoral thresholds are often perceived as violating the equality of elections. For instance, in the 2015 elections, the coalition of left-wing parties received 7.55 per cent of the vote and thus did not reach the 8 per cent threshold required for coalition party lists. As a consequence, over one million votes were not taken into account in the distribution of seats.[22]

Proportionality of the elections for the Chamber of Deputies is reflected in the way in which votes are converted to seats. The elections take place in 41 electoral districts with between 7 and 20 seats each. Voters have one vote and select one candidate from a range of available party lists. Seats are then allocated to parties in proportion to the overall number of votes awarded to candidates on their lists in each district. Within lists, the candidates with the highest number of votes will have priority in the allocation of the seats that their party list has won.[23] The precise method for seat allocation has been changed frequently. Since 2005, the D'Hondt method, an algorithm of mapping votes into a limited number of seats, has been applied. On balance, it somewhat favours larger parties over smaller ones.

Minimum vote thresholds were first introduced in 1993 in response to the elections to the Chamber of Deputies of 1991, in which almost 30 different political parties won at least one seat in the chamber. Such a high number of political parties hindered the formation of a stable coalition, and led to two consecutive and ultimately unsuccessful minority governments and overall political instability. Since 2001, the minimum share of valid votes nationwide that a party list must gain in order to take part in the proportional allocation of seats has been five per cent. As was indicated earlier, in the case of party coalition lists, this threshold

[22] See http://parlament2015.pkw.gov.pl/pliki/1445898069_Komunikat-pkw-zbiorcze-wyniki-glosowania.pdf.

[23] Article 227 of the Electoral Code.

increases to eight per cent of valid votes. However, these thresholds are waived for electoral committees created by recognised minorities, such as the German minority in Poland, which regularly wins one seat in the Chamber of Deputies despite falling well short of five per cent nationally.

Nonetheless, in practice, the thresholds present an effective obstacle to the election of a multi-party Chamber of Deputies. For example, in the 2011 elections, of 18 electoral committees that registered, only five gained enough votes to pass the thresholds; in the 2015 elections, only six out of 26 electoral committees entered parliament.[24] The election thresholds thus represent yet another reason for the tendency towards majority governments in Poland.

In the Senate, during the period between its reconstitution in 1989 and 2001, the election districts were quite mechanically designed to overlap with the administrative areas called voivodeships (of which there were 49 in total) with two or three seats available in each. This system was first reformed in 2001, with the number of districts reduced to 40 with 2–4 senators in each. Until 2011, seats within each district were allocated by plurality block voting, in which voters had one vote for each available seat in their district and could allocate the votes to their preferred candidates. The most recent reform of 2011 then introduced 100 single-member districts, elected via a first-past-the-post system.

In recent history, both chambers of parliament tended to have a similar party composition. On the face of it, some manner of differentiation could have been expected from the different electoral systems applicable to the two chambers, namely proportional and majoritarian. However, in practice, whichever party won in the Chamber of Deputies in the two recent elections of 2011 and 2015 also dominated the Senate, be it the Civic Platform or the Law and Justice party. This may be partly due to the fact that elections to both chambers take place at the same time. Furthermore, features such as minimum thresholds and the D'Hondt rule make the proportional Chamber of Deputies elections more favourable towards bigger parties and thus more similar to the majoritarian system of the Senate elections. In sum, the election methods have tended to undermine Polish bicameralism by providing for relatively congruent chambers.

The legality of elections is safeguarded by a system of electoral bodies headed by the National Electoral Commission. This is a permanent

[24] See the elections outcome at http://wybory2011.pkw.gov.pl/wsw/pl/000000.html for 2011 and at http://parlament2015.pkw.gov.pl/349_Wyniki_Sejm for 2015.

organ tasked with holding elections and referendums.[25] It consists of nine judges, three from each of Poland's highest courts: the Constitutional Court, the Supreme Court and the Supreme Administrative Court. The President appoints all members of the National Electoral Commission. Its membership will change after the 2019 parliamentary elections. The National Electoral Commission will then encompass two judges (one from the Constitutional Court and one from the Supreme Administrative Court) and seven other persons merely qualified to exercise a judicial office elected by the Chamber of Deputies. In practice, politicians will gain the decisive impact on the composition of the National Electoral Commission. The change in its construction should be perceived negatively as it departs from the 'judicial model' of electoral oversight, which worked well in practice.

In sum, elections in Poland follow established electoral principles. This concerns all types of elections: presidential, parliamentary (including the European Parliament), as well as those to local authorities.[26] If any irregularities take place (for instance, a delay in opening of a polling station), they are corrected in real time; the opening hours of the polling station will be accordingly extended. However, such minor irregularities would not have any impact on the outcome of elections. The Supreme Court has confirmed the legality of all parliamentary and presidential elections that have taken place under the 1997 Constitution. Ordinary courts confirm the legality of local elections, and in practice have in a limited number of individual cases refused to certify local elections.

C. The Constitutional Status of MPs and Senators

According to the Constitution, the MPs and senators are 'representatives of the Nation' and 'shall not be bound by any instructions of the electorate'.[27] This means that their mandate is general, independent and irrevocable. The general character of the mandate implies that the MPs and senators express the will of the whole nation and not only that of the voters of their electoral district or party or of a specific group. In the exercise of their mandate, they should pursue the 'good of the nation'.[28] The independence of the mandate denotes that the MPs and the senators

[25] Article 177 of the Electoral Code.

[26] See also chs 4, 6 and 7.

[27] Articles 104 and 108 of the Constitution.

[28] Law of 9 May 1996 on the Exercise of the Mandate of a Member of Parliament and a Senator, JL 2018 Pos 1799.

are not legally bound by the will of the voters, meaning that the representatives do not have to explain any of their actions or votes to voters. In other words, the elections do not create a contractual relationship between the MPs or senators and the voters. Nonetheless, it is expected that the parliamentarians keep voters informed about their work and the functioning of the chambers. Finally, the mandate is irrevocable, since the voters cannot withdraw the support granted in the elections. Voters cannot recall an MP or senator.

The Constitution establishes strong legal safeguards for the independence of parliamentarians. Specifically, MPs and senators are equipped with formal and material immunity and their integrity is protected under the Constitution.[29] Material immunity forbids holding the MPs and senators accountable for any activity performed within the scope of their mandate during the parliamentary term. This type of immunity is permanent and extends until the death of the parliamentarian in question. The MPs and senators cannot renounce the immunity and the chambers cannot deprive their members of it. In cases where an MP or senator has infringed the rights of third parties, he or she may be held accountable before a court only with the prior agreement of the respective chamber (so-called quasi-formal immunity). In turn, the formal immunity guarantees that a parliamentarian cannot be held accountable for any criminal act, including one outside the scope of his or her mandate, without the prior consent of the relevant chamber. However, this type of immunity does not have a permanent character and it expires at the end of the mandate. Finally, the Constitution grants personal inviolability to parliamentarians. They cannot be detained or arrested without the consent of their chamber, unless they were apprehended in the commission of an offence and the detention is necessary to ensure that proceedings take their proper course.

Moreover, the Constitution indicates a number of activities that are considered incompatible with being an MP or a senator.[30] These include holding of certain positions, such as President of the National Bank of Poland, Ombudsman or ambassador. Other categories of incompatibility include the positions of judge, public prosecutor, officer of the civil service, soldier on active military service, or functionary of the police or of the services of state protection. An interesting case illustrating difficulties that may arise in practice concerned an MP who participated in

[29] Article 105 of the Constitution.

[30] ibid arts 103 and 108. See M Zubik, 'Ustrojowe założenia niepołączalności mandatu parlamentarnego' (2008) 87 *Przegląd Sejmowy* 103.

175 votes in the Chamber of Deputies after being appointed ambassador to Italy.[31] The question at stake was the moment of expiration of an MP's mandate in cases of appointment to another office. The case had no further consequences, as the votes of the MP in question were not decisive in any of the debated issues.

At times, the prohibitions in question are difficult to implement, as some exceptions are foreseen. The Constitution does allow for an MP or senator to hold a ministerial position (such as prime minister, minister or secretary of state). This possibility – widely used by all cabinets – softens the principle of incompatibility.[32] Seen from this perspective, the system of separation of powers seems inconsequential.

In principle, parliamentarians are not restricted from engaging in business activity. However, this cannot involve any benefit derived from the property of the State Treasury or the local self-government, nor can such property be acquired.[33] The sanction for a violation is constitutional accountability before the Tribunal of State. Under such circumstances, the Tribunal of State imposes only one penalty – stripping the parliamentarian of his or her mandate. In practice, a case of an MP or senator being held accountable before the Tribunal of State has not occurred thus far. Those parliamentarians who do not conduct businesses receive a full monthly salary, instead of a reduced one, and are traditionally referred to as 'professional parliamentarians'.

MPs and senators come with a varying experience to the parliament. At the beginning of the eighth term of the Chamber of Deputies (2015 to present) 44 per cent of the newly elected members were first-time members, 13 per cent had been a member for one term, 14 per cent had already served two terms, 17 per cent three terms, 7 per cent four terms, and the remaining 3 per cent between five and seven terms.[34] In the case of the Senate (ninth term, 2015 to present), 41 per cent of the newly elected members had never been senators, 29 per cent during one term, 15 per cent had served two terms, 14 per cent three terms, and 1 per cent had served four terms.[35] Interestingly, however, 26 per cent of senators have previously served as members of the Chamber of Deputies.

[31] 'O ambasadorze, który głosował jako poseł' *Rzeczpospolita* (25 July 2018).

[32] For examples, see ch 4.

[33] Article 107(1) of the Constitution.

[34] Authors' own interpretation based on the information available at: www.sejm.gov.pl/Sejm8.nsf/page.xsp/poslowie_poczatek_kad.

[35] Authors' own calculation based on www.senat.gov.pl/o-senacie/senat-wspolczesny/dane-o-senatorach-wg-stanu-na-dzien-wyborow.

This data highlights the 'kinship' between the Chamber of Deputies and the Senate.

III. THE IMPACT OF POLITICAL PARTIES ON THE PARLIAMENT

Political parties are critical for the quality and the character of the Polish parliament, and, as explained in Chapter 2, they form an important element of the system of parliamentary government. Parties play a crucial part in the election process. Although the Constitution states that both political parties and the voters themselves can nominate candidates for MPs and senators, in practice the former play the main role in nominations.[36] Political parties create electoral committees, which undertake activities on behalf of the party, such as the selection of candidates, and manage the electoral campaign. In the elections to the Chamber of Deputies, electoral committees can put forward one candidate list in each of the 41 electoral districts. The list must be supported by at least 5,000 voters living in the district in question. In practice, it is important to present candidate lists in as many districts as possible, due to the minimum thresholds applicable in the elections to the Chamber of Deputies discussed earlier. The situation is different in Senate elections, which take place in single-member districts. There are no lists and each electoral committee can put forward only one candidate. A Senate candidacy requires the support of at least 2,000 voters living in the district.

The Electoral Code imposes gender quotas and demands that candidate lists for the Chamber of Deputies consist of at least 35 per cent female and at least 35 per cent male candidates.[37] The gender quotas are a necessary requirement for registration of the lists and are applicable to all types of elections where lists are required. Currently, in the Chamber of Deputies of the eighth term, female MPs hold 27 per cent of the mandates.[38] This shortfall can be explained by the absence of any requirement to rank women high on party lists as well as the open list electoral system in which voters can influence which members of the list are awarded seats in parliament.

Political parties also influence the functioning of the parliament after the elections. Although the mandate of a parliamentarian is free and the

[36] Article 100(3) of the Constitution.

[37] Article 211 §3 of the Electoral Code.

[38] Authors' own estimation based on the date available at: www.sejm.gov.pl/Sejm8.nsf/page.xsp/poslowie_poczatek_kad.

Constitution guarantees the independent execution of this mandate, political parties influence parliamentarians through so-called 'clubs' (at least 15 MPs or seven senators) and smaller 'circles' of parliamentarians. Each MP or senator can belong to only one club or circle. These groups are forms of self-organisation in parliament, but in practice, they tend to represent associations of parliamentarians in accordance with their political party colours. They exert influence, for example, by putting forward their members for posts in the parliament and its organs, such as the Marshal of the chamber or the chairperson of a parliamentary committee.

The clubs and circles offer a way to impose the discipline necessary to support the execution of policies pursued by the political parties. Insubordination displayed by MPs and senators within parties usually results in their removal from the particular club and marginalisation. This guarantees strong party discipline in the Chamber of Deputies.[39] Similarly, party discipline remains strong in the Senate. Examples include senators voting along strict party lines on the amendment of the pension funds system in 2013[40] and on state budget for 2018 and 2019,[41] or the controversial Law on the Constitutional Court of 22 July 2016.[42] These examples shows that the Senate does not appear to offer a more independent view than the Chamber of Deputies, arguably undermining one of the rationales of a bicameral structure.

IV. THE FUNCTIONING OF PARLIAMENT IN THE PRESENCE OF MAJORITY GOVERNMENTS AND WEAK BICAMERALISM

A. Legislative Procedures

According to the Constitution, the legislative process encompasses four main phases: legislative initiative; proceedings in the Chamber of Deputies; proceedings in the Senate; and the President's signature.

[39] See votes taken on the floor of the Chamber of Deputies, eg, in its seventh term, available at: www.sejm.gov.pl/sejm7.nsf/agent.xsp?symbol=posglos&NrKadencji=7.

[40] See Senate's vote No 3 on 11 December 2013, available at: https://www.senat.gov.pl/sklad/senatorowie/szczegoly-glosowania,88,4,8.html.

[41] See Senate's Vote No 2 on 19 January 2018, available at: https://www.senat.gov.pl/sklad/senatorowie/szczegoly-glosowania,300,2,9.html; and Senate's Vote No 11 on 24 January 2019, available at: https://www.senat.gov.pl/sklad/senatorowie/szczegoly-glosowania,345,13,9.html.

[42] See Senate's Vote No 51 (and other votes) on 21 July 2016, available at: www.senat.gov.pl/prace/senat/posiedzenia/przebieg,467,2,glosowania.html.

Both the Chamber of Deputies and the Senate participate in the legislative process, but only the former adopts statutes.[43]

i. Initiation of the Legislation

The Constitution invests the right to introduce legislation to MPs, the Senate, the President, the Council of Ministers and any group of 100,000 citizens on the basis of a citizens' initiative.[44] In practice, most legislative initiatives originate in the Chamber of Deputies. For example, during the seventh legislative term of the Chamber of Deputies (2011–15), more than half of all bills were initiated by MPs, while the government put forward one-third of the total number of proposals.[45] However, this data does not reflect the complexity of the process. In this regard, parliamentary practice indicates that the decisive aspect for the ability to legislate is the political circumstances. In the Chamber of Deputies of the eighth legislative term in particular, one can observe the practice that legislative proposals stemming from the government are put forward by the MPs as their own. For example, this concerned the laws reforming the judiciary.[46] This is explained by the faster pace of proposals brought in by MPs in comparison to those initiated by the government. Notably, the Senate, which in the eighth legislative term (2011–15) accounted for only eight per cent of the proposed legislation, does not act as a 'motor' of the legislative process. Again, this highlights the inequality of the bicameral structure within the legislative process. Finally, bills proposed by the President as well as under a citizens' initiative make up only a small share of the proposals overall.

The diagram below presents data on the origin of legislation during the seventh legislative term of the Chamber of Deputies. It seems that the data for the eighth term of the Chamber of Deputies does not differ substantially from the previous term. Nonetheless, some of the legislative initiatives of the President – for instance, the proposal concerning the Supreme Court – had a far-reaching, negative impact on the independence of courts and judges.[47]

[43] Article 120 of the Constitution.

[44] ibid art 118(1) and (2).

[45] A total of 31 per cent of government's bills were implementing EU law (see further section V below).

[46] See, eg, Law of 20 July 2018 amending Law on the Ordinary Courts and other laws, JL 2018 Pos 1443. See also ch 5.

[47] Chamber of Deputies, Print No 2003, 26 September 2017. See also ch 5.

Figure 3.1 Origin of legislation

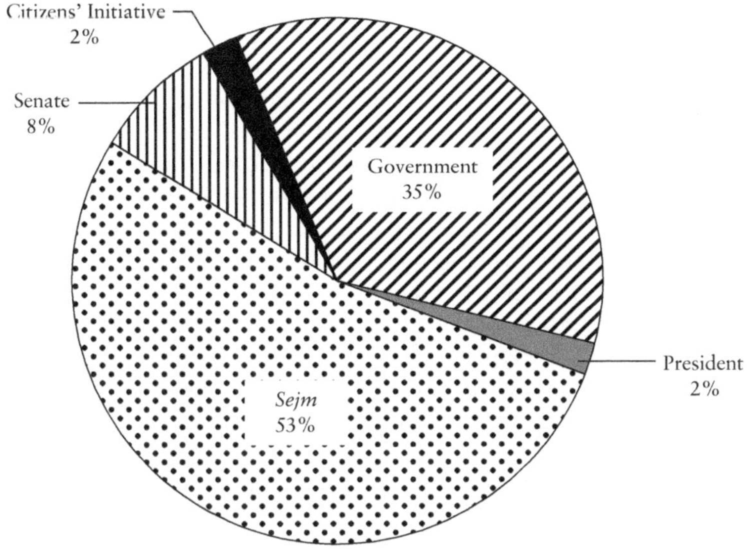

Source: authors' calculations based on data available from the website of the Chamber of Deputies of the seventh legislative term (2011–15)[48]

The citizens' initiative was introduced into the Polish legal system as a form of direct democracy for the first time by the Constitution of 1997. This institution differs from petitioner's rights that allow individuals to submit petitions, proposals and complaints in the public or own interest to organs of public authority, or organisations and social institutions whose duties fall within the field of public administration.[49] Launching a citizens' initiative requires the creation of a committee by at least 15 Polish citizens with active voting rights.[50] This committee must then initially collect 1,000 votes in favour of the proposal in order to gain official notification of the initiative by the Marshal of the Chamber of Deputies. With this notification, the committee becomes a legal person, and then has three months to collect the 100,000 signatures required for the initiative to succeed. If successful, the initiative will then go through all stages of the legislative process just like a normal bill brought by the government. However, a citizens' initiative is privileged in some respects. For instance, a legislative procedure relating thereto will not be

[48] See www.sejm.gov.pl/sejm7.nsf/page.xsp/przeglad_projust.

[49] Article 63 of the Constitution; Law of 11 July 2014 on Petitions, JL 2018 Pos 870.

[50] Act of 24 June 1999 on the Exercise of the Citizens' Initiative, JL 2018 Pos 2120.

discontinued at the end of the term of the parliament, as would be the case for other types of initiatives.

Successful citizens' initiatives concern a wide range of topics, including the environment, education and social security. One of the most controversial initiatives concerned the introduction of a complete ban on abortion.[51] This initiative was rejected in the Chamber of Deputies. A subsequent citizens' initiative aimed to exclude the possibility of terminating pregnancy in cases where there is a high probability of severe and irreversible foetal defect or incurable illness endangering the life of the foetus.[52] This proposal remains under deliberation.

Although some proposals originating from citizens' initiatives have become binding law, in practice the procedure has certain flaws. For example, the final act approved by parliament may differ substantially from the original initiative and, in contrast to, for example, the Latvian system, does not need to be submitted to a national referendum.[53] Consider, for example, the citizens' initiative on electoral gender parity discussed earlier, which was put forward by the Congress of Women. Even though it became binding law, it differs from the original initiative in that it introduced a 35 per cent gender quota instead of full equality as demanded in the original proposal.[54]

ii. Proceedings in the Chamber of Deputies

In the second phase of the legislative procedure, the Chamber of Deputies debates the draft bill in three readings.[55] The first reading usually takes place in one of the chamber's committees, while the remaining two take place on the floor of the chamber.

Committees are composed of a small number of members on the basis of a proportional representation of all parties elected to the chamber, thus also including opposition parties. The expertise of the members is second only to their political affiliation. Committees are organized on a thematic basis, roughly corresponding to governmental departments.

[51] Chamber of Deputies, Print No 784, available at: www.sejm.gov.pl/Sejm8.nsf/druk.xsp?nr=784.

[52] Chamber of Deputies, Print No 2146, available at: www.sejm.gov.pl/Sejm8.nsf/druk.xsp?nr=2146. See also ch 7.

[53] Article 1 of the Law of 20 April 1994 on National Referendums, Initiation of Laws and European Citizens' Initiative.

[54] A Śledzińska-Simon and A Bodnar, 'Gender Equality from Beneath: Electoral Gender Quotas in Poland' (2013) 28 *Canadian Journal of Law and Society* 151.

[55] The legislative procedure in the Chamber of Deputies and the Senate is set out in arts 119–23 of the Constitution.

Currently, the Rules of Procedure of the chamber provide for 29 standing committees concerning issues such as internal affairs, foreign affairs, public finance, culture, defence, agriculture and health.[56] MPs may sit in up to two permanent committees, and in practice the majority of the parliamentarians belong to two such committees. However, in the two most recent parliamentary terms (in 2011–15 and the ongoing term), some of the MPs belonged to three standing committees, which is only permitted with the approval of the chamber's Presidium.[57] MPs who are government ministers or secretaries of state in the government administration cannot be members of a standing committee, except for the committee for constitutional amendment. Beyond the standing committees, the chamber may create special ad hoc committees, for example, to debate drafts of legal codes.

The main task of the committees is to discuss and opine on proposed bills. Committees can request that government ministers or directors of organs of state and other state institutions submit a report or provide information and participate in the committee meeting concerning areas falling under their departmental powers.

The core support offered to the committees comes from the Bureau of Legislation and the Bureau of Research in the Chamber of Deputies. The former analyses every step of the legislative procedure with regard to procedural issues and also reviews legislative proposals on their merits. The activities of the latter are more research-oriented, often providing the MPs with the opinions of scholars who are experts on the issue at stake, as well as advising on the compliance of legislative proposals with the Constitution and EU law.

In general, committee meetings are undertaken in public. However, the list of eligible participants is limited. For example, members of other committees and Members of the European Parliament (MEPs) can participate in discussions during committee meetings, but cannot vote. Lobbyists and invited representatives of professional and social organisations, experts and, in some cases, the staff of the MPs, as well as journalists, can also participate in the committee meetings. In some cases, the committee can decide to hold a closed meeting, and information from a meeting might be declared as classified. Otherwise, protocols of committee meetings, draft statutes, resolutions and other documents

[56] For the relevant provisions on the chamber's committees, see arts 17–20 and 149–68 of the Rules of Procedure of the Chamber of Deputies of 30 July 1992, MP 2018 Pos 729.

[57] See www.sejm.gov.pl/Sejm7.nsf/page.xsp/udzial and www.sejm.gov.pl/Sejm8.nsf/page.xsp/udzial.

are made public via publication in the chamber's official Information System.

During a committee meeting, the chair can call upon MPs who are drifting off topic to talk on the matter at hand and even strip a member of his or her speaking rights. In addition, the chair can call the MP to order if he or she further disrupts the meeting. Finally, MPs can be expelled from the meeting.

Following the first reading in committee, the second reading of a draft bill takes place on the floor of the chamber, followed by a third reading that is de facto a vote on the draft bill. A bill approved in the Chamber of Deputies becomes a statute. In order for a bill to be approved and to pass for consideration by the Senate, it requires a simple majority vote with a quorum of at least half of the statutory number of MPs. In certain cases, greater majorities are required, as discussed in Chapter 2 with regard to bills amending the Constitution and for statutes granting consent for the ratification of some types of international agreements. At the end of the legislative procedure, the Chamber of Deputies adopts a statute.

iii. Proceedings in the Senate

A statute adopted by the Chamber of Deputies is subsequently forwarded to the Senate. The Senate can choose between three options: it can adopt a statute as it is, adopt amendments to the statute or reject it entirely.[58] The Senate has 30 days regardless of which option it decides to choose. If it does not take any resolution within that period, the statute is considered to be adopted with the wording submitted by the Chamber of Deputies. If the Senate rejects the statute or introduces amendments, these statutes (together with the changes) return to the Chamber of Deputies.

Work in the Senate on all of the three options mentioned earlier encompasses three readings. As is the case in the Chamber of Deputies, the first reading takes place in committee and the following two on the floor of the chamber. The Senate's committees are designed in a manner similar to those in the Chamber of Deputies. The Senate also has similar rules regarding the participants of the meetings, including the participation of ministers. Senators are supported by their own Legislative Bureau and Bureau of Analysis and Documentation. There are both standing committees established for the full four-year term of the Senate (16 in total) and special committees. A senator's membership is limited to two committees.

[58] Article 121(2) of the Constitution.

In practice, recent terms of the Senate show that the chamber appears to prefer to adopt amendments and rarely rejects a statute outright. For example, during the Senate's fifth term (2001–05), out of 899 statutes adopted by the Chamber of Deputies, the Senate opted to reject only six, proposed amendments to 495 and adopted 398 statutes without amendment.[59] In response, the Chamber of Deputies adopted 83.1 per cent of the amendments proposed by the Senate and followed the Senate's resolution for total rejection of a statute in only one case. In the other five cases, the Chamber of Deputies overrode the Senate's veto. The percentage of the Senate's amendments approved by the Chamber of Deputies in the following two terms (2005–07 and 2007–11) remained at similar levels – 81.8 per cent and 86 per cent, respectively. This was accompanied by a very low number of rejections of statutes by the Senate (four during each term).[60]

Although this data shows that the Senate exercises a degree of control over statutes adopted by the Chamber of Deputies, in particular through amendments, in fact such amendments rarely concern the merits of the act in question and instead focus on rather minor editorial issues.[61] Their main contribution to the legislative process lies in reducing the need for later review by the Constitutional Court.[62]

The weak position of the Senate derives from the fact that the Chamber of Deputies can discard any of the Senate's amendments or rejections. The Chamber of Deputies acts by absolute majority vote in the presence of at least half of the statutory number of members. In addition, the vote of the Chamber of Deputies always has a negative character. The MPs vote only on the question whether to *reject* the Senate's amendments or the Senate's veto. This gives the Chamber of Deputies an advantage in the legislative procedure. This relationship between the Chamber of Deputies and the Senate – a design whereby the former votes down the latter chamber – stems from late 1980s and the Round Table talks. In this way, the Chamber of Deputies, dominated by the post-Communist powers, was granted an advantage over the Senate that stemmed from

[59] See http://ww2.senat.pl/k5/pos/inf.HTM.

[60] See data for the sixth term at http://ww2.senat.pl/k6/pos/inf.htm and for seventh term at http://ww2.senat.pl/k7/pos/inf.pdf.

[61] K Skotnicki, 'Senat III RP – nieprzemyślany czy niepotrzebny?' in M Zubik (ed), *Dwadzieścia lat transformacji ustrojowej w Polsce* (Warsaw, Wydawnictwo Sejmowe, 2010) 225 ff.

[62] B Banaszak, 'Przesłanki istnienia Senatu w Polsce' in A Bisztyga and P Zientarski (eds), *Kierunki zmian pozycji ustrojowej i funkcji Senatu RP* (Warsaw, Kancelaria Senatu, 2014) 20.

free elections. The lack of any reform of the Senate in the subsequent constitutions – the Small Constitution (1992) and the 'big' 1997 Constitution – led to the consolidation of that approach.

Another mark of the weak position of the Senate in the legislative process can be seen in the fact that there is no procedure for reconciling differences between the two chambers. For example, in Germany, in cases of discord between the *Bundestag* and the *Bundesrat*, a bill can be referred to a Joint Mediation committee.[63] In Poland, such proposals were put forward at the beginning of 1990s.[64] However, the Small Constitution did not provide for such a possibility, nor was it adopted by the 1997 Constitution. As a consequence, the Chamber of Deputies can quite easily overrule the Senate.

iv. The Role of the President

In the final stage, legislation adopted by the Chamber of Deputies and the Senate is signed by the President within 21 days of its submission and published in the official journal – the *Journal of Laws of the Republic of Poland* (*Dziennik Ustaw* or DzU). The President has some room for manoeuvre regarding this signature. The Constitution foresees two different instruments – a legal one and a political one.[65] First, before signing an adopted statute, the President may submit it for constitutional review to the Constitutional Court. However, if the statute is declared to be in compliance with the Constitution, the President cannot refuse to sign it. Second, the Constitution furnishes the President with the option of returning the statute to the Chamber of Deputies (legislative veto). The Chamber of Deputies can overturn the veto with a three-fifths supermajority vote, forcing the President to sign the statute within seven days.

In practice, the legislative veto is normally used when the President and the parliamentary majority represent different political colours. For example, both President Lech Kaczyński (2005–10) and President Bronisław Komorowski (2010–15) vetoed only a small number of statutes (one and five respectively) when the parliamentary majority was of the same political colour as the President. However, the number of vetoes by President Lech Kaczyński was significantly higher (16) when the party

[63] Article 77 of the Grundgesetz für die Bundesrepublik Deutschland vom 23. Mai 1949 (BGBl. S. 1), zuletzt geändert durch Artikel 1 des Gesetzes vom 13. Juli 2017 (BGBl. I S. 2347) ('German Basic Law').

[64] P Sarnecki, *Senat RP i jego relacje z Sejmem, lata 1989–1993* (Warsaw, Wydawnictwo Sejmowe, 1995) 148.

[65] Article 122(3) and (5) of the Constitution.

to which Kaczyński was connected was in parliamentary opposition. This was the case between 2007 and 2010. The Chamber of Deputies successfully reapproved only half of these statutes with the necessary supermajority, showing that the presidential veto has some bite.[66]

v. Accelerated Procedure

Beyond the legislative procedure discussed above – traditionally referred to as 'ordinary legislative procedure' – the Constitution also provides for an accelerated legislative procedure for urgent cases, which can be launched only on the initiative of the Council of Ministers.[67] It features shorter periods for deliberation by the Chamber of Deputies. The Senate has 14 days to take one of the three positions discussed earlier. In turn, the President has seven days to sign the statute or forward it to the Constitutional Court. This procedure is not available for tax bills; bills governing elections for the President, the Chamber of Deputies, the Senate and to organs of local government; bills governing the structure and jurisdiction of public authorities; or the drafts of law codes. In practice, the accelerated procedure has only been invoked for a very small number of bills. For example, only three per cent of all the government's bills proposed in the seventh term of the Chamber of Deputies were adopted in the accelerated procedure.[68] The accelerated procedure was employed, for instance, for the amendment of the social security system to protect an important state interest that was at stake. This statute aimed to decrease the state's debt, and the accelerated procedure allowed the act to enter into force in a timely manner.[69] So far in the eighth term of the Chamber of Deputies, this legislative procedure has not been used, except for the amendment of the Law on the Institute of National Remembrance, which introduced penalties, including imprisonment, for anyone who publicly ascribes blame to the Polish nation or state for crimes committed by Nazi Germany.[70] However, following international pressure, the amendment was overturned.[71]

[66] See http://orka.sejm.gov.pl/proc6.nsf/0/4A3FA8F1CE69378AC12577BA004A72A7?OpenDocument.

[67] Article 123 of the Constitution.

[68] Authors' own calculation on the basis of data referred to in n 48.

[69] See the government's bill on the Amendment of the Social Security System, Print No 84, 16 December 2011.

[70] Law of 18 December 1998 on the Institute of National Remembrance – Commission for the Prosecution of Crimes against the Polish Nation, JL 2018 Pos 2032.

[71] 'Poland's Holocaust Law Weakened after "Storm and Consternation"' *New York Times* (27 June 2018).

vi. Budgetary Procedure

The budget is a legislative act adopted via a slightly modified legislative procedure.[72] It can only be initiated by the Council of Ministers, but still involves both parliamentary chambers, granting the Senate a shorter 20-day decision period. The President signs the budget within seven days or forwards it for constitutional review. However, the legislative veto is not available to the President for the budget. Another important difference between a regular statute and the budget concerns their respective consequences for the parliamentary term in the case of a failure of adoption. Specifically, if the parliament does not adopt the budget within four months of the submission of its draft to the Chamber of Deputies, the Constitution permits the President to shorten the chamber's term of office at any time within the subsequent 14 days, thereby triggering new elections.

The Council of Ministers executes the budget and presents a report to the Chamber of Deputies on its implementation, together with information on the state's debt, within five months of the end of the fiscal year. The chamber considers the report within the next 90 days and, after seeking the opinion of the Supreme Chamber of Control, passes a resolution on whether to grant approval of the financial accounts submitted by the Council of Ministers, the so-called *absolutorium*. However, the position of the Chamber of Deputies is relatively weak in this respect, since the government is not obliged to resign if no approval is granted.

In sum, the ordinary legislative procedure is the primary means of passing laws. Beyond this procedure, the Constitution and the Rules of Procedure of the Chamber of Deputies indicate a number of special procedures, each with their own characteristic elements discussed above. The law-makers had high hopes for the accelerated procedure; however, in practice, it does not play any major role. Finally, in practice, the characteristic feature of the legislative procedures discussed in this chapter is their flexibility. All of them are regulated in the Rules of Procedure of the Chamber of Deputies (1991), which is frequently amended. In contrast, only the main principles governing these procedures – regulated in the 1997 Constitution – remain constant: statutes are adopted only by the Chamber of Deputies (and not the Senate); the Chamber of Deputies passes laws by simple majority of votes; and the Senate only cooperates in the adoption of laws.

[72] Articles 221–25 of the Constitution.

B. Oversight of the Executive Branch

The Constitution endows only the Chamber of Deputies (as a whole, its committees and individual deputies) with control over the executive.[73] These control rights concern the functioning and dismissal of the government, as well as the execution of the budget described earlier.

The Prime Minister may request a confidence motion in the government's policies at any time.[74] This is a risky move for the Prime Minister, since a lack of majority support in the Chamber of Deputies in the presence of at least half of the statutory number of MPs will force the government to resign.[75]

The government and its members are politically accountable and can be dismissed by the Chamber of Deputies in a vote of no confidence, addressed either to the government as a whole or to individual members.[76] However, the Chamber of Deputies has no ability to hold the President politically accountable. The political position of the head of state chosen in direct and universal elections is independent from parliamentary majority. The President is only constitutionally accountable before the Tribunal of State.[77]

The committees of the Chamber of Deputies also play a role in the oversight of the executive branch. Committees can issue written recommendations (*dezyderaty*) and opinions directed at the government, which oblige it to take a stance on a specific issue, which is then discussed at the next meeting of the committee. Most importantly, the Constitution provides that a parliamentary committee of inquiry can be established to examine 'a specific case'.[78] This notion is defined neither in the Constitution nor in the relevant statute.[79] The Constitutional Court filled this void by specifying rigorous positive and negative requirements with regard to the scope of inquiry.[80] The positive requirement demands that a 'specific case' has an individual and concrete character. The negative requirement forbids an inquiry into the legality of court judgments and controlling independent organs, such as courts or the National Central

[73] On the possible role of the Senate in this regard, see P Sarnecki, 'Kompetencje kontrolne Senatu Rzeczypospolitej Polskiej' (2000) 41 *Przegląd Sejmowy* 9.

[74] Aricle 160 of the Constitution.

[75] On the practice, see ch 4.

[76] Articles 158–59 of the Constitution. On the practice, see ch 4.

[77] See ch 4.

[78] Article 111(1) of the Constitution.

[79] Law of 21 January 1999 on the Committee of Inquiry, JL 2016 Pos 1024.

[80] Constitutional Court, judgment of 14 April 1999, K 8/99, OTK ZU 3/1999, poz 41.

Bank, as well as private parties who do not exercise any function of the public administration.

The limits set by the Constitutional Court seek to find some balance between the openness of the Constitution with regard to the scope of inquiry and the political feasibility of the proceedings. The membership of the inquiry committee reflects the representation of political parties in the Chamber of Deputies, which as a consequence means that the division between majority and opposition remains intact. The committee is equipped with the right to interrogate and can request the Public Prosecutor to conduct an investigation. As a consequence of its report, the committee can bring a motion to hold the person at stake constitutionally accountable before the Tribunal of State. Since the entry into force of the Constitution, the Chamber of Deputies has established 10 committees of inquiry to deal with issues that had an important impact on the public sphere and their proceedings enjoyed a good deal of public interest. For example, the first inquiry committee (2003–04) dealt with allegations of corruption during the process of amending the law on public media. Its final, negative report, in practice, led to the fall of the left-wing government, also reducing the impact of left-wing parties in Polish politics in the long term.[81]

Finally, the MPs may individually submit questions in writing to ministers concerning specific aspects of the government's (current) policy or address an interpellation regarding more fundamental issues. Ministers might also be requested to present information on issues of current and vital political interest on the floor of the chamber. This is not done on a systematic basis, but is rather ad hoc in character: an MP informs in writing the Marshal of the Chamber about the addressee and topic of the intended question by 9 pm on the day preceding the parliament's sitting.[82] In general, the replies to questions and interpellations are prepared by civil servants. All of these tools are very popular with MPs. For example, in the seventh term of the Chamber of Deputies, they directed 34,895 interpellations, 8,627 written questions at the government and 975 questions concerning current matters, with a similar level of activity evident during the previous terms.[83] Nonetheless, their impact as an oversight tool is very low. This exchange does not offer any

[81] Chamber of Deputies, Resolution of 24 September 2004, PM 2004 No 1 Pos 711, available at: http://prawo.sejm.gov.pl/isap.nsf/DocDetails.xsp?id=WMP20040410711.

[82] Article 115(2) of the Constitution; art 194 of the Rules of Procedure of the Chamber of Deputies.

[83] See www.sejm.gov.pl/Sejm7.nsf/page.xsp/prace_sejmu.

profound debate on the issues of controversy and is rather a way for the MPs to show to the voters that they actively exercise their mandate. In practice, the more the government and parliamentary majority dominate the parliament, the more the power of these oversight tools is reduced.

C. Independent Functions of the Senate

Two new functions, not foreseen in the Constitution, but rather developed via parliamentary practice, allow the Senate to complement the work of the Chamber of Deputies. First, the Senate engages in the execution of judgments of the Constitutional Court within its competence to initiate legislation. In fact, proposals executing such judgments constitute a large share of the Senate's legislative drafts. For example, in the Senate's eighth term, 60 per cent of bills concerned the execution of judgments of the Constitutional Court.[84] Since the start of the constitutional crisis in 2015, this function of the Senate lost some of its importance.[85] This is connected to the fact that the Constitutional Court issues far fewer judgments when compared to previous years.[86] Second, the Senate is involved in maintaining contacts with Poles living abroad. This role as guardian of the Polish diaspora (so-called 'Polonia') is connected to the symbolic position of the Senate as the institution that was re-established and fully and freely elected after the fall of Communism. In this capacity, the Senate finances the promotion of Polish culture and the protection of national heritage through its budget. These functions of the Senate demonstrate the capability of the upper house to share parliamentary duties.

V. THE PARLIAMENT AND EUROPEAN INTEGRATION

The involvement of the Polish parliament in the process of European integration began during the pre-accession period. The parliament was engaged in the significant task of approximation of national law to EU law. Only with the amendment of the rules of procedure of the chambers in 2000 and the creation of a European Legislation Committee to deal

[84] Authors' own calculation based on Senate's data, available at: https://www.senat.gov.pl/gfx/senat/userfiles/_public/k8/statystyki/podstawowe_dane_1-8/11_podstawowe_statystyki_8.pdf.

[85] See ch 6.

[86] ibid.

with those proposals in a speedy manner did the backlog in the transposition of EU law diminish to a sufficient degree to allow Poland to fulfil all of the Copenhagen criteria in time.[87]

The implementation of EU law remains one of the key tasks of the Polish parliament today. The government submits proposals for acts transposing EU directives to the Chamber of Deputies not later than three months before the deadline for their implementation prescribed by the relevant EU measure.[88] The proceedings concerning such proposals are quicker, and the rights of the MPs and senators to amend such proposals are limited in comparison to the regular legislative process. Moreover, the government is obliged to present information to the parliament on the current state of implementation of EU law at least once every six months. During the seventh legislative term, 22.6 per cent of statutes adopted by the Chamber of Deputies were implementing EU law.[89] Despite the established procedures, Poland is not faring well in its transposition efforts: at the end of 2017, it had a total of 39 open cases for late transposition, placing it in fifth position in the Commission ranking of late transposition cases in the EU-28, with only Belgium, Cyprus, Portugal and the Czech Republic having a worse record in this regard.[90] Nonetheless, the blame for late implementation lies with the government rather than the parliament, as the former tends to submit the relevant proposals so late that there is no chance for parliament's approval before the deadline set by the EU.[91]

The process of European integration posed new challenges for national parliaments that led to them often being perceived as the losers in the EU legislative process due to the central role of national executives in the Council of the EU. In order to overcome this deficit, the Act on Cooperation of 2010 grants the Chamber of Deputies *and* the Senate

[87] A Łazowski, 'The Polish Parliament and EU Affairs: An Effective Actor or an Accidental Hero?' in J O'Brennan and T Raunio (eds), *National Parliaments within the Enlarged European Union: From 'Victims' of Integration to Competitive Actors* (Abingdon, Routledge, 2007) 204 ff.

[88] Article 18 of the Act of 8 October 2010 on the Cooperation of the Council of Ministers with the Chamber of Deputies and the Senate in matters relating to the Republic of Poland's membership of the European Union, JL 2010 No 213 Pos 1395, further as the Act on Cooperation of 2010.

[89] J Maśnicki, 'Ustawy wykonujące prawo Unii Europejskiej przyjęte przez Sejm VII kadencji' (2017) 101 *Przegląd Legislacyjny* 67, 71.

[90] European Commission, Annual report on monitoring the application of EU law, Commission staff working document, general statistical overview, SWD(2018)377, 16.

[91] J Sokołowski and D Stolicki, 'Przyczyny uchybień w transpozycji dyrektyw europejskich do polskiego porządku prawnego w świetle analizy ilościowej krajowego procesu legislacyjnego' (2017) 22 *Przegląd Politologiczny* 39, 50.

the right to opine the government's position on a draft EU legislative act which the Council of Ministers intends to take at the Council of the EU or the European Council.[92] This is certainly an improvement of the Senate's position. Originally, the government was not obliged to seek the Senate's opinion on the position of the government before Council of the EU meetings.[93] However, the Constitutional Court found this provision unconstitutional because the Senate was not exercising a control function over the government, a role reserved to the Chamber of Deputies, but a legislative function, which demands equal status between the chambers.[94] In the view of the Court, both chambers should participate equally in the shaping of the government's position in EU affairs.

Although both chambers are asked for an opinion, only the opinion of the Chamber of Deputies, if issued, becomes the basis of the negotiating position of the government for the meeting of the Council of the EU or the European Council.[95] If the government does not follow the opinion of the Chamber of Deputies, it must give reasons for so doing, but no further consequences arise. In sum, the scrutiny mechanisms available to the Polish parliament vis-a-vis the government in EU affairs are relatively strong, placing Poland high within the EU-28 on this scale, not far behind the archetypical, particularly rigorous Danish model.[96]

Finally, the Early Warning System (EWS) established in Protocol No 2 to the Lisbon Treaty of 2009 in response to the perceived democratic deficit of the EU strengthened the role of national parliaments in the EU legislative process.[97] Under this mechanism, national parliaments review EU draft legislative acts for their compliance with the EU subsidiarity principle and can object in the form of a reasoned opinion. Depending on the number of reasoned opinions issued by parliaments, the EU legislature may decide to stop considering the draft act in question.

In this respect, the Constitutional Court in its Lisbon Treaty judgment positively assessed the EWS as empowering the Polish parliament to shape the content of EU law 'to the extent … that it is possible to narrow

[92] See arts 11 and 12 of the Act on Cooperation of 2010.

[93] Article 9 of the Act of 11 March 2004 on Cooperation of the Council of Ministers with the Sejm and the Senate on matters related to Poland's membership in the European Union, JL 2015 No 160 Pos 1342.

[94] Constitutional Court, judgment of 12 January 2005, K 24/04, OTK ZU 1A/2005, poz 3, para III, points 8–11.

[95] Article 13 of the Act on Cooperation of 2010.

[96] J Karlas, 'National Parliamentary Control of EU Affairs: Institutional Design after Enlargement' (2012) 35 *West European Politics* 1095, 1102.

[97] K Granat, *The Principle of Subsidiarity and its Enforcement in the EU Legal Order* (Oxford, Hart Publishing, 2018).

down the scope of its "external character" in relation to the Polish state'.[98] Following the entry into force of the Lisbon Treaty, national procedures for subsidiarity review under the EWS were introduced in the Rules of Procedure of each of the chambers. The Chamber of Deputies applies a centralised model of subsidiarity scrutiny where the European Affairs Committee remains the main actor, whereas the Senate uses a mixed system, where the European Affairs Committee and other standing committees cooperate on drafting a reasoned opinion.[99] As of July 2019, under the EWS, the Chamber of Deputies and the Senate issued 16 and 17 reasoned opinions, respectively.[100] Both chambers were among the most active parliaments in 2010 and 2011, the first two years of the functioning of the EWS.[101] This practice shows that the Lisbon Treaty and national provisions for subsidiarity scrutiny have placed the Senate on an equal footing with the Chamber of Deputies.

VI. THE FUTURE OF POLAND'S SECOND CHAMBER

Abandoned under the Communist regime, the Senate played an important role as a symbol of an independent Poland, since its members were elected in the first free elections in 1989 and the organ itself was re-established in 1990. In turn, the first free elections to the Chamber of Deputies took place only in 1991. For this reason, the Senate expresses the aspirations for freedom of the Polish people. Still, in each parliamentary election, the idea of eliminating the Senate arises. However, except for the absence of federalism, none of the factors that studies of parliamentarism correlate with unicameralism – for instance, small populations and small countries – is present in Poland.[102] As a consequence, one may look for ways to reform Polish bicameralism rather than abandoning it outright. In some areas, the Senate's role has already been reformed and improved, for example, in EU affairs, as discussed above. Since 1990, the electoral system underwent only one major change, namely the 2011 reform that introduced single-member districts for the

[98] Constitutional Court, judgment of 24 November 2010, K 32/09, OTK ZU 9A/2010, poz 108, para III 2.3.

[99] Granat (n 97) 104–06.

[100] See www.ipex.eu.

[101] European Commission, Annual Report 2010 on relations between the European Commission and National Parliaments, COM(2011)345, 3.

[102] L Massicotte, 'Legislative Unicameralism: A Global Survey and a Few Case Studies' (2001) 7 *Journal of Legislative Studies* 151, 152.

election of the members of the Senate. However, this reform did not bring about any political differentiation of the chambers. The election results in single-member constituencies that overlap with the outcomes in the majoritarian elections for the Chamber of Deputies. Thus, another method would be necessary to achieve more diversity in terms of political membership between the chambers.

One of the reasons why breakthrough reform of the Senate has not taken place thus far is a lack of clarity over the ultimate purpose of the chamber, which seems to be a common problem of bicameral systems.[103] Instead, loose, ad hoc proposals are put forward. One idea is to include the representatives of the Polish communities abroad into the Senate's membership in order to diversify its composition and help better fulfil its role as a link with 'Polonia'.[104] Another proposal suggests the differentiation of the terms of the chambers to limit the congruence between the Chamber of Deputies and the Senate.[105] Indirect election of the senators remains out of the question. Therefore, proposals that the senators would be elected by the organs of local self-government (conceiving of the Senate as a 'chamber of local self-government') are unrealistic.[106] Upholding direct elections to the Senate is important for maintaining the political legitimacy of the chamber, especially as it presents a factor contributing to 'strong' bicameralism.[107] It seems that a major reform of the Senate would not be possible without a profound change of the Constitution as such. It is quite telling that none of the questions of the 2018 referendum proposed by President concerned the bicameral structure of the parliament.[108] This indicates that the Senate will likely remain in its current shape for the foreseeable future.

VII. CONCLUSION

The Polish parliament was reborn after the fall of Communism as a fully fledged, bicameral parliament, which regained its position within the

[103] M Russell and M Sanford, 'Why are Second Chambers So Difficult to Reform?' (2002) 8 *Journal of Legislative Studies* 79, 81.

[104] M Granat, M Dobrowolski, 'Jaka reforma Senatu?' (2005) *Państwo i Prawo*, 79.

[105] M Dobrowolski, 'W sprawie potrzeby reformy dwuizbowości polskiego parlamentu' (2009) 91 *Przegląd Sejmowy* 31, 50.

[106] See https://www.psl.pl/wp-content/uploads/2018/01/Rzeczpospolita-Samorządowa.pdf; KM Ujazdowski, 'Senat: więcej niż "izba refleksji"' *Rzeczpospolita* (3 May 2017).

[107] Russell and Sanford (n 103) 81.

[108] See ch 9.

system of separation and balance of powers. The current constitutional framework in the form of the 1997 Constitution has had a twofold effect on the position of the parliament.

First, the design of the electoral system enabled the creation of quite strong parliamentary coalitions. On the one hand, in addition to the disciplinary impact of the political parties, they have allowed for a smooth legislative procedure, without lengthy negotiations with the opposition parties. On the other hand, the Chamber of Deputies has very little incentive to exercise its oversight powers. The governments that sought support of the parliament have always been granted a vote of confidence, while the opposition has always been unsuccessful in the constructive vote of no confidence procedure, as well as in holding the members of government politically accountable. It was the committees of inquiry that have had a real impact as a control tool, while questions and interpellations served as proof of activity of the MPs for their voters. In contrast, Poland's membership of the EU incentivised the establishment of strong control powers over the decisions taken by the government at the EU level.

The second effect of the Constitution of 1997 on the parliamentary system is visible in the unequal position of the Senate in the bicameral structure, apart from some improvement of its status due to the impact of EU law on the national order. The parallel term of office with the Chamber of Deputies, domination by the same political parties and strong party discipline in the Senate disable the latter from offering a more independent view vis-a-vis the Chamber of Deputies. Moreover, the Senate barely fulfils the role of a veto player, since the Chamber of Deputies can easily reject its amendments. In addition, the Senate has no function within the oversight procedure. Overall, the Senate occupies a weak position within the bicameral system and this status has led to recent, unfruitful debates over the reform of the chamber.

FURTHER READING

Barcz, J and Pudło, A, 'The Polish Parliament and EU Affairs', in C Neuhold, O Rozenberg, J Smith and C Hefftler (eds), *The Palgrave Handbook of National Parliaments and the European Union* (Basingstoke, Palgrave Macmillan, 2015) 594–612.

Goetz, KH and Zubek, R, 'Government, Parliament and Law-Making in Poland' (2007) 13 *Journal of Legislative Studies* 517–38.

Granat, K, 'The Future of Poland's Second Chamber: Is the Senate Still Needed?' in R Albert, A Baraggia and C Fasone (eds), *Constitutional Reform of*

National Legislatures: Bicameralism under Pressure (Cheltenham, Edward Elgar, 2019) 210–77.

Ka-Lok Chan, K, 'Idealism versus Realism in Institutional Choice: Explaining Electoral Reform in Poland' (2001) 24 *West European Politics* 65–88.

Markowski, R, 'The Polish Elections of 2005: Pure Chaos or a Restructuring of the Party System?' (2006) 29 *West European Politics* 814–32.

——. 'The 2007 Polish Parliamentary Election: Some Structuring, Still a Lot of Chaos' (2008) 31 *West European Politics* 1055–68.

Olson, D, van der Meer-Krok-Paszkowska, A, Simon, MD and Jackiewicz, I, 'Committees in the Post-Communist Polish Sejm: Structure, Activity and Members' (1998) 4 *Journal of Legislative Studies* 101–23.

Pełczyński, Z, 'Parliamentarism in Poland' (1956) 4 *Parliamentary Affairs* 495–504.

Pudło, A, 'A New Role of the Polish Senate's EU Affairs Committee in European Integration' (2010) 16 *European Public Law* 223–30.

4

The Executive

President – Prime Minister – Minister – Council of Ministers – Government – Government Administration – Civil Service

I. INTRODUCTION

ONE OF THE most important characteristics of the 1997 Constitution is its division of the executive power into two arms. The first of them is the President, elected by the nation in universal and direct elections, and the second is the Council of Ministers, led by the Prime Minister. This chapter deals with the origin, characteristic features and practice of this double headed-executive.

The design of the executive power in Poland stems from the principle of parliamentary government. However, since the early 1990s, this design has undergone significant modifications. First, the Small Constitution of 1992 introduced the presidential-parliamentary system. The President was the most important arm of the executive, while the position of the government was weaker. The ongoing work on the executive power that became the 1997 Constitution was disturbed by the results of the 1995 presidential election. Initially the constitution-makers aimed to weaken the President's position, fearing the election of Lech Wałęsa who had been in office since 1990. After Wałęsa's electoral loss – defeated by Aleksander Kwaśniewski – the constitution-makers partially enhanced the competences of the President. The main political forces behind the 1997 Constitution were left-wing parties and Kwaśniewski was one of their leaders. This flipping of competences from the President onto the government when the victory of Wałęsa was still a possibility, and then from the government onto the President when Kwaśniewski won led to inconsistent and sometimes unclear legal concepts. Twenty years of applying the 1997 Constitution only partially smoothed these rough edges. One such rough edge can be seen in the Constitutional Court's decision on the division of competences between the President and Prime

Minister in foreign affairs, including EU matters, which is discussed in this chapter. In short, the origin and design of the executive is among the most interesting problems of the current Constitution.

Another interesting aspect is the introduction of executive institutions from two different models of government – the German chancellor system and the French semi-presidential system – which modify the shape of the executive in the Constitution. The model of the relationship between the parliament, the President and the Council of Ministers to a large extent mirrors the design of the German Basic Law.[1] Similarities are evident in the limited influence of the President on day-to-day politics, and the parallel strengthened position of the government in respect of responsibility for home and foreign affairs. The Prime Minister also has a significant role in forming the government, presenting its programme and leading the Council of Ministers on a daily basis. In turn, the impact of the French semi-presidential system is visible in the universal and direct election of the President by the nation.[2] This chapter explores the extent and success of these received models.

The shape of the executive is one of most disputable aspects of the Constitution. However, it is unclear whether the problematic character of the executive is a consequence of constitutional design or of political practice over the past two decades. For instance, in its draft constitution, the Law and Justice party proposed a strong presidency with a President who would be the head of the whole executive, yet since 2015, when the party won the parliamentary elections, it has supported strengthening the Council of Ministers and the Prime Minister.[3] The changing approaches to the executive power can probably be explained from a party political perspective, yet the executive offers an interesting arena for legal analysis of the Constitution.

II. THE PRESIDENT

A. The Concept of the Presidency

The presidency was resurrected as a direct consequence of the Round Table Agreement of 5 April 1989. Specifically, the amendment of 7 April

[1] M Grzybowski, 'Wpływ europejskich rozwiązań konstytucyjnych na unormowania Konstytucji RP z 1997 r. Zagadnienia wybrane' (2017) *Przegląd Sejmowy* 43, 57.

[2] ibid.

[3] The Constitution of Poland, draft prepared by the Law and Justice party, January 2010.

1989 to the Constitution of the Polish People's Republic of 1952 replaced the Council of State with the office of the President of the Polish People's Republic. The Council of State was a multi-person, Soviet-type body. For this reason, the abolition of the Council of State and the creation of the office of President (between April 1989 and December 1989 'President of the Polish People's Republic') was a major change. The President of the Polish People's Republic was elected in July 1989 by the Chamber of Deputies and Senate, acting jointly as the National Assembly. However, such a solution was not satisfactory even after 1989, shortly after the fall of Communism. General Wojciech Jaruzelski, who introduced martial law in Poland in 1981 and led the Communist Party, was elected President of the Polish People's Republic. At the time, the position of the President was perceived as one that would ensure Communist influence over state power. This was evident in the competences that the President maintained with regard to the parliament and in the area of national security. For example, the President was responsible for political and military alliances with other states, which preserved the dependence of Poland upon the Soviet Union. In this sense, in 1989 the presidency remained an institution of the Communist past.

Against this background, the development of the present-day presidency took the following course. The 1990 amendment of the Constitution of the Polish People's Republic achieved a breakthrough: the nation was to elect the President in universal and direct elections. This was a consequence of the proposals of anti-Communist opposition that had called for the acceleration of political changes that had stopped after the Round Table talks of 1989. One of these proposals advanced a new model of presidency. The President – the guarantor of the Round Table Agreement – chosen indirectly by the Parliament was to be replaced by an officeholder universally elected by the nation. The first elections took place in December 1990. Lech Wałęsa was elected as President to serve a five-year term. The President received a strong democratic mandate. For the first time, the President (the head of state) was elected directly by the nation. Neither in the March Constitution (1921) nor in the April Constitution (1935) was the President elected according to such a method. Under the March Constitution, the President was elected indirectly, by the National Assembly.[4] In turn, under the April Constitution, the President was elected by the Council of Electors. However, the outgoing President could designate his or her own successor, who would

[4] Article 39 of the March Constitution of 1921.

compete in popular elections against a candidate chosen by the Council of Electors.[5]

The President was vested with limited competences typical of a head of state in a parliamentary system. However, in practice, the President extended these competences, which was facilitated by the ambiguity of the constitutional provisions at that time. Although the amended Constitution of 1952 was still in force, its provisions were treated as transitional. In addition, the personality of the President Wałęsa, who had little consideration for the letter of the law, facilitated an extensive reading of his competences.

The next stage in the development of the presidency concept is connected to the Small Constitution of 1992, which introduced a presidential-parliamentary system of government. For the first time, the constitution made the appointment of crucial government ministers (defence, foreign affairs and internal affairs) dependent de facto on the President's consent.[6] Moreover, the President was vested with general leadership in foreign affairs.[7] Finally, the President gained competence to dissolve the Chamber of Deputies under a number of circumstances, and indeed took advantage of it by dissolving the parliament in 1993.[8] In practice, this system tilted the balance towards a presidential system of government, yet, as it transpired, this was only a temporary alteration.

The Constitutional Commission of the National Assembly (1992–97), endowed with the task of drafting a new constitution, could draw inspiration from a number of past experiences when designing the presidency. Specifically, the interbellum constitutions offered two drastically different concepts of the office. Before its 1926 amendment, the March Constitution adopted the office of President in the shape typical of the parliamentary system of government, while the April Constitution offered an authoritarian vision of the presidency. However, these two models wielded no influence. The political strategy of the time prevailed in the decision over the shape of the presidency. As has been mentioned, in the presidential elections of 1995, Lech Wałęsa's competitor won, which influenced the direction taken by the Constitutional Commission. As a consequence, the competences of the President under the Constitution of 1997 and his or her position within the system of separation and balance of powers largely reflect the political circumstances at the time of drafting. The drafters pondered whether it was best to include the

[5] Article 16 of the April Constitution of 1935.
[6] Article 61 of the Small Constitution of 1992.
[7] ibid art 32(1).
[8] ibid art 4(5).

President among the organs of the executive power – which was the case under the Small Constitution – as this model would complicate the vision of a neutral presidency and endanger the President's function as political referee in cases of disagreement between the parliamentary majority and the Council of Ministers.[9] The difficulties of the drafters are evident in the Constitution's unclear division of tasks and competences between the President, the Prime Minister and two of the ministers (foreign affairs and defence).[10] In addition, the adopted model of the executive reflects a mix between the French semi-presidential system and the German chancellor system, raising questions about their compatibility.[11] Such an approach has its advantages and disadvantages, as will be discussed in this chapter.

B. The Direct Election of the President by the People

Without doubt, the system of election of the Polish President adopted in 1990 is inspired by the method of election of the President in the French Fifth Republic.[12] The systems share a number of striking similarities.[13] The nation elects the President for a five-year term in universal, equal and direct elections by secret ballot.[14] The candidate who receives more than half of the valid votes becomes the President. In cases where none of the candidates has amassed the required majority of votes in the first round, a second round between the two candidates with the largest number of votes is held within 14 days of the first vote. The candidate with the higher number of votes in the second round is elected President. Thus far, the second round has been necessary in all but one out of the presidential elections under the Constitution of 1997. In 2000, Aleksander Kwaśniewski, who was running for re-election, won the presidential elections in the first round.

The Supreme Court confirms the validity of elections.[15] The President assumes the office after taking an oath before the National Assembly,

[9] P Sarnecki, *Prezydent Rzeczypospolitej Polskiej. Komentarz do przepisów* (Kraków, Zakamycze, 2000) 28.

[10] Grzybowski (n 1) 60.

[11] ibid.

[12] S Boyron, *The Constitution of France: A Contextual Analysis* (Oxford, Hart Publishing, 2013) 58.

[13] ibid 57. Compare art 7 of the Constitution de la République française du 4 octobre 1958 ('Constitution of France').

[14] Article 127 of the Constitution. On these principles, see ch 3.

[15] Article 129(1) of the Constitution.

which also marks the first day of the five-year presidency, with a possibility of re-election for one more term.[16] It is not possible for the same individual to become President for a third term, even with a break in between terms. In practice, only Aleksander Kwaśniewski, who served as the President between 1995 and 2000, was re-elected in 2000.

The Constitution specifies that presidential elections should take place at least 100 days and at most 75 days before the end of the term of the President in office.[17] In case of the office becoming vacant, within 14 days, the Marshal of the Chamber of Deputies orders new elections to take place within 60 days.

The electoral system is as follows: Polish citizens of 35 years of age, who have full electoral franchise for the Chamber of Deputies, have the passive right to vote and can stand as a candidate in the elections if supported by at least 100,000 citizens who themselves have the right to vote in the elections for the Chamber of Deputies.[18] Citizens who wish to put forward a presidential candidate and run a presidential campaign for him or her are required to create an electoral committee for that candidate.[19] These candidates must be proposed at least 45 days before the election day.[20] In practice, neither the requirement of forming an electoral committee nor that of collecting 100,000 signatures has proven a particular obstacle to the number of candidates participating in the elections. In the six presidential elections between 1990 and 2015, the lowest number of candidates was six (in 1990), while in other years the number varied between 10 and 17.

The formal requirements are not particularly demanding in comparison to the presidential election. For example, in France potential candidates must receive signed nominations from a minimum of 500 elected representatives from at least 30 departments.[21] First, the Electoral Code does not set any particular conditions concerning the educational background or residency of the candidate.[22] Second, the electoral system does not prevent the emergence of random candidates. For instance, in the second round of the 1990 elections, a candidate, Stan Tymiński, arrived in the country just before the elections. The Electoral Code does not foresee any type of pre-selection process such as primaries in

[16] ibid art 130.
[17] ibid art 128(1) of the Constitution.
[18] ibid art 127(3) of the Constitution.
[19] Article 297 § 1 of the Electoral Code.
[20] ibid art 303 §1.
[21] See Boyron (n 12) 65.
[22] Article 297 §1 of the Electoral Code.

political parties. Finally, there is no parity requirement and the number of female presidential candidates remains very low. There was only one female candidate in the 2005 and 2015 elections, while no women ran in the remaining elections (1990,1995 and 2000).

Any Polish citizen of 18 years of age, who has not been deprived of his or her right to vote, has the active right to vote in the presidential elections.[23] The electoral turnout oscillates around 50 per cent.[24] The elections are preceded by an electoral campaign, which is usually interesting and animates the political life of the state.

Electoral committees are eligible for limited unpaid political advertisement of their candidates on public television and radio.[25] A rule of electoral silence bans political campaigning on election day. A presidential campaign can be financed from a number of sources, including the funds of the political party, bank credit as well as (capped) contributions from Polish citizens who reside in Poland.[26] The electoral committee can start collecting and spending funds to finance the candidate as soon as the National Electoral Commission registers that committee. In recent campaigns, social media such as Twitter or Facebook – whose use by politicians remains unregulated in Poland – served the running candidates to promote their platforms and communicate with the electorate.[27]

The Constitution also indicates two situations where the office of the President can become vacant.[28] The first concerns cases where the President is temporarily unable to exercise his or her duties and informs the Marshal of the Chamber of Deputies of this fact, who then takes over the President's duties. If the President is unable to inform the Marshal, then the Constitutional Court, upon the Marshal's request, determines whether there is an impediment to the exercise of the office by the President. Such a situation has never arisen. The second concerns cases such as the death of the President, resignation from office, invalidity of the presidential elections, a declaration by the National Assembly that the President is permanently incapable of exercising his or her duties based on the state of his or her health, and dismissal of the President by the

[23] See ch 4.

[24] For example, in the 2015 presidential elections, 48.96 per cent of voters voted in the first round and 55.34 per cent voted in the second round. In comparison, in 2015, 50.92 per cent of voters voted in the parliamentary elections for the Chamber of Deputies and 50.91 per cent in those for the Senate.

[25] Article 326 of the Electoral Code.

[26] ibid art 327.

[27] 'Szefernaker: Potrzebne są regulacje korzystania z mediów społecznościowych' *Dziennik Gazeta Prawna* (21 March 2018).

[28] Article 131 of the Constitution.

Tribunal of State. Again, in all these cases, the Marshal of the Chamber of Deputies (or if the latter is unable to do so, the Marshal of the Senate) assumes the duties of the President until the next elections. Indeed, this was the case in April 2010 after the crash of the presidential plane and the death of President Lech Kaczyński in Smoleńsk, Russia. The Marshal of the Chamber of the Deputies at the time, Bronisław Komorowski, assumed the duties of the President. Under these circumstances, the Constitution forbids the acting President from shortening the term of office of the Chamber of Deputies.[29] Following new elections in July 2010, Bronisław Komorowski became the President.

C. The President in the System of Separation and Balance of Powers

The position of the President under the Constitution of 1997 is circumscribed from three perspectives. First, the Constitution assigns to the President a set of specific tasks as the head of state.[30] Second, the President acts as a part of the double-headed executive with the Prime Minister. In fulfilling this function, the exercise of the President's competences demands either a countersignature – a formal action where the Prime Minister undersigns any official act of the President (*akt urzędowy*) – or is part of the presidential prerogative (an exclusive right of the President). Third, the President exercises the function of political referee. The position of the President has been shaped over time by political practice and by the jurisprudence of the superior courts.

The responsibilities of the President indicated in the Constitution reflect his or her general role as the head of state. Specifically, the Constitution identifies the President as the 'supreme representative of the Republic of Poland, and the guarantor of the continuity of state authority'.[31] Moreover, the President 'ensures observance of the Constitution, [and] safeguards the sovereignty and security of the state as well as the inviolability and integrity of its territory'.[32] The Constitutional Court has recognised these constitutional tasks of the President as functions or aims of the presidency.[33] The fundamental function of the head

[29] ibid art 131(4).
[30] ibid art 126.
[31] ibid art 126(1).
[32] ibid art 126(2).
[33] Constitutional Court, decision of 20 May 2009, Kpt 2/08, OTK ZU 5A/2009, poz. 78, point 5.7.

of state implies that the President is the guardian of all constitutional processes in the state. As head of state, the President exercises competences that are crucial for the functioning of each of the branches of government.[34] All the Presidents who have held the office since 1997 – Aleksander Kwaśniewski, Lech Kaczyński, Bronisław Komorowski and Andrzej Duda – attached great importance to the provisions regarding these competences and highlighted the role of the President, often referred to as the first person in the country. Such a perception of the function of the President has not raised controversy in scholarship or political practice.[35]

The competences concerning the executive power have a crucial significance for the functioning of the state. For instance, the President nominates and appoints the Prime Minister, appoints and dismisses the Council of Ministers, and executes changes with regard to the membership of the Council of Ministers at the request of the Prime Minister.[36] In practice, the mode of exercise of these competences depends on the political forces in power. If the President and the governing majority are politically homogeneous, no issues arise. The process of appointing and dismissing the government remains an internal matter for the governing party. This may look different in cases of cohabitation. For instance, this was the situation between 2007 and 2010, when the President and the Council of Ministers represented opposing political camps. In 2007, President Lech Kaczyński hesitated, on political-personal grounds, to appoint the Foreign Affairs Minister proposed by the Prime Minister Donald Tusk, but finally the appointment was made.[37]

The functions enshrined in Article 126 of the Constitution enable the President to act as a political referee. This is facilitated by the fact that the President is not politically responsible before parliament and, as a consequence, does not participate in political conflicts, generally remaining above them. This independence from parliament, together with a ban on holding any other office or public function with the exception of those connected to the office of the President, allows the President to maintain some distance from day-to-day politics while nonetheless wielding a certain degree of influence.[38] An example is the President's competence

[34] For the President's competences vis-a-vis the legislative and the judicial powers, see chs 3 and 5, respectively.

[35] Sarnecki (n 9) 43.

[36] See section III.A below.

[37] 'J. Kaczyński: nikt nie zbiera haków na Sikorskiego' *Dziennik Gazeta Prawna* (15 February 2010).

[38] Article 132 of the Constitution.

to call and chair the Cabinet Council which deals with state issues of particular importance, although it does not exercise the executive power.[39] The Cabinet Council was summoned prior to crucial political events, such as Poland's accession to the North Atlantic Treaty Organization (NATO) (1999). Similarly, a series of Cabinet Council meetings before 2004 chaired by President Aleksander Kwaśniewski concerned the progress of preparations for Poland's accession to the EU.

The exercise of the function of a political referee depends on a number of factors and it is hard to indicate specific circumstances in which it is likely to work best. For instance, the Cabinet Council was called when the President and the Prime Minister originated from the same political affiliation. One such example was the Cabinet Council summoned in 2013 concerning Poland's strategy in advance of its possible accession to the eurozone. However, it is significant that the Cabinet Council also met when the relevant state organs represented different political colours. The Cabinet Councils of 2008 concerning public health policy and the eurozone are apt examples. Finally, calling a Cabinet Council may lead to political tension between the President and the Prime Minister. For instance, in 2015, the Prime Minister asked the President to summon a Cabinet Council to debate the political priorities of the government in the upcoming months.[40] The President, originally from an opposition party, rejected this request.[41] Set against this background, the Cabinet Council is perceived as having a symbolic meaning.[42] Still, it is worth maintaining the Cabinet Council as it is never known in advance when a constitutional institution may turn out to be useful.[43]

The functions of the President may overlap with each other. Sometimes the President simultaneously exercises the function of the head of state and the chief of the executive power, for example, with regard to state finances. The President does not decide upon the deficit level of the state budget, yet he or she acts as a safeguard to ensure the timely approval of the budget bill by the Chamber of Deputies.[44] In principle,

[39] ibid art 141.

[40] 'Ewa Kopacz prosi Andrzeja Dudę o zwołanie Rady Gabinetowej' *Rzeczpospolita* (6 August 2015).

[41] See www.prezydent.pl/aktualnosci/wypowiedzi-prezydenta-rp/wywiady/art,10,polityka-zagraniczna-wymaga-profesjonalizmu-i-spokoju.html.

[42] D Dudek, *Autorytet Prezydenta a Konstytucja RP* (Lublin, Wydawnictwo KUL, 2013) 52–53.

[43] M Granat, *Prawo Konstytucyjne. Pytania i odpowiedzi* (Warsaw, Wolters Kluwer, 2018) 302.

[44] Articles 224–25 of the Constitution.

the President signs the budget or interim budget within seven days of its receipt from the Chamber of Deputies. If, within four months of the submission of the government's budget bill, the Chamber of Deputies fails to adopt the budget or submit it to the President to sign, the President may decide (within 14 days) to shorten the term of office of the Chamber of Deputies. In 2006, the Chamber of Deputies failed to find a sufficient majority to adopt the budget bill in that timeframe. Still, the President did not decide to use his prerogative to shorten the parliament's term, arguing that the coalition agreement that had been adopted in the meantime guaranteed the necessary majority to the government.[45]

The President is assisted in his or her duties by an office, the Presidential Chancellery (*Kancelaria Prezydenta*). The President appoints and dismisses the chief of the Presidential Chancellery and establishes its terms of reference, thereby deciding on its tasks.[46] The office – funded from state budget – organises and supports the President's activities, and provides legal and technical aid to the President.

D. The Problematic Double-Headed Executive: The Functions and Competences of the President

The above-noted double-headed design of the executive may lead to tension between the President and the Prime Minister with his or her cabinet. The grand functions of the presidency discussed earlier – namely, acting as head of state, exercising the executive power and being a political referee – do not directly reflect the rather moderate competences of the President foreseen in the Constitution. Traditionally, the competences of the President are ordered into four groups, concerning the parliament, the government, the armed forces, and the traditional competences of the head of state. The disjunction between the functions of the President and his or her constitutional competences reflects the difficulties encountered by the constitutional drafters, who struggled to find a suitable position for the President in the system of government.[47] This was evident in the two following examples. The first concerns the influence of the President on foreign affairs, including Poland's policy-making vis-a-vis the EU, while the second example illustrates the role of the President in defence policy.

[45] See www.prezydent.pl/archiwum-lecha-kaczynskiego/aktualnosci/rok-2006/art,150,146,wystapienie-prezydenta-rp.html.

[46] Article 143 of the Constitution.

[47] Grzybowski (n 1) 60. See section IIA above.

First, the President is the supreme representative of the state and guardian of the continuity of state authority.[48] However, the competences of the President in foreign policy are limited. In the area of foreign affairs, the President should cooperate with the Prime Minister and the relevant minister in each case.[49] In practice, this cooperation can be troublesome and usually depends on whether the President and the Foreign Affairs Minister are attached to the same political powers, or whether their relationship is based on cohabitation. Their cooperation relates to the choice of ambassadors and other important functionaries of the diplomatic corps. For instance, in 2008 the President declined to appoint the ambassador to Slovakia recommended by the Foreign Affairs Minister due to 'loyalty issues' and delayed decisions with regard to other appointments.[50] In comparison, it is worth highlighting that the 1992 Small Constitution was more consistent in this respect. The President exercised general leadership in the area of foreign affairs, while the role of the Foreign Affairs Minister was limited to aiding the President in contacts with other states.[51] Individual decisions of the President, such as not to appoint an ambassador, a public servant or a judge, could not (under the 1992 Constitution) and cannot (under the 1997 Constitution) be challenged before the courts (administrative or ordinary) or before the Constitutional Court. The case discussed below, in which the Constitutional Court was competent to intervene in this area, had a different legal character.

Until 2009, it remained unclear whether Poland's EU policy belonged to foreign affairs or whether it was a separate policy matter. In the end, the Constitutional Court solved this issue in the most prominent competence conflict case to date.[52] The so-called 'chair dispute' concerned the situation in which both the President and the Prime Minister interpreted the Constitution as allowing each of them to represent Poland at the European Council meetings that gather heads of state or government of the EU Member States to define the general direction and priorities of the EU.[53] At the time, the President (Lech Kaczyński) and the Prime Minister (Donald Tusk) were affiliated to different political powers – Law and Justice, and Civic Platform, respectively – raising the possibility of them

[48] Article 126(1) of the Constitution.
[49] ibid art 133(3).
[50] 'Dyplomaci odblokowani' *Rzeczpospolita* (1 September 2008).
[51] Article 32 of the Small Constitution.
[52] Constitutional Court, Kpt 2/08.
[53] Article 15 TFEU.

wishing to present different visions of Poland's position at the European Council. The Constitutional Court, which was called by the Prime Minister to adjudicate concerning this competence conflict, indicated that it is for the Council of Ministers to determine the stance of Poland at the European Council meeting, and that the Prime Minister represents Poland at those meetings and presents the agreed stance. The President, as the supreme representative of Poland, can decide to participate in a specific European Council meeting if the President sees it as useful for the exercise of his or her constitutional tasks indicated in the Constitution. The President and the Prime Minister (and competent government minister) should cooperate to enable the President's participation in specific European Council meetings. The aim of the cooperation is to safeguard the uniformity of actions taken on behalf of Poland vis-a-vis the EU. This cooperation should enable the President to refer to the position adopted by the Polish government, as well as the extent and manner in which the President intends to participate in the European Council meeting in question. This judgment of the Constitutional Court exemplifies the interpretation of the general provisions of the Constitution on the functions of the President and competences of the Council of Ministers.[54] In practice, this interpretation has now been consolidated and is respected by the political powers.[55]

Second, the President ensures observance of the Constitution and safeguards the sovereignty and security of the state, as well as the inviolability and integrity of its territory.[56] To this extent, although the President is the Supreme Commander of the Armed Forces, in peace time this competence is exercised through the Defence Minister.[57] In this capacity, the President is aided by the Council of National Security, an advisory body. In practice, the notion of 'exercise through' has raised certain controversies. For instance, the President remains the Supreme Commander of the Armed Forces, but, as it transpired, was unable to influence or dismiss the Defence Minister. Accordingly, in an attempt to exert some power over the Defence Minister, in 2017 the President refused to promote the officers put forward by that minister to the post of general. This conflict was solved a year later only after the Defence Minister was dismissed due to the reorganisation of the Council of

[54] Articles 126 and 146 of the Constitution.

[55] P Sarnecki, 'Spory kompetencyjne przed Trybunałem Konstytucyjnym' (2009) *Przegląd Sejmowy* 9.

[56] Article 126(2) of the Constitution.

[57] ibid art 134(2).

Ministers.[58] In contrast, the Small Constitution offered more clarity in this area. The President exercised general leadership in the area of internal and external security of the state.[59]

It must be highlighted that the position of the President is quite dynamic. Article 126 of the Constitution offers a rather broad framework for the President's actions, as long as they fall within the scope of, and are in accordance with, the Constitution. Although this rather pompous-sounding provision does not confer any competence on the President, it is not merely symbolic. In fact, its indeterminate contours benefit the President, permitting the extension of his or her political presence. In this, the President is also helped by the system of countersignature and the lack of political responsibility before parliament, which separates the President from ongoing political issues and enables the exercise of an additional function as a political referee.[60] Finally, the constitutional boundaries of the presidency do not limit the esteem of this office. The President, as the 'first person of the Republic of Poland' and its 'supreme representative', combines the personal and institutional dimensions of the presidency.

In sum, the President cannot be described simply as one component of the executive. The constitutional system of Poland designates the President as the most important organ of state power. Despite this constitutional importance of the presidency, the position can be exercised in a weak or a strong manner. Accordingly, the President's role can be merely ceremonial. Putting it more figuratively, the President can be so weak that his or her role could be compared to the 'guardian of the chandeliers' of the Presidential Palace. But it can also be strong. For example, in 2017, the Law and Justice government proposed a set of bills reforming the judiciary. After days of demonstrations and threats that EU institutions would trigger the so-called 'Article 7 TEU procedure' against Poland for breaches of EU values, President Andrzej Duda – also formerly affiliated to the Law and Justice party – vetoed the proposed bills concerning the Supreme Court and National Council of the Judiciary.[61] The President's veto was welcomed by the wider society, highlighting the importance of the President's competences as exercised vis-a-vis the government

[58] 'Rekonstrukcja rządu. Antoni Macierewicz straci stanowisko' *Rzeczpospolita* (9 January 2018).

[59] Article 34 of the Small Constitution of 1992.

[60] See section II.E below.

[61] 'Poland's President Duda Vetoes Judicial Reforms after Protests' *BBC News* (24 July 2017).

and parliament. Nonetheless, the veto did not halt Poland's collision course with the rule of law. Ultimately, new laws introducing in-depth changes into the court system were adopted and signed into law by the President.[62]

E. Countersignature and Presidential Prerogatives

Although the Constitution vests the President with a set of grand functions (see above), it simultaneously strengthens the system of countersignature, making the acts of the President dependent on the consent of the Prime Minister.[63] The notion of countersignature is central for explaining the position of the President in the Polish system of government. Technically, the Constitution uses neither the notions of countersignature nor prerogative, although they are both key instruments of presidential power.[64] The countersignature is given by the Prime Minister to an official act of the President which can have the legal form of a regulation (*rozporządzenie*) or an executive order (*zarządzenie*).[65] Although the Constitution does not determine when the President needs to obtain a countersignature for an official act, countersignature is always presumed. Without a countersignature, any official presidential act is void; this thereby limits the President within the executive power, as the President cannot act without the knowledge of the Prime Minister. The countersignature implies that the President and the Prime Minister cooperate, simultaneously transferring the responsibility for an official act from the head of state to parliament and making the Prime Minister, who signs President's official acts, fully responsible for the act in question.[66] Beyond this legal function of the countersignature, politically, the countersignature leads to a weakening of the independent position of the President in the system of rationalised parliamentarism under the Constitution of 1997.[67]

This design of countersignature stands in contrast to its construction in a classic parliamentary system. In the case of the March Constitution of 1921, the countersignature encompassed every governing act of

[62] See ch 5.

[63] See S Patyra, *Prawnoustrojowy status Prezesa Rady Ministrów w świetle Konstytucji z 2 kwietnia 1997* (Warsaw, Wydawnictwo Sejmowe, 2002) 138–39.

[64] Article 144 of the Constitution.

[65] ibid art 142.

[66] See Dudek (n 42) 63 ff.

[67] See ch 2.

the President.[68] The government was required to have knowledge of the content of the acts of the President. The governing acts of the President received a countersignature of two organs: the Prime Minister and the relevant minister. In this way, the countersignature completely excluded the President from independent decision-making.[69] In contrast, the Small Constitution adopted a different concept of countersignature, thereby reflecting the idea of a strong presidency. The President's acts required the signature of the Prime Minister or the relevant minister.[70] This construction enabled the President to choose between the Prime Minister and a minister, and thus to 'play' with the government in this regard, even more so in the light of coalition governments at the time.

Presidential prerogatives present an exception from the requirement (and principle) of a countersignature. The Constitution lists 30 prerogatives of the President.[71] If the President's official act concerns a subject from that list, a signature of the Prime Minister is not required. In general, the prerogatives can be grouped into four clusters. First, the President can act independently on issues that concern relations with the parliament (for instance, calling parliamentary elections or proposing new legislation). Second, issues connected with the appointment and responsibility of the government, such as nomination and appointment of the Prime Minister, belong to the President's prerogatives. The third group of prerogatives concerns the appointment of other state institutions, such as the President and Vice President of the Constitutional Court, or of two members of the National Council of Broadcasting and Television. The last group of prerogatives includes what can be seen as the traditional tasks of the head of state: pardoning, appointing judges of all types of courts, and conferring awards and decorations. Therefore, on those four types of issues, the President decides without the political scrutiny of the Prime Minister and thus of the parliament.

Each of the prerogatives of the President is important for the functioning of the state. The best example of this importance is that the President appoints judges to all courts at the request of the National Council of the Judiciary (the Council).[72] In some cases, this model of judicial appointments has caused problems. The request of the Council is a necessary element of the appointment procedure, yet it is not

[68] Article 44 of the March Constitution of 1921.
[69] See Sarnecki (n 9).
[70] Article 47 of the Small Constitution of 1992.
[71] Article 144(3) of the Constitution.
[72] ibid art 179.

binding for the President. In 2007, for the first time, President Lech Kaczyński refused the appointment of nine candidates, while in 2016 President Andrzej Duda declined to appoint 10 candidates.[73] As a consequence, the individuals involved, who were already judges, could not take the higher judicial position to which they aspired. Although the President can refuse to make a judicial appointment, he or she cannot put forward his or her own candidate.[74] At the same time, the President cannot leave the request of the Council unanswered.[75] The Supreme Administrative Court found that in the process of appointing judges, the President does not exercise a public administrative function that could be questioned in a complaint before an administrative court.[76] The judicial nominees not appointed by the President attempted to launch proceedings before the Constitutional Court. However, the Constitutional Court found their constitutional complaints inadmissible.[77] In practice, the relationship between the President (who appoints judges) and the Council (which puts forward the candidates) has sometimes had a conflictual character. Since 2015, the nature and scope of the President's prerogative to appoint judges has represented one of the most contested issues, as is discussed in the following chapter on the judiciary. The question of judicial nominations also raises other problems linked to the composition of the Council and its disputed compliance with the Constitution.[78]

Another example of the controversial exercise of prerogatives by the President to date has been the pardoning of the head of the Central Anti-Corruption Office and three high functionaries of this office who had links to the governing party.[79] In 2015, the court of first instance found these persons guilty of transgression of competence and illegal activities, and sentenced them to prison. Shortly thereafter, President Andrzej Duda pardoned the individuals in question, arguing that he wished to 'free the

[73] 'Prezydent Andrzej Duda odmówił nominacji 10 sędziom' *Rzeczpospolita* (29 June 2016).

[74] Constitutional Court, decision of 23 June 2008, Kpt 1/08, OTK ZU 5A/2008, poz 97.

[75] Between 2009 and 2012, the Law on Ordinary Courts offered the President one month to decide on the nomination. However, the Constitutional Court has declared this limitation to be unconstitutional. Constitutional Court, judgment of 5 June 2012, K 18/09, OTK ZU 6A/2012, poz 63.

[76] Supreme Administrative Court, decision of 9 October 2012, I OSK 1872/12, maintained in 2017: judgment of 7 December 2017, I OSK 857/17.

[77] See Constitutional Court, decision of 19 June 2012, SK 37/08, OTK ZU 6A/2012, poz 69.

[78] See ch 5.

[79] R Piotrowski, 'Stosowanie prawa łaski w świetle Konstytucji RP' (2006) 45 *Studia Iuridica* 165.

courts from the problems involved in deciding this case'.[80] The Supreme Court rightly decided that the power of pardon can apply only where an individual was convicted in a final court judgment.[81] For this reason, the exercise of the right to pardon before a final court judgment did not trigger any procedural consequences. In other words, the President may pardon whoever he or she wishes, but the procedure of pardoning has to follow the formal requirements indicated by the Supreme Court, one of them being a final, convicting court judgment in the case at hand. Thus, the President can exercise his or her prerogative to pardon, yet must act within the legal boundaries of the Constitution and statutes.[82] However, in a later decision, the Constitutional Court adopted a different view and decided that the President's right to pardon cannot be limited by statutory law.[83] Both judicial decisions indicate the profound and alarming changes within the judiciary.[84]

F. The Constitutional Accountability of the President

One of the consequences of the parliamentary system of government is a lack of political responsibility of the President before the parliament. In the system of separation of powers, political differences between the Chamber of Deputies and the President do not have any negative impact on the President's mandate. The Chamber of Deputies has no tools at hand that would enable holding the President politically accountable. The Constitution instead foresees that the President is constitutionally responsible before the Tribunal of State for infringement of the Constitution.[85] This form of constitutional accountability is quite typical in the Polish constitutional tradition, having already been a feature of the March Constitution. In contrast, under the April Constitution, the President was not politically or constitutionally accountable before the parliament or any other organ, but was responsible only 'before God and history'.[86]

[80] See www.prezydent.pl/aktualnosci/wydarzenia/art,69,postanowilem-uwolnic-wymiar-sprawiedliwosci-od-sprawy-m-kaminskiego.html.

[81] Supreme Court, resolution of 31 May 2017, I KZP 4/17.

[82] Article 126(3) of the Constitution.

[83] Constitutional Court, judgment of 17 July 2018, K 9/17, OTK ZU A/2018, poz 48.

[84] See chs 5 and 6.

[85] Article 145 of the Constitution. See J Ciapała, 'Zagadnienie odpowiedzialności prawnej Prezydenta Rzeczypospolitej Polskiej' (2005) *Przegląd Sejmowy* 101. On the Tribunal of State, see ch 6.

[86] Articles 15 and 71 of the April Constitution.

The procedure is launched through a motion by 140 members of the National Assembly (both chambers of the parliament). Next, to put the President before the Tribunal of State requires a resolution supported by at least two-thirds of the National Assembly (374 members). At that moment, the President is suspended from exercising his or her office. If the Tribunal of State finds the President accountable for the constitutional delict, he or she loses active and passive voting rights for all types of elections, cannot hold any directorial position or function of particular responsibility in state organs or social organisations, is stripped of all decorations and honorary titles, and is ultimately removed from office.[87]

Beyond constitutional delicts, the Constitution also foresees criminal responsibility for committing a crime, again before the Tribunal of State.[88] Therefore, the President can be held accountable before the Tribunal of State for a constitutional delict or for a crime, or for both at the same time. The fact that the President is called before the Tribunal of State instead of a criminal court in the event that a crime is committed is a substitute for the formal immunity existing in other systems.[89] For example, the President was covered by formal immunity under the April Constitution.[90]

In practice, none of the previous Presidents has been called before or held accountable by the Tribunal of State as of 2019. So far, the institution of constitutional accountability in the case of the President, as well as other relevant state organs, has not been put into practice.[91]

III. THE COUNCIL OF MINISTERS AND GOVERNMENT ADMINISTRATION

A. The Formation and Accountability of the Council of Ministers

In the parliamentary system of government, the head of state appoints the Council of Ministers (the government or cabinet), which is politically

[87] Article 25 of the Law of 26 March 1982 on Tribunal of State, JL 2016 Pos 2050.

[88] This includes also fiscal crimes on the basis of Law of 29 August 2003 amending the Law on the Tribunal of State, JL 2003 No 175 Pos 1692.

[89] K Grajewski, 'O pojęciu i rodzajach immunitetu w świetle Konstytucji RP (parlamentarny immunitet materialny i procesowy, przywilej nietykalności oraz szczególny immunitet głowy państwa)' in M Kłopocka-Jasińska and M Filipowska-Tuthill (eds), *Immunitet parlamentarny i immunitet głowy państwa z perspektywy konstytucyjnej i karnoprocesowej* (Warsaw, Elipsa, 2018) 29–30.

[90] Article 15(2) of the April Constitution.

[91] See ch 6.

accountable to the parliament. This principle has been present in the Polish system of government since 1989. The process of forming the government is the same as in a classic parliamentary system, with added elements from rationalised parliamentarism.[92] This process foresees up to three attempts to form a government, resembling the relevant procedure in the German Basic Law.[93]

Under the first procedure, the President nominates a candidate for Prime Minister, who then proposes the composition of a Council of Ministers. The President appoints the Prime Minister and his or her cabinet, and accepts their oaths of office. This appointment has to take place within 14 days since the first sitting of the Chamber of Deputies or, if the previous Council of Ministers resigned, within 14 days since the President's acceptance of that resignation. Next, the Prime Minister presents to the Chamber of Deputies his or her programme of government (exposé) requesting a vote of confidence. This requires the support of an absolute majority of votes in the presence of at least half of the statutory number of MPs.

If the first procedure fails – the government did not receive sufficient support – the second procedure is triggered. Within 14 days, the Chamber of Deputies itself choses a Prime Minister with ministers proposed by him or her. The same parliamentary majority as in the first procedure needs to support the proposed government. The President then appoints the government and accepts the oath of office from its members.

Should this second procedure fail too, a third attempt is launched. The third procedure is identical to the first, with the exception that the Chamber of Deputies grants the vote of confidence with only a simple majority of votes in the presence of at least half of the statutory number of MPs. However, in the event that this procedure should also fail, the Constitution obliges the President to shorten the term of the Chamber of Deputies and order new elections. Thus far, all but one of the governments existing under the Constitution of 1997 were formed on the first attempt, the exception being the minority government of Marek Belka in 2004, which succeeded only at the third attempt.

The Constitution allows the MPs and senators to be a member of the Council of Ministers and secretaries of state in government administration simultaneously.[94] Indeed, many of the government ministers remain MPs.

[92] See ch 2.

[93] Articles 154–55 of the Constitution. Compare art 63 of Grundgesetz für die Bundesrepublik Deutschland vom 23. Mai 1949 (BGBl. S. 1), zuletzt geändert durch Artikel 1 des Gesetzes vom 13. Juli 2017 (BGBl. I S. 2347) ('German Basic Law').

[94] Article 103 of the Constitution.

This design tends to weaken the principle of the separation of powers.[95] Moreover, it impedes possibilities through which the persons in question can be held accountable as they may use parliamentary immunity as a shield. For instance, in 2016, the Secretary of State in the Ministry of Justice, an MP of the governing majority, attempted to use his parliamentary immunity to protect himself from a civil lawsuit from local activists who felt offended by his statements in a radio interview.[96] The minister argued that his statements were made in his capacity as an MP, so he was protected by parliamentary immunity. The relevant court agreed with the minister, but halted the proceedings to await the decision of the Chamber of Deputies on waiving the immunity.

Another drawback of holding positions simultaneously is that ministers may miss parliamentary votes or cause problems when a quorum is needed to proceed with parliamentary business due to their ministerial obligations. For instance, in the Chamber of Deputies of the eighth term, the predominance of members of the Council of Ministers remain MPs.[97] This is problematic in the light of the narrow majority of the governing party. The presence of the ministers during the votes in the Chamber of Deputies is thus often a condition of accomplishing of its political aims.

The Council of Ministers is politically accountable to the Chamber of Deputies, both collectively and individually. Political accountability is collective in cases where there is a political discrepancy between the parliamentary majority and the Council of Ministers. In those instances, the Constitution foresees that the Chamber of Deputies, acting by a majority of the statutory number of MPs, can pass a vote of no confidence.[98] The vote of no confidence is triggered by a motion of at least 46 MPs, which must be constructive in character: it is obliged to name a new candidate for Prime Minister. This construction is again inspired by the relevant German regulation of the Basic Law and replaced the simple no confidence vote of the Small Constitution.[99] The vote can be held no earlier than seven days after the motion is put forward. If the vote of no confidence succeeds, the President appoints the new Prime Minister and then the ministers. If the vote of no confidence fails, the next such motion

[95] See ch 3.

[96] 'Patryk Jaki straci immunitet? "Sejmowa arytmetyka jest jednak nieubłagana"' *Gazeta Wyborcza Opole* (25 September 2017).

[97] As of July 2019, 15 out of 23 ministers of the Mateusz Morawiecki government remain simultaneously MPs.

[98] Article 158 of the Constitution.

[99] Grzybowski (n 1) 62. Compare art 67 of the German Basic Law.

can be put to a vote no sooner than three months after the submission of the previous motion, unless a higher threshold of 115 MPs supports the new motion. Holding the government collectively accountable is the only avenue provided by the 1997 Constitution to replace the Prime Minister or the government. In practice, under the current Constitution, the Chamber of Deputies has considered a constructive vote of no confidence for the Council of Ministers on four occasions: in March 2013 and July 2014 against Donald Tusk's government, in April 2017 against Beata Szydło's government and in December 2018 against Mateusz Morawiecki's government, in all cases triggered by the strongest opposition parties. None of those attempts to change the government was successful.

Naturally, beyond collective accountability, the Constitution attributes political accountability to individual members of the government.[100] This concerns cases of political disagreement between the Chamber of Deputies and a specific government minister. At least 69 MPs must put forward a motion for a vote of no confidence for the minister in question, with the vote held no sooner than seven days after the initial motion. The Chamber of Deputies then decides by a majority of the statutory number of MPs on the political accountability of the minister at stake. If successful, the President recalls the relevant minister. If, however, the vote of no confidence fails, the procedure can again be repeated no sooner than three months after the submission of the previous motion, unless 115 MPs support that motion. In practice, multiple motions of no confidence in individual ministers have failed. Only twice (in 1999 and 2004) was the opposition close to reaching the relevant majority.[101]

In sum, the procedures to hold ministers politically accountable, both individually and collectively, illustrate the characteristics of rationalised parliamentarism.[102] They are designed, in terms of thresholds and timing, to prevent frequent government change, while at the same time preserving a strong position for the Prime Minister and his or her ministers.

Besides political accountability for the activities of the Council of Ministers, the Prime Minister and the ministers can be held constitutionally accountable before the Tribunal of State for infringements of the Constitution or statutes (constitutional delicts), as well as for committing an offence connected with the duties of the office.[103] On a motion

[100] Article 159 of the Constitution.

[101] J Kuciński, *Sejmowa kontrola działalności rządu z perspektywy prawnoustrojowej i praktyki politycznej* (Warsaw, Elipsa, 2017) 445.

[102] See ch 2.

[103] Article 156 of the Constitution.

of the President or 115 MPs, the Chamber of Deputies decides by a three-fifths majority of the statutory number of MPs whether to hold a member of the Council of Ministers accountable before the Tribunal of State.[104] So far, none of the motions to launch proceedings before the Tribunal of State has attracted sufficient support in the Chamber of Deputies. There were only two – failed – motions, in 2012, against the former Prime Minister Jarosław Kaczyński and the Minister of Justice Zbigniew Ziobro. The only successful example of a case where a group of ministers were brought before the Tribunal of State took place in the 1990s under the Small Constitution, which provided for an analogous model of constitutional accountability.

The Constitution also foresees a vote of confidence in the Council of Ministers.[105] In that case, it is the Prime Minister rather than the MPs who, at any time during the parliamentary term, puts forward a suitable motion. The Chamber of Deputies decides on the motion at a forthcoming sitting or even during an ongoing sitting if the motion was made then. During the debate, the Prime Minister answers the questions posed by the MPs. Thereafter, the Chamber of Deputies grants a motion of confidence in the Council of Ministers by a majority of votes in the presence of at least half of the statutory number of MPs. If the vote of confidence is not successful, the Prime Minister must submit a letter of resignation to the President. In practice, the Chamber of Deputies granted a vote of confidence to all of the governments that requested it: in 2003 (the minority Leszek Miller government), in 2004 (the Marek Belka government), in 2012 and 2014 (the Donald Tusk government) and in 2018 (the Mateusz Morawiecki government). In Tusk's case, the Prime Minister argued before the Chamber of Deputies that the vote of confidence was necessary after the eavesdropping scandal in which some of the ministers were illegally recorded in a restaurant.[106] The recordings were made public, casting a shadow over some of the ministers. The aim of this vote, and the other ones, was to confirm the political mandate of the government in the face of strong criticism or in order to seek support for its policies. For instance, in the eavesdropping scandal, the Prime Minister contended that he needed to confirm the mandate of his government before difficult talks in Brussels.

The Constitution requires that the outgoing Prime Minister should submit the resignation of the Council of Ministers at the first sitting of

[104] On the particularities of the procedure, see ch 6.

[105] Article 160 of the Constitution.

[106] 'Afera podsłuchowa nie obaliła rządu. Donald Tusk uzyskał wotum zaufania' *Dziennik Gazeta Prawna* (25 June 2014).

a newly elected Chamber of Deputies.[107] This natural consequence of parliamentary elections illustrates the legal and political link between the government and the term of the Chamber of Deputies (parliamentary majority). However, as mentioned earlier, the failure to pass a vote of confidence in the Council of Ministers or a successfully passed motion of no confidence obliges the President to accept the resignation of the government. The President, after accepting the resignation of the Council of Ministers, obliges it to continue its duties until the appointment of a new government. If, however, the Prime Minister himself or herself resigns from office, the President may refuse that resignation.

The President's acceptance of the Council of Ministers' resignation affects the wider government administration. The secretaries of state, undersecretaries of state, voivodes[108] and vice voivodes must also submit their respective resignations. The newly elected Prime Minister will then decide within three months whether to keep those officials in office. On the one hand, this allows for some continuity in the government administration, while, on the other hand, the new Prime Minister has the opportunity to make his or her own appointments to the bureaucracy. This link between the legal status of the government and the government administration is a manifestation of rationalised parliamentarism.

B. The Prime Minister in Rationalised Parliamentarism

The 1997 Constitution introduced the system of parliamentary government, 'rationalising' some of its elements.[109] One of the manifestations of rationalised parliamentarism is the strengthening of the role of the Prime Minister as the key actor of the government. The position of the Prime Minister is often characterised as that of a 'semi-chancellor', being close to that of the German chancellor. The Prime Minister's position is strong but has been adapted to the national constitutional context. It is worth highlighting that in Poland the government, especially in recent years, has been led by women – Ewa Kopacz (Civic Platform, 2014–15) and Beata Szydło (Law and Justice, 2015–17). Before this, in the 1990s Hanna Suchocka (Democratic Union, 1992–93) became the first female Prime Minister.

[107] Article 162 of the Constitution.
[108] Voivode is the representative of the Council of Ministers in a voivodeship. See ch 6.
[109] See ch 2.

The office of Prime Minister has four main components.[110] First, the Prime Minister represents the Council of Ministers: he or she requests the President to carry out changes in the membership of the Council of Ministers, and decides on the fate of the government by handing in the resignation of the entire Council. Second, the Prime Minister is vested with the tools to wield the executive power. He or she manages the work of the government, ensures the implementation of its policies and specifies the manner in which that implementation takes place. To this extent, the Prime Minister coordinates and controls the work of the ministers and sets their tasks. This competence resembles the power of the German chancellor to determine the general policy guidelines of its cabinet.[111] Therefore, the Prime Minister is not 'first among equals', as is the case in a classic parliamentary system, but is rather the undisputed leader of the Council of Ministers. Moreover, the Prime Minister, within the limits and by means specified by the Constitution, supervises the local self-government.[112] Lastly, he or she is the official superior officer of the employees of the wider government administration. The third characteristic feature of the Polish rationalised parliamentarism is that the Prime Minister has a decisive voice on the political direction taken by the cabinet. For instance, first the government of Beata Szydło and then of her successor, Mateusz Morawiecki, focused on the implementation of extensive social programmes, offering financial support for each consecutive child, or for school supplies at the beginning of a new school year. The fourth element is the mechanism of a constructive vote of no confidence, representing the sole admissible avenue to introduce a new Prime Minister. Overthrowing the Prime Minister means the end for the Council of Ministers in office. In addition, as mentioned earlier, the Prime Minister can decide to submit the resignation of the cabinet *en bloc*. In principle, such a situation does not present the President with a prerequisite to order new elections.

The Chancellery of the Prime Minister serves the Prime Minister and the Council of Ministers.[113] Its tasks include, inter alia, the supervision of activities of the government, coordination with regard to the cooperation with the parliament and the President, as well as publishing the official journals containing universally and internally binding laws, the

[110] Article 148 of the Constitution.
[111] Grzybowski (n 1) 62. Compare art 65, first sentence of the German Basic Law.
[112] See ch 7.
[113] Article 26 of the Law of 8 August 1996 on the Council of Ministers, JL 2012 Pos 392, JL 2015 Pos 1064, JL 2018 Pos 1669.

'Dziennik Ustaw' (DzU, *Journal of Laws of the Republic of Poland*) and the 'Monitor Polski' (MP, *Polish Monitor*), respectively.[114]

C. The Council of Ministers

The Council of Ministers is not only a multi-person body, but is in fact a body that potentially encompasses a whole system of governing the state. As an executive arm, the Council of Ministers is linked to the parliament, especially to the parliamentary majority. As was already mentioned, MPs and senators qualify for the Council of Ministers; however, ministers can also originate from outside of parliament.

Primarily, the Council of Ministers consists of the Prime Minister and ministers.[115] In addition, Deputy Prime Ministers and presidents of 'committees specified in statutes' can be appointed to the Council of Ministers. For example, the Chairperson of the Committee of European Integration was a member of the government between 1996 and 2009. In practice, since the early 2000s, such committees are no longer being created. Thus, in principle, the Council of Ministers consists of the Prime Minister, Deputy Prime Ministers and ministers. All governments formed under the 1997 Constitution were coalition governments formed by at least two cooperating political parties.[116]

The Constitution differentiates the legal status of ministers.[117] Ministers may either lead a particular department of government administration (eg, labour, health or foreign affairs), may perform a specific task allocated to them by the Prime Minister or may exercise both functions contemporaneously. In practice, the position of a minister who leads a department of government administration is stronger in legal and political terms: he or she belongs to the group of chief institutions of government administration and can issue regulations, an essential instrument of governing. The ministers who perform a task allocated by the Prime Minister – ministers without portfolio – do not possess such competences. The Constitution demands a statutory regulation of the scope of responsibility of ministers. However, in this respect, the relevant statute offers only a framework for the functioning of the government and delegates power to the Prime Minister to set the specific tasks of the

[114] See ch 3.
[115] Article 147 of the Constitution.
[116] See ch 3.
[117] Article 149 of the Constitution.

ministers.[118] To this extent, the Prime Minister issues so-called attributing regulations, which expire automatically when a minister is recalled or when a new cabinet is established. Until a new regulation enters into force, the Prime Minister himself or herself exercises the tasks of the minister in question.[119]

The Prime Minister can also appoint Deputy Prime Ministers at his or her own discretion. In practice, this is usually connected to the establishment of a coalition government, and such positions are frequently granted to the leaders of the coalition parties, cementing the agreement, or to a particular minister to enhance his or her dossier. For instance, the leader of the Agreement Party (*Porozumienie*), which has been part of the coalition government established in 2015, holds the position of Deputy Prime Minister. A Deputy Prime Minister does not have his or her own competences, but instead executes, on behalf of the Prime Minister, those specifically indicated by the Prime Minister. The Prime Minister and his or her deputies may simultaneously be ministers. Frequently, the position of Finance Minister is combined with that of a Deputy Prime Minister.[120] In this way, the position of the Finance Minister is politically and administratively strengthened. The Deputy Prime Minister directs the work of the government only in the case of the absence of the Prime Minister or a temporary impediment to the exercise of his or her function.[121]

i. Competences of the Council of Ministers

The 1997 Constitution vests the Council of Ministers with competences that are typical for a parliamentary system.[122] Thus, the Council of Ministers conducts the internal affairs and foreign policy of the Polish state.[123] The Constitution also presumes that the Council of Ministers is responsible for any state affairs not reserved for any other state organ or local self-government.[124] The Constitution then lists the specific competences of the Council of Ministers.[125]

[118] Article 5(1) of the Law on Council of Ministers.
[119] ibid art 33(3).
[120] For instance, Leszek Balcerowicz, Marek Belka, Grzegorz Kołodko, Zyta Gilowska, Jacek Rostowski and Mateusz Morawiecki held the two positions simultaneously.
[121] Article 6 of the Law on Council of Ministers.
[122] See J Stembrowicz, *Rząd w systemie parlamentarnym* (Warsaw, Państwowe Wydawnictwo Naukowe, 1982).
[123] Article 146(1) of the Constitution.
[124] ibid art 146(2).
[125] ibid art 146(4).

First, the government ensures the implementation of statutes in the form of regulations and executive orders. This represents the key competence of the government. The Council of Ministers also has a right to initiate legislation and generally actively uses this competence.[126] In some areas, the Council of Ministers even possesses an exclusive competence to initiate legislation, as in the case of the budget. In addition, only the Council of Ministers can employ the accelerated legislative procedure.[127]

The Council of Ministers coordinates and controls the work of organs of government administration.[128] Furthermore, the Council of Ministers protects the interests of the State Treasury. In this regard, the government is aided by a central organ of government administration, the General Counsel to the Republic of Poland (*Prokuratoria Generalna Rzeczypospolitej Polskiej*).[129]

Another constitutional competence of the Council of Ministers is to adopt a draft state budget and to supervise its implementation after its adoption by the parliament.[130] Within five months from the end of the fiscal year, the Council of Ministers presents a report for approval by the Chamber of Deputies on the implementation of the budget and information on state debt.[131]

Moreover, the Council of Ministers ensures the internal and external security of the state and public order, and exercises control with regard to national defence. The government performs these tasks through central organs of government administration such as the Head of Civil Defence, the Chief Commander of the Fire Brigade and the Chief Commander of the Border Patrol. Within the integrated administration, there are also provincial police commanders and military district commanders.

Finally, the Council of Ministers handles relations with other states and international organisations. To this end, the government concludes and renounces international agreements.[132] Nowadays, the competences of the government in the area of foreign affairs predominantly concern the relationship with the EU. In particular, the participation in the

[126] See ch 3.

[127] ibid.

[128] See section III.D below.

[129] Between 2006 and 2016, this organ existed as the General Counsel of State Treasury (*Pokuratoria Generalna Skarbu Państwa*).

[130] See ch 3.

[131] Article 147 of the Constitution.

[132] See Law of 14 April 2000 on International Agreements, JL 2000 No 39 Pos 443, JL 2002 No 216 Pos 1824, JL 2010 No 213 Pos 1395, JL 2011 No 117 Pos 676.

Council and European Council meetings presents an important aspect of the government's activities in this field.[133]

The Constitution offers a clear concept of the position and competences of the Council of Ministers, even though some critical voices are also present.[134] Still, it is worth noting that since 1997, there has been no cabinet (government) crisis that would have paralysed the life of the state. The competences granted to the government appear to enable an efficient running of state affairs. This is evident in Poland's successful joining of the EU, its successful handling of the financial crisis (2008–11) and the enforcement of social reforms.

D. Government Administration

In the mid-1990s, the structure of the central government administration underwent thorough reform to adjust it to the new reality of the democratic state after the Communist era, as well as to enhance its functioning. In 1997, government departments called *resorty* which existed in the Polish People's Republic were replaced with a newer, more flexible structure of departments of government administration (*działy administracji rządowej*). As was mentioned earlier, the Prime Minister freely assigns ministers to the different departments.[135] Ministers are supported in their tasks by a ministry. The number and names of the ministries often change as they are created or abolished in a regulation issued by the Council of Ministers itself.

The structure of the government administration in Poland is as follows: the government administration at the central level consists of chief organs that are appointed by the President and the Chamber of Deputies, and central organs that are appointed and recalled by the Prime Minister, the Council of Ministers or individual ministers. The chief organs comprise the Council of Ministers, the Prime Minister, the ministers and the heads of committees which are part of the government. In turn, the central organs include, for example, the General

[133] See K Pomorska, 'The Impact of Enlargement: Europeanization of Polish Foreign Policy? Tracking Adaptation and Change in the Polish Ministry of Foreign Affairs' (2007) 2 *The Hague Journal of Diplomacy* 25.

[134] See, eg, B Banaszak, 'Egzekutywa w Polsce -stan obecny i uwagi de lege fundamentali ferenda' (2006) *Przegląd Sejmowy*, 9, 21–24.

[135] As of July 2019, there are 35 departments. See art 5 of the Law of 4 September 1997 on the Departments of Government Administration, JL 2019 Pos 945.

Treasury Inspectorate and the Chief Commander of the Fire Brigade. In contrast to the central level, at the local level the government administration can be divided into an integrated administration, which is subordinate to a voivode, and a non-integrated administration, which is subordinate to the chief and central organs of administration.

The Constitution does not regulate the functioning of all organs of government administration. In cases where the Constitution is silent, the position and the functions of these organs can be changed in a statute rather than demanding a constitutional amendment, making such changes susceptible to political influence. One such example of a political struggle within the government administration concerns the Prosecutor's Office. Due to the crucial role played by the prosecution in the state, the Prosecutor's Office is one of the most important organs of state administration. Its trajectory is indicative of problems in the development of the Polish legal system. Between 1950 and 1990, the Prosecutor's Office was a separate institution under the supervision of the Justice Minister, who simultaneously held the office of Public Prosecutor. This design was a direct consequence of the Soviet model of the Prosecutor's Office and was tightly bound to the Communist Party. Between 1990 and 2010, the Prosecutor's Office remained under the Justice Ministry, though during this period, the Public Prosecutor acted as intermediary between them. In 2010, the positions of Justice Minister and Public Prosecutor were separated in an attempt to shield the prosecution from the influence of the government administration, as well from politics more generally. The Public Prosecutor was to be appointed by the President from among a list of candidates shortlisted by the National Council of Judiciary and the National Council of Prosecution. However, in 2016, with a new majority in parliament, the positions of the Justice Minister and the Public Prosecutor were once again merged.[136] The Public Prosecutor now leads the Prosecutor's Office personally or through a National Prosecutor. The Prime Minister appoints the National Prosecutor who is nominated by the Public Prosecutor. These continuous reforms of the Prosecutor's Office demonstrate the extreme flexibility caused by the failure to anchor this institution in the Constitution, leading as a result to frequent changes.

Another issue is the rather low, but still increasing, extent to which government policy is delivered through private sector organisations.[137]

[136] Article 1 of the Law of 28 January 2016 on Prosecution, JL 2017 Pos 1767, JL 2018 Pos 5, 1000, 1443, 1669.

[137] J Zimmermann, *Prawo Administracyjne* (Warsaw, Wolters Kluwer, 2016) 212.

The delivery of policies through private entities (natural or legal persons) is possible only when allowed by a statute. For instance, the 1996 Law on municipal management enables communes to commission private entities for public tasks such as managing a marketplace or rubbish collection.[138] Another requirement is the obligation of closing a contract between the public (state or local body) and the private entity. Such a contract is similar to civil law contracts in its character and effects, such as responsibility for failure to comply with the contract. Public-private partnership, discussed in Chapter 7, presents an integral part of privatisation.

In some policy areas, such as notary services, the privatisation of public tasks has been complete and successful. Some public tasks are harder to privatise because of their social significance (eg, managing population records), state security (eg, managing prisons and military service) or state property (eg managing cultural heritage objects).[139] A significant barrier for the privatisation of public tasks are the constraints stemming from the principles of equality and social justice; for example, privatisation of health care or education can only be partial because of this.

i. Civil Service

The notion of the executive, as has been discussed in this chapter, encompasses the Council of Ministers and the government administration. A civil service has been developing in Poland since the 1990s, with the aim of replacing the bureaucracy of the Communist state. The civil service corps comprises around 118,000 servants (including 7,500 highly qualified 'nominated' civil servants).[140] It is estimated that the civil service encompasses around one-quarter of government administration and around 15 per cent of the whole public administration.[141] It is impossible to compare the civil service corps with the Communist bureaucracy, and such an analysis would be misleading in terms of size and quality.

The Constitution establishes a general framework for the civil service, while its functioning is regulated in a statute.[142] Accordingly, the Constitution indicates that the civil service ensures the 'professional, diligent,

[138] Article 3 of the Law of 20 December 1996, JL 2019 Pos 712.

[139] Zimmermann (n 137) 210–12.

[140] See https://dsc.kprm.gov.pl/analizy-i-statystyki.

[141] G Makowski, 'Dla państwa i obywateli. Diagnoza i propozycje reformy służby cywilnej, Fundacja im. S. Batorego', 4 available at www.batory.org.pl/upload/files/Programy%20operacyjne/Forum%20Idei/Dla%20panstwa%20i%20obywateli_Makowski.pdf.

[142] Law of 21 November 2008 on Civil Service, JL 2018 Pos 1559.

impartial and politically neutral exercise of state obligations'.[143] Its professional character implies a permanent type of service, especially on the part of the civil servants appointed for an indefinite period. The permanent work contract is the main form of employment, and the relevant law on the civil service limits the circumstances under which the employment may be terminated.

The relationship between the government in power and the civil service is not without ambiguity. Political neutrality, as a principle of the civil service, implies that the civil servants are recruited in open competition on a competitive basis. Although the civil servants work in offices of state administration, the government does not manage matters of human resources, which is a task of a general director of an office. However, the influence of the governing power is visible in the higher-ranking civil servants who are politically nominated. Specifically, in 2016 the Law on Civil Service was amended, abolishing open competition for higher positions in the civil service.[144]

A government minister is the head of an office, but is not superior vis-a-vis the civil servants employed in it. The supervisory function is exercised by a general director of the relevant office, who is nominated and recalled by the minister. Government ministers – and not the members of the civil service – are politically responsible for failed policies. Civil servants bear only disciplinary responsibility for infringement of their professional duties, or financial liability for issuing an administrative decision in gross violation of the law.

In practice, in recent years, the civil service has been suffering from political nominations to the highest positions of the civil service, organisational and management problems, low salaries and the comparative attractiveness of new private sector jobs.[145] In the long run, these developments can impede the ability to implement government policy and even endanger public security.[146]

IV. CONCLUSION

The double-headed executive under the 1997 Constitution consists of the President and the Council of Ministers, led by the Prime Minister.

[143] Article 153(1) of the Constitution.

[144] Law of 30 December 2015 amending Law on Civil Service and some other Laws, JL 2016 Pos 34.

[145] Makowski (n 141).

[146] 'Nie ma państwa bez urzędnika' *Rzeczpospolita* (28 March 2019).

The President is endowed with a strong democratic mandate and is assigned a number of constitutional functions typical of a formal head of state, acting as a political referee and wielding some executive power. However, the President remains to a large extent dependent upon the government formed by a parliamentary majority. In this configuration, it is the Prime Minister who maintains the central position within the government and government administration.

The problematic position of the President is exacerbated by the constitutional strengthening of the position of the Prime Minister and of the Council of Ministers as organs of the executive power. Thus, one of the main problems of the constitutional system of Poland today is that, on the one hand, the Constitution introduces a presidency with a strong democratic mandate, while, on the other hand, it places the Prime Minister in a powerful position in respect of the exercise of governmental power. The constitutional design of the executive results in an overlap of powers between the President and the Prime Minister, especially with regard to foreign affairs and defence policy. Over the last 20 years, in cases where the President and the Prime Minister represented different political forces, a Polish version of cohabitation between those organs was largely observed. These constitutional organs were capable of cooperating without major disagreement. However, political crises were not absent, as was clear during the 'chair crisis' and the delays in the nomination of ambassadors or generals, discussed in this chapter. Such conflicts are resolved by ad hoc solutions, despite a general perception that constitutional amendment is necessary. Thus far, reforms have been subject to political discussion only, while no legal debate over what would constitute reasonable reform has taken place.[147]

Finally, the design of the executive exhibits a mix of elements. This includes features specific to the Polish system (for instance, requirements for countersignature and the scope of the President's prerogatives), elements of a chancellor system (the marginal role of the President, except for crisis situations) and of semi-presidential systems (direct election of the President by the nation). This has led to the establishment of an interesting and quite effective government. The post-1997 governments have been particularly stable, with cases of governments falling or being dismissed remaining rare.

[147] See ch 9.

FURTHER READING

Bałaban, A (ed), *Rada Ministrów – organizacja i funkcjonowanie* (Kraków, Zakamycze, 2002).

Banaszak, B and Nowacki, K, 'The Model of Executive Power in Poland: Outline of Political Evolution' (2009) 15 *European Public Law* 171–82.

Dudek, D, *Autorytet Prezydenta a Konstytucja RP* (Lublin, Wydawnictwo KUL, 2013).

Frankiewicz, A, *Kontrasygnata aktów urzędowych Prezydenta Rzeczypospolitej Polskiej* (Kraków, Zakamycze, 2004).

Patyra, S, *Prawnoustrojowy status Prezesa Rady Ministrów* (Warsaw, Wydawnictwo Sejmowe, 2002).

Wyrzykowski, M and Cieleń, A, 'Presidential Elements in Government Poland – semi-presidentialism or 'rationalised parliamentarianism'?' (2006) 2 *European Constitutional Law Review* 253–67.

5

Judicial Power

Judges – Judiciary – Independent Courts – National Council of the Judiciary – Ordinary Courts – Administrative Courts – Supreme Court – Judicial Crisis – Rule of Law – European Integration – Preliminary Reference

I. INTRODUCTION

DESIGNING THE JUDICIAL power in a state that rebuilds its institutions after a period under Communism was a daunting task, yet was arguably essential for establishing a democratic system of government. In the Polish case, the judicial power underwent in-depth reforms after 1989 that rejected the undemocratic Soviet legal structures. The crucial point of reference in this matter is quite telling: judges had to submit to the Communist Party in power at that time. With the overthrow of Communism, Poland began to introduce the principle of division of state powers into legislative, executive and judicial branches, guided by the mechanisms of separation and balance of powers.[1] Within that system, the judicial power and its organs have gained a special position, as they have been perceived as bulwarks against the return of undemocratic practices, be it under the Polish People's Republic or stemming from other sources.

Under the Constitution of 1997, the judicial branch has a strong position, 'separate and independent' from the other branches of government.[2] The Constitution assigns the administration of justice to the Supreme Court (*Sąd Najwyższy*), the ordinary courts (*sądy powszechne*), administrative courts (*sądy administracyjne*) and military courts (*sądy wojskowe*).[3] This function of courts – adjudication of legal disputes in

[1] See ch 2.
[2] Article 173 of the Constitution.
[3] ibid art 175(1).

which at least one party is a natural or legal person with a right of access to court – does not exhaust the constitutional notion of the judicial power. The Constitution also includes tribunals in the judicial branch, which will be discussed in Chapter 6.

Following the presidential elections of May 2015 and the parliamentary elections of October 2015, the political party that had recently taken power, Law and Justice, which was distrustful of an independent judiciary, began a process of weakening the judicial branch. The changes in the autumn of 2015 began with an assault by the parliamentary majority on the independence of the Constitutional Court (discussed in Chapter 6), followed by new laws concerning the Supreme Court and the National Council of the Judiciary. In 2017, the Chamber of Deputies, following the popular slogans of 'amending the judiciary' and 'bringing the courts closer to ordinary people', adopted laws that substantially impact on the court system in Poland. The governing majority argued that judges are an isolated 'social caste' that was lavishly remunerated for its mediocre work (as seen in lengthy court proceedings) and was not accountable to society. At the time, following national protests, the President vetoed the laws concerning the Supreme Court and the National Council of the Judiciary.[4] However, in December 2017, the President proposed new statutes containing similar content, which were adopted by parliament and signed into law by the head of state, and entered into force in 2018. Around these developments, in December 2017 the European Commission, in an unprecedented move, launched the 'Article 7(1) TEU procedure' against Poland.[5]

The aim of this chapter is to present, on the one hand, the post-1989 shape of the judiciary in the context of the Constitution of 1997: its principles, organs and main functions. On the other hand, it discusses the deep changes to judicial power that started in 2015, in particular their form – through statutes instead of constitutional amendments – and their content – often conflicting with the substance of the Constitution. These changes were labelled by the governing party as 'reforms' of the judiciary. However, in fact, they have created major dysfunction in the judiciary. Section II deals with the structure of the court system, section III then discusses the principle of independence of courts and

[4] 'Poland's President to Veto Controversial Laws on Judges' *Financial Times* (24 July 2017). See M Matczak, 'Who's Next? On the Future of the Rule of Law in Poland, and Why President Duda Will Not Save it' *Verfassungsblog* (19 July 2017).

[5] On this and other ongoing proceedings against Poland, see ch 9.

judges, and section IV highlights the important role of Polish judges as EU judges, acting as 'first responders' to the rule of law crisis.

II. THE CONSTITUTIONAL STRUCTURE OF THE POLISH COURTS

The Polish court system consists of two main parts: ordinary courts and administrative courts.[6] Beyond these two parts, the Constitution also establishes the Supreme Court.[7] However, the Supreme Court belongs neither to the ordinary nor the administrative judiciary. Its position is specified in the way that the Constitution vests the Supreme Court with the function of judicial supervision over the court system. Moreover, the Constitution also enlists military courts as part of the court system, but their role is very limited in practice. Military courts are competent only in criminal cases concerning soldiers in active service and, exceptionally, with regard to civil employees of the military. In the past, proposals to abolish the military courts and to instead include military matters in the jurisdiction of ordinary courts were put forward. However, the constitutional status of the military courts shields them from being eliminated from the court system.

The Constitution includes a number of principles concerning the functioning of the courts. The most important of these are the uniformity of courts, two instance court proceedings, and the right to appeal a first-instance judgment or decision, which will be discussed in turn below.[8]

The uniformity of the courts expresses the idea that the courts create a system in which each court pronounces its judgments in the name of the same subject, namely the Republic of Poland. The judicial proceedings must consist of (at least) two instances, allowing the parties to question the judgment in a court of second instance. Initially, the principle of two-instance judicial proceedings did not apply in the administrative courts, but since their 2004 reform and the introduction of the cassation complaint to the Supreme Administrative Court (*Naczelny Sąd Administracyjny*), two-tier proceedings have taken effect in both ordinary and administrative courts. Finally, the right to appeal a first-instance judgment or decision expressed is broader than the principle of two-instance court proceedings, as it includes proceedings before courts, but also

[6] Article 175(1) of the Constitution.
[7] ibid art 183.
[8] ibid arts 174, 176(1) and 78, respectively.

before the organs of state administration and other proceedings, offering a strong safeguard for individuals.

A. The Design of Ordinary Courts

The heaviest case load is placed upon the ordinary court system, consisting of 318 district (*sądy rejonowe*), 45 regional (*sądy okręgowe*) and 11 appeals (*sądy apelacyjne*) courts.[9] The Minister of Justice establishes the ordinary courts, their seat (the office of the court) and the scope of their jurisdiction by regulation after seeking the opinion of the National Council of the Judiciary on this matter. Ordinary courts typically deal with civil and criminal matters, family law, labour law and social security, and economic law, while in the case of regional courts, they can also administer land and mortgage registers. The regional courts, created for a territory covering at least two district courts, can decide both as courts of first instance (eg, with regard to felonies) and as appeals courts from the decisions of district courts. The appeals courts are created for a territory of at least two district courts and decide on appeals from the judgments of the regional courts in which they acted as a first instance court. In addition, the Warsaw Regional Court is competent in cases concerning competition law and consumer protection (*Sąd Ochrony Konkurencji i Konsumentów*).

Part of the 'reforms' of the governing majority was the amendment of 12 July 2017 to the 2001 Law on Ordinary Courts Organisation, which enabled the Justice Minister to make radical changes to the leadership of all of the ordinary courts. For six months, the Justice Minister gained an extraordinary right to remove from office the presidents and vice presidents of ordinary courts, without prior consultation on the decision with representatives of the judiciary, especially with the National Council of the Judiciary, and without stating any reasons for this removal. The Justice Minister has taken advantage of this right in practice, massively changing the leadership of many of the ordinary courts.[10] In addition, changes in the retirement regime were introduced.

[9] As of 31 December 2017. See Statistics Poland, *Mały Rocznik Statystyczny Polski* (Warsaw, 2018) 81, available at: https://stat.gov.pl/files/gfx/portalinformacyjny/pl/defaultaktualnosci/5515/1/19/1/maly_rocznik_statystyczny_polski_2018.pdf.

[10] A total of 66 presidents and 63 vice presidents of the ordinary courts were removed. See 'Ziobro szybko wymienia prezesów i wiceprezesów sądów' *Rzeczpospolita* (7 February 2018).

The amendment of 12 July 2017 to the Law on Ordinary Courts Organisation and other statutes reduced the retirement age from 67 to 65 years for male judges and 60 years for female judges. The Justice Minister could prolong the term of a judge up to 70 years of age depending on the needs of the court system. In the first couple of months after the entry into force of the law in question, the term of a significant number of judges of ordinary courts was not prolonged, affecting female judges in particular, who had to seek the consent of the Justice Minister much earlier as compared to their male peers.[11] However, these rules were softened over the subsequent months. According to the amendment of 12 April 2018, judges will retire at 65, while female judges may request to retire as early as 60. The National Council of the Judiciary may agree that a judge maintains his or her office until the age of 70, conditional on the outcome of a medical examination and in the interests of the judicial system or the public interest.

B. The Design of Administrative Courts

Administrative courts exercise control over the acts of public administration, and review compliance with statutes of acts of local law issued by the organs of local self-government and government administration.[12] The system of administrative judiciary was first established on the basis of the March Constitution of 1921 and the Law of 1922 on the Supreme Administrative Court. This Court was initially included within the executive branch of government, and only the April Constitution (1935) incorporated it into the judicial branch under the supervision of the Prime Minister. The administrative judiciary did not exist after the Second World War. The Supreme Administrative Court as a one-tier court judicially supervised by the Supreme Court was only established in 1980. The entry into force of the Constitution of 1997 with its requirement for two instances in court proceedings initiated a thorough reform of the administrative judiciary in 2004. The first instance now consists of 16 voivode administrative courts, one per voivodeship. The second instance is the Supreme Administrative Court, a kind of cassation court. It is presided over by the President of the Supreme Administrative Court, who is appointed for a six-year term by the head of state from among two candidates put forward by the general assembly of the judges of

[11] 'To nie jest kraj dla starszych sędziów' *Dziennik Gazeta Prawna* (17 January 2018).
[12] Article 184 of the Constitution. See also ch 7.

that court. In contrast to ordinary courts, the administrative courts are created by the President rather than the Minister of Justice. Another difference concerns the supervision of administrative courts. This is conducted by the President of the Supreme Administrative Court and there is thus no internal and external supervision, as is the case for ordinary courts.

Administrative courts deal with individual complaints against administrative decisions and orders issued in administrative, enforcement and security proceedings. Anyone with a legal interest can lodge a complaint on a final decision of an organ of public administration within 30 days of its delivery. The complaint is lodged in the court through the intermediary of the relevant organ of public administration. Moreover, administrative courts deal with complaints concerning failure to act or excessive length of proceedings before an administrative organ. Another competence of the administrative courts is to review compliance with statutes of acts of local law issued by the organs of self-local government and government administration.[13] Administrative courts also decide on controversies between local self-government and government administration, as well as jurisdictional controversies between the organs of local government. Finally, the Supreme Administrative Court issues resolutions to clarify discrepancies in the legal interpretation of administrative courts.

In 2017, the voivodeship administrative courts decided a total of 77,567 complaints (around 75 per cent of all pending complaints), which was 4.1 per cent more than the year before.[14] The administrative courts tend to function effectively, deciding cases in a timely manner: around 42 per cent of complaints are decided within three months, 56 per cent of cases in four months and 73 per cent in six months. In turn, in 2017, the Supreme Administrative Court decided 19,192 cassation complaints, 40 per cent of which concerned tax and financial issues. Almost 50 per cent of cases of the Supreme Administrative Court were decided within a year, and 86 per cent within two years. However, only 28 per cent of cassation complaints were decided within a year. The Supreme Administrative Court also deals with other issues: in 2017, for instance, it issued 20 resolutions clarifying legal provisions, settled 479 motions regarding local competence conflicts and decided on other types of complaints.

[13] See ch 7.

[14] Supreme Administrative Court, *Informacja o działalności sądów administracyjnych w 2017 roku* (Warsaw, 2018) – for data on the voivodeship courts, see at 17–18, and on the Supreme Administrative Court, see at 21–30.

C. The Supreme Court: Before and after Changes

Each of the two limbs of the Polish court system – the ordinary and administrative courts – has its own 'supreme court'. The Supreme Administrative Court, discussed earlier, fulfils the function of a 'supreme court' for administrative courts. In turn, the Supreme Court exercises certain functions vis-a-vis the ordinary courts. These are presented in this section. As such, the Supreme Court and the Supreme Administrative Court maintain a cooperative relationship and any conflicts are avoided.[15]

The Constitution, on the one hand, places the Supreme Court outside the system of ordinary and administrative courts. On the other hand, the Supreme Court exercises judicial supervision over the judgments of ordinary courts. The Supreme Court safeguards the legality and uniformity of the case law of ordinary courts, but not of the administrative courts; this function is fulfilled by the Supreme Administrative Court. The Supreme Court decides on cassation complaints (*skargi kasacyjne*) on the final judgments of ordinary courts. In this capacity, it is restricted to reviewing points of law and does not review the facts of the case. To safeguard the uniformity of the case law of ordinary courts, and of the Supreme Court itself, the Supreme Court takes resolutions to clear arising discrepancies in the interpretation of law. Under some circumstances, these resolutions become legal principles (*zasady prawne*) with a binding effect on all cases and not only concerning the case in the context of which they were taken. Some of these principles are relevant in constitutional terms as they may concern human rights protection – for instance, the right to access to courts.[16]

Beyond its main function – judicial supervision over the jurisprudence of ordinary courts – the Supreme Court also performs other constitutionally relevant functions. These include deciding on complaints on formal irregularities during elections, as well as confirming the validity of parliamentary and presidential elections, and nationwide and constitutional referendums. Besides, the Supreme Court opines on legislative proposals concerning the judiciary and, when necessary, on other drafts.

The Law on the Supreme Court of 8 December 2017 introduced crucial changes to the court's functioning, as it gained the competence of 'extraordinary review' of final court judgments with the broadly termed

[15] L Garlicki, *Polskie Prawo Konstytucyjne. Zarys wykładu* (Warsaw, Wolters Kluwer, 2017) 393–94.

[16] See, eg, Supreme Court, decision of 18 October 2001, I KZP 25/01.

aim of safeguarding the rule of law and social justice. Specifically, an extraordinary complaint (*skarga nadzwyczajna*) can be lodged, in principle, within five years from a final judgment on the request of, among others, the Public Prosecutor or the Ombudsman. Additionally, in the first three years following the entry into force of the Law on the Supreme Court (3 April 2018), an extraordinary complaint can be lodged against any final court judgment issued since the entry into force of the Constitution (17 October 1997). The introduction of the extraordinary complaint is extremely controversial, as it opens up the possibility to verify past (and future) judgments causing legal uncertainty and puts into question the *res iudicata* principle.

Since the entry into force of the Law on the Supreme Court, the Ombudsman[17] and the Public Prosecutor have received vast amounts of applications from individuals requesting the extraordinary complaint procedure be launched on their behalf.[18] Both bodies have already lodged their first extraordinary complaints.[19] The newly established Extraordinary Control and Public Affairs Chamber of the Supreme Court – whose members were appointed by the head of state in October 2018 – is competent to review these extraordinary complaints. In March 2019, for the first time the Supreme Court decided on an extraordinary complaint brought by the Ombudsman concerning two contrary inheritance decisions of an ordinary court that were in force for almost 20 years.[20] On the one hand, the extraordinary revision of final court judgments, including past judgments issued within the last 20 years, can upset the stability of court judgments (and of law more generally), an important value in a state subject to the rule of law. On the other hand, the amount of applications seeking to launch an extraordinary complaint, and the fact that the Ombudsman submitted a number of them to the Supreme Court, indicates that this tool may transpire to be useful.

The Supreme Court is led and represented by the First President of the Supreme Court, appointed by the President for a six-year term, from among the candidates put forward by the General Assembly of the

[17] See ch 8.

[18] In 2018, the Ombudsman received a total of 2,991 applications, while the Public Prosecutor had received 3,240 applications as of February 2019. See 'RPO kieruje do SN piątą skargę nadzwyczajną – chodzi o sprawę spadkową' *Dziennik Gazeta Prawna* (2 February 2019); 'Tysiące wniosków, ale mało skarg nadzwyczajnych do Sądu Najwyższego' *Rzeczpospolita* (5 February 2019).

[19] ibid. As of February 2019, each of them had lodged five extraordinary complaints.

[20] Supreme Court, decision of 26 March 2019, I NSNc 1/19.

Judges of the Supreme Court.[21] This method of election does not raise any concerns relating to the independence of the Supreme Court's First President. There are also further presidents of the Supreme Court leading each of the chambers of the Supreme Court: civil; criminal; labour law and social security; extraordinary control and public affairs; and the disciplinary chamber. The establishment of the two latter chambers by the 2017 Law on the Supreme Court led to the introduction of 'lay members of the Supreme Court' elected by the Senate for a four-year term.

The head of state appoints Supreme Court judges on the motion of the National Council of the Judiciary. Before 3 April 2018, the appointment was made for an indefinite term until the judge reached 70 years of age. Between 3 April 2018 and 1 January 2019, the retirement age was set at 65 years of age.[22] Female judges could retire at the age of 60. A judge could apply to have his or her term prolonged by three years. The head of state received an opinion on the application to prolong from the First President of the Supreme Court and from the National Council of the Judiciary, and could agree to the prolongation of a judge's term (although no more than twice). Following the interim measures order by the Luxembourg Court, in October 2018 the retirement rules were amended.[23] All Supreme Court judges will now retire at 65.[24] There is no possibility to prolong the term of a judge. These rules apply only to judges who were appointed after 1 January 2019 and thus do not encompass the so-called 'old judges' whose terms are perceived to have been uninterrupted.

The Law of 8 December 2017 on the Supreme Court presents an in-depth change in the status of the Supreme Court judges. Since its entry into force, the Supreme Court can potentially consist of as many as 120 judges, as compared to around 80 members before the changes were made. Crucially, as a consequence of the provision on retirement at 65 years, around 38 per cent of judges were supposed to leave the Supreme Court.[25] This regulation was extremely controversial, as it introduced

[21] Article 183(3) of the Constitution.

[22] This retirement regime also encompassed the judges of the Supreme Administrative Court.

[23] CJEU, Order of 19 October 2018 of the Vice President of the Court in Case C-619/18 R, EU:C:2018:852. See ch 9.

[24] Law of 21 November 2018 amending the law on the Supreme Court, JL 2018 Pos 2507.

[25] European Commission, 'Rule of Law: European Commission Refers Poland to the European Court of Justice to Protect the Independence of the Polish Supreme Court', press release, 24 September 2018.

a retirement age requirement with retroactive effect. First, from the constitutional perspective, it was doubtful whether the President had the competence to agree to extend the term of a judge. Certainly, the President has the right to appoint judges, but it was doubtful whether this prerogative encompassed the prolongation of judges' terms.[26] The competence of consenting to extend judge's term only 'pretended' to be a prerogative. Second, the competence of the head of state to agree to extend the term of a Supreme Court judge also raised formal issues. The President issued 'notifications' (*zawiadomienie*) addressed to judges. However, in fact, the actions of the President should have had the form of a 'decision' (*postanowienie*) and thus an act with a countersignature of the Prime Minister, as indicated in the constitutional competences of the President.[27] Third, the regulation of the conditions of service of a judge naturally depends on the legislature, but this does not imply that a statute can submit judges to the unlimited power of the parliament and the President. In practice, there was a discrepancy in the perception of the position of the judges whose term was not extended by the President. The judges in question maintained that they were still active judges, while according to the government those judges have already retired.

Finally, the 2017 Law on the Supreme Court introduced a stricter disciplinary procedure for all judges. Judges are held accountable before a new Disciplinary Chamber of the Supreme Court, as mentioned earlier. This chamber has an autonomous position within the Supreme Court. In addition, its members have salaries that are 40 per cent higher than those of other Supreme Court judges.

In the summer of 2018, the governing majority violated the constitutional principle of a six-year term of the First President of the Supreme Court (Małgorzata Gersdorf) under the pretext of reaching retirement age.[28] However, the continuity of the six-year term of the First President was confirmed by the interim relief of the CJEU ordering Poland to refrain from adopting any measure concerning the appointment of a new First President of the Supreme Court.[29] The effects of the CJEU's interim measures on the Supreme Court are discussed further in Chapter 9.

[26] Article 144(3), point 17 of the Constitution.

[27] Article 144(2) of the Constitution. See also 'Zabłocki z SN: Według prawa jestem sędzią w stanie czynnym' *Dziennik Gazeta Prawna* (13 September 2018). See ch 4.

[28] Article 183(3) of the Constitution.

[29] CJEU, Order of 19 October 2018 of the Vice-President of the Court in Case C-619/18 R.

III. INDEPENDENT COURTS AND INDEPENDENT JUDGES AS THE BACKBONE OF JUDICIAL POWER

Judicial power – independent from other powers – remains separated from other branches of government by a double wall. The first of these barriers is the institutional separation that is a consequence of the constitutional principle of the separation and balance of powers. The second wall is created by the particular position of judges, especially by the principle of the irremovability of judges.

A. The Status of a Judge and its Guarantees

These principles, which are fundamental to the functioning of a democratic state ruled by law, are often mistakenly taken to mean the same thing, but are nonetheless distinct.[30] The independence of the courts concerns the autonomous position of the courts within the structure of the state and the fact that only courts can issue judgments.[31] This first principle then conditions the second principle of the independence of judges, which, instead, concerns the freedom of a judge in issuing judgments. Both principles fulfil the same function: separating judgments of the courts from the legislative and executive powers. The other branches of government cannot influence the functioning of the courts, unless such a possibility is explicitly provided for in the Constitution or in statute, yet even then, this influence can never concern a court's ruling. For example, the presidents of the administrative courts exercise internal control over the functioning of the administrative courts, while the Justice Minister exercises external control, which covers, inter alia, an assessment of the effectiveness of internal control. The Constitutional Court has confirmed this combination of ministerial supervision and protection of courts' independence in issuing judgments to be in compliance with the Constitution.[32]

The independence of judges implies that within the exercise of their office, judges are subject only to the Constitution and statutes.[33] Judges

[30] However, it should be noted that the Polish Constitution uses two different words to describe independence: *niezależność* with regard to courts and *niezawisłość* with regard to judges. Compare arts 173 and 178(1) of the Constitution.

[31] Constitutional Court, judgment of 7 November 2013, K 31/12, OTK ZU 8A/2013, poz 1433.

[32] ibid; judgment of 15 January 2009, K 45/07, OTK ZU 1A/2009, poz 3.

[33] Article 178(1) of the Constitution.

are not bound by infra-statutory law.[34] When applying infra-statutory law, judges can, on their own, assess if such law complies with statutes and in the event of incompatibility, they can set such acts aside, but not invalidate them. In a positive sense, the principle of judges' independence implies that a judge is under the obligation to issue judgments in accordance with law and his or her own conscience. As such, judicial independence is not a judge's privilege, but rather an obligation that an independent judge 'serves' the people and the rule of law. In its negative sense, judicial independence means that a judge should remain free from any type of pressure or threats, such as a possibility to be ordered into retirement, from parties to proceedings, state institutions or politicians. Judicial independence does not forbid judges to have views on political, social or other issues, but the judge must maintain rationality and objectivity when deciding a case. Judges cannot be members of political parties and should remain apolitical: they cannot be involved in any public activity that is incompatible with the principles of independence of the courts and judges.

Candidates for judges need to possess impeccable personal traits and have passed the judicial exam. The President appoints judges upon the request of the National Council of the Judiciary for an indeterminate period.[35] Polish judges are professional judges. They are educated in a two-stage system of five-year university studies in law and a three-year training (*aplikacja sędziowska*) that ends with an exam. Poland has around 10,000 judges.[36] Poland ranks relatively high among its EU peers as regards the number of judges.[37] With regard to gender equality in the judiciary, Poland's performance is mixed, with a share of over 50 per cent of female professional judges at the first and second instance courts, but fewer than 30 per cent at the Supreme Court level.[38] These figures place the country roughly at the median of the distribution across EU countries.

Judicial independence is further guaranteed by the irremovability of judges.[39] However, a judge can be recalled from office, suspended, or

[34] See ch 2.

[35] Article 179 of the Constitution.

[36] As of 31 December 2017 there were 9,719 judges of ordinary courts. See Statistics Poland (n 9) 82.

[37] European Commission, Communication from the Commission to the European Parliament, the Council, the European Central Bank, the European Economic and Social Committee and the Committee of the Regions, The 2018 EU Justice Scoreboard, COM(2018) 364, 31.

[38] ibid 32.

[39] Article 180 of the Constitution.

transferred to another bench or position against his or her will by virtue of a court judgment and in cases indicated in a statute. Such recalls do not violate the principle of removability of judges. In practice, they concern disciplinary offences and the subsequent disciplinary accountability of judges. Transfer to another position can take place only on the basis of the decision of the Justice Minister, since transfers could negatively influence the perception of stability of the position or even influence the jurisdictional freedom of the judge.[40]

In sum, judges enjoy a number of guarantees of their independence. The post-2015 discussion concerned the question whether the regulation of the status of a judge represents guarantees of judicial independence or privileges of the judicial caste, as argued by the governing majority. Certainly, the regulation of judicial status presented above presents guarantees of judicial independence that is integral to a democratic state ruled by law. In particular, this concerns judicial immunity: a judge cannot without prior court consent be held criminally responsible or deprived of his or her liberty.[41] Judges should be provided with appropriate conditions for work and granted remuneration consistent with the dignity of their office and the scope of their duties.[42] The aim is to safeguard the dignity of the office of a judge. This provision does not aim to protect the welfare of the judges or the principle of social justice. As such, the Constitutional Court sees the dignity of the judicial office as a crucial aspect of the judicial system. Still, the Constitutional Court has found the freeze on the remuneration of judges for 2012 to be compatible with the Constitution. The Court reasoned that the freeze had an incidental character, in the face of danger that not doing so would pose to a balanced state budget.[43]

B. The National Council of the Judiciary and its Destruction

To safeguard the independence of the courts and judges, the Constitution provides for the National Council of the Judiciary (hereinafter 'the Council').[44] The Council, which was first introduced in 1989 as

[40] Supreme Court, resolution of 28 January 2014, BSA-4110-4/13.
[41] Article 181 of the Constitution.
[42] ibid art 178(2).
[43] See Constitutional Court, judgment of 12 December 2012, K 1/12, OTK ZU 11A/2012, poz 134.
[44] Article 186(1) of the Constitution.

an amendment to the Constitution of the Polish People's Republic of 1952, expressed the ideal of beginning the process of establishing an independent judiciary. Under the Constitution of 1997, the Council is now the highest representative of the judicial milieu and its functions are closely bound to the judicial power.[45] Formally, the Constitution does not include the Council among the organs of the judicial power, yet it sits between the three branches of government, in close proximity to the judicial power.[46]

The constitutional composition of the Council reflects the idea that all three branches of government can influence its structure and functioning. Each governmental branch chooses its own representatives for the Council. In addition, the Council has a special, 'balancing' position combining the representatives of the three branches of government. The Constitution does not foresee any other organ constructed in such a way. In this light, the number of judge-members in the Council is less important than the Constitution's attempt to balance the tensions between the government branches with respect to judicial appointments.

The Constitution prescribes that the composition of the Council is mixed: its 25 members represent all three branches of government, with the majority (15) representing the judiciary and elected for a four-year term which cannot be shortened by statute.[47] The judge-members are chosen from amongst the judges of the Supreme Court, as well as the ordinary, administrative and military courts. In addition to the 15 judge-members, the Council consists of the heads of the Supreme Administrative Court and the Supreme Court, the Justice Minister, and one member appointed by the head of state. Finally, four MPs chosen by the Chamber of Deputies and two senators chosen by the Senate round out the membership.

The amendment of 8 December 2017 to the Law on the National Council of the Judiciary changed the procedure through which judges' representatives in the Council were selected in a manner that was unquestionably contrary to Article 187 of the Constitution. The interpretation of this provision presented above implies that the representatives of the judges should be elected by the judges themselves. This is the

[45] See Constitutional Court, judgment of 18 February 2004, K 12/03, OTK ZU 2A/2004, poz 8; judgment of 15 December 1999, P 6/99, OTK ZU 7/1999, poz 164; and judgment of 16 April 2008, K 40/07, OTK ZU 3A/2008, poz 44.

[46] Article 10(2) of the Constitution. See Constitutional Court, K 40/07.

[47] Article 187 of the Constitution.

understanding that dominates academic scholarship on this issue.[48] In contrast, in the amendment, the Chamber of Deputies decided that the seats would instead be filled by judges chosen by the legislature. The 15 judge-members previously chosen by the judiciary are now elected by the parliament: a three-fifths majority of votes in the Chamber of Deputies or a simple majority if that higher threshold is not reached. The consequences of this change are far-reaching. The legislature moved away from the letter of the Constitution, made the appointment process dependent upon the parliamentary majority in office and shortened the terms of the current members of the Council, set by the Constitution at four years. The new method of staffing the 15 positions reserved for judges' representatives destroyed the structure of the Council as a body balancing the three branches of government. Even if the Council maintains the same number of representatives of the judiciary, the influence of these representatives will be determined by a political organ – the Parliament. In practice, in March 2018, the Chamber of Deputies elected 15 judge-members.[49] All three types of membership in the Council are now dependent upon the political powers or are part of these powers themselves, like the Justice Minister.

It is crucial to address the Council and the changes to its structure because the Constitution vests in this organ a number of important competences. First, the Council presents to the President the candidates to be appointed as judges.[50] In this regard, the Council assesses the candidates and approves a list of recommended candidates. The candidates can appeal the decision before the Supreme Court, which can then assess the legality of the Council's procedure. The second function is the Council's competence to request a constitutional review of normative acts concerning the independence of courts and judges.[51] Prior to the reforms conducted by the Law and Justice party, the Council had lodged a number of such requests.[52] The Council also opines on normative acts concerning courts and judges, as well as deciding on issues concerning the status of the judicial office, such as setting criteria for the assessment

[48] Garlicki (n 15) 396–97; M Safjan and L Bosek (eds), *Konstytucja RP, Komentarz, t.II, art. 87-243* (Warsaw, CH Beck, 2016) 1121.

[49] Resolution of the Chamber of Deputies of 6 March 2018 on the election of members of the National Council of the Judiciary. See also W Sadurski, 'Bad Response to a Tragic Choice: The Case of Polish Council of the Judiciary' *Verfassungsblog* (16 April 2018).

[50] Article 179 of the Constitution.

[51] ibid art 186(2).

[52] See www.krs.pl/pl/dzialalnosc/wystapienia-do-tk/p,1.

of judicial candidates or assessing the judicial training programmes. A crucial task of the Council is adopting a code of judicial ethics.

In 2019, the Constitutional Court reviewed the constitutionality of electing the 15 judge-members by the Chamber of Deputies.[53] This review was launched on the request of the Council itself, in the face of criticism that its members were illegally elected. The Constitutional Court declared the 2017 amendment to the Law on the National Council of the Judiciary as compliant with the Constitution. However, this judgment does not clarify the status of the Council; on the contrary, it creates even more uncertainty. For instance, the judgment was issued by the Constitutional Court including a judge who was not eligible to adjudicate.[54] In sum, the judgment issued on the request of the Council presents a 'confirmation' of its status rather than a decision on the merits of the case.

IV. NATIONAL JUDGES AS EU JUDGES

The system of preliminary references[55] enabled a discourse – often called a 'judicial dialogue' – between national courts and the CJEU on the application and validity of EU law in the Member States.[56] In this respect, compared to other EU Member States, Polish judges consider themselves relatively knowledgeable about EU law, which might be explained by the training they received around the time of Poland's accession to the EU.[57] Between 2004 and 2018, Polish courts made 158 requests for a preliminary ruling to the CJEU – the second-highest number of requests after Hungary from among Member States that acceded to the EU in 2004.[58] Almost 50 per cent of those references were lodged by Poland's Supreme Administrative Court and the Supreme Court, with the other half submitted by the ordinary and administrative courts.[59]

[53] Constitutional Court, judgment of 25 March 2019, K 12/18, OTK ZU A/2019, poz 17.

[54] See ch 6.

[55] Article 267 TFEU.

[56] G Martinico and O Pollicino, *The Interaction between Europe's Legal Systems: Judicial Dialogue and the Creation of Supranational Laws* (Cheltenham, Edward Elgar, 2012) 17.

[57] JA Mayoral, U Jaremba and T Nowak, 'Creating EU Law Judges: The Role of Generational Differences, Legal Education and Judicial Career Paths in National Judges' Assessment Regarding EU Law Knowledge' (2014) 21 *Journal of European Public Policy* 1120, 1134.

[58] Authors' own calculation based on CJEU, Annual Report 2018, 143, https://curia.europa.eu/jcms/upload/docs/application/pdf/2019-04/_ra_2018_en.pdf.

[59] ibid 145.

Crucially, the preliminary reference mechanism enabled Polish courts to seek the help of the CJEU in defending the rule of law in Poland. In this sense, from the Member States' perspective, national courts adopted the role of 'first responders' to the rule of law crisis by being the first Member State institutions on the scene and by reacting in a timely manner. Accordingly, the Polish Supreme Court referred eight preliminary references to the Luxembourg Court.[60] The Supreme Court enquired whether the national law lowering the retirement age of active judges and making the prolongation of a judge's term dependent on the executive violated the EU principle of judicial independence and effective judicial protection. Other references concerned the new chambers staffed with judges chosen exclusively by the politicised National Council of the Judiciary – that is, whether the chambers remain an independent court within the meaning of EU law. Awaiting the response of the Luxembourg Court, the Supreme Court decided to halt the application of the controversial retirement provisions and the implementation of the relevant resolutions of the National Council of the Judiciary. Nonetheless, the Council and the President continued to apply the national law in question. Finally, the Supreme Administrative Court also referred a case regarding appeals to the resolutions of the National Council of the Judiciary to the CJEU and questioned the political composition of that organ in the light of EU law.[61]

In addition, three Polish lower-instance courts turned to the CJEU in the preliminary reference procedure.[62] Their questions focused on the excessive influence of the executive on the initiation and enforcement of disciplinary proceedings, and on the establishment of the disciplinary chamber of the Supreme Court. Two of the courts expressed the concern that if they were to deliver a judgment that was unfavourable to the state, they might face disciplinary proceedings.[63] In their view, the threat posed by the disciplinary provisions to judicial independence, which is protected under EU law, deprived an individual of effective judicial protection.

The preliminary references from Polish courts came as a surprise to the national executive and met with a backlash. This was visible

[60] CJEU, C-522/18 *Zakład Ubezpieczeń Społecznych*; C-537/18 *Krajowa Rada Sądownictwa*; C-585/18 *Krajowa Rada Sądownictwa and Others*; C-624/18 *CP*; Case C-625/18 *DO*; Case C-668/18 *Uniparts*; Case C-487/19 *Prokurator Prokuratury Krajowej Bożena Górecka and Others*; Case C-508/19 *Prokurator Generalny*.

[61] Supreme Administrative Court, Decision of 21 November 2018, II GOK 2/18; registered as CJEU, C-824/18, *Krajowa Rada Sądownictwa*, pending; Decision of 26 June 2019, II GOK 2/18 containing additional questions.

[62] CJEU, C-558/18, *Miasto Łowicz*, pending; C-563/18, *Prokuratura Okręgowa w Płocku*, pending; C-623/18, *Prokuratura Rejonowa w Słubicach*, pending.

[63] For facts of the cases, see CJEU, Order of the President of the Court of 1 October 2018, EU:C:2018:923 (concerning Cases C-558/18 and C-563/18).

in the Public Prosecutor's call on the regional court in Warsaw to withdraw its reference, or in a disciplinary representative's questioning of a judge from Łódź who sent a reference to Luxembourg.[64] Clearly, acting as 'first responder' subjected some of the national judges to more scrutiny. The government maintained that some of the references to Luxembourg were inadmissible as the questions were not connected to the subject matter of the proceedings, but to the work status of the judges involved.[65] At the same time, the Public Prosecutor requested the Constitutional Court to review the constitutionality of the Supreme Court's decision to halt the application of the relevant national laws.[66] Crucially, the motion also enquires whether Article 267 of the Treaty on the Functioning of the European Union (TFEU) complies with the Constitution to the extent that it enables preliminary requests on issues of the court system and its organisation, and on the procedures before the organs of the Member State's judiciary.[67] This clearly attempts to undermine the mechanisms that are at the core of Poland's membership in the EU and to further intimidate national judges. In the past, when reviewing the Accession Treaty and the Lisbon Treaty as ratified international agreements, the Constitutional Court indicated that in cases of an ultimate, irresolvable collision between EU law and the Constitution, the Polish legislature can decide to either amend the Constitution, or argue for a change in EU law, or ultimately withdraw from the EU.[68] If such a case is acknowledged by the Constitutional Court, the scope of manoeuvre is limited and any of the three options poses clear difficulties.

Finally, the European Commission found that the exposure of judges to disciplinary sanctions for directing preliminary references to the Luxembourg Court created 'a chilling effect' on the Polish courts for making use of this tool.[69] As a consequence, the Commission started a treaty infringement procedure against Poland for violation of its obligations under Article 267 TFEU.

[64] 'Prokuratura wystąpi do Sądu Okręgowego o cofnięcie pytania do TSUE' *Rzeczpospolita* (7 September 2018); 'Sędzia zadała pytania do TSUE wezwał ją rzecznik dyscypliny. Teraz sprawdzą jej akta na trzy lata wstecz' *Rzeczpospolita* (15 September 2018).

[65] See S Biernat and M Kawczyńska, 'Czy pytanie prejudycjalne jest niedopuszczalne?' *Rzeczpospolita* (4 September 2018).

[66] Constitutional Court, K 7/18.

[67] Public Prosecutor, Application of 4 October 2018.

[68] See ch 2.

[69] European Commission, 'Rule of Law: European Commission Launches Infringement Procedure to Protect Judges in Poland from Political Control', press release, 3 April 2019. See ch 9.

V. CONCLUSION

Under the Constitution of 1997, the judicial branch in Poland is formed by the ordinary and administrative courts and the Supreme Court. Up to 2015, this system generally functioned well. However, since then, the judiciary has faced strong criticism from the new governing majority led by the Law and Justice party, aimed first at the Constitutional Court and subsequently at the ordinary courts, the Supreme Court and the National Council of the Judiciary. A range of legislative changes has moved the judicial branch towards the legislative and executive power. This is best exemplified by the new election system for judge-members of the National Council of the Judiciary, who are now elected by the Chamber of Deputies instead of by the judges themselves. This system, as well as the interruption of the constitutional term of the First President of the Supreme Court, clearly violates the Constitution. In addition, the new statutes – undermining the principle of the independence of courts and judges – were adopted by the Parliament within hours. Such a legislative practice lowers rule of law standards.

In December 2017, the process of undermining of the Supreme Court began. The term of its First President was interrupted, judges were forced into retirement and profound changes were made to its structure. The interim relief ordered by the CJEU in 2018 and the subsequent, seventh amendment of the Law on the Supreme Court has raised the hope that at least in some ways, the ongoing crisis can be stopped. The EU's response to the judicial crisis in Poland is further discussed in Chapter 9.

Finally, the changes within the system of ordinary courts, the Supreme Court and the National Council of the Judiciary do not exhaust the overhaul of the judiciary by the governing majority. The functioning of the Constitutional Court has also been affected, as will be highlighted in the next chapter. The latest data indicates that the average length of ordinary court proceedings in first instance increased from 4.2 months in 2015 to 5.4 months in 2018.[70] Unsurprisingly, the backlog at the Supreme Court is also growing: for instance, in 2018, the number of undecided cases in the criminal chamber doubled within nine months.[71] What is evident after three years since the launch of the changes of the governing

[70] *cf* Informator Wymiaru Sprawiedliwości, 'Sprawność postępowań sądowych – czas trwania postępowania sądowego w latach 2011–2018', available at: https://isws.ms.gov.pl/pl/baza-statystyczna/opracowania-wieloletnie.

[71] 'Zabłocki o sporze wokół SN: liczby nie kłamią, czyli mój bilans zamknięcia' *Rzeczpospolita* (5 October 2018).

majority is that they did not lead to an improvement of the situation in the judiciary, but instead appear to have worsened it.

FURTHER READING

Bobek, M, 'The Fortress of Judicial Independence and the Mental Transitions of the Central European Judiciaries' (2008) 14 *European Public Law* 99–123.

Jaremba, U, *National Judges as EU Law Judges: The Polish Civil Law System* (Leiden, Martinus Nijhoff, 2014).

Śledzińska-Simon, A, 'The Rise and Fall of Judicial Self-Government in Poland: On Judicial Reform Reversing Democratic Tradition' 19 *German Law Journal* 1839–1869.

6

Constitutional Review and Constitutional Accountability

Constitutional Court – Tribunal of State – Judicial Appointments – Constitutional Review – Constitutional Interpretation – Constitutional Crisis – European Integration – Rule of Law

I. INTRODUCTION

THE CONSTITUTION INCLUDES in the judicial branch, in addition to the courts, two tribunals – the Constitutional Court (*Trybunał Konstytucyjny*) and the Tribunal of State (*Trybunał Stanu*) – which deal with constitutional review and constitutional accountability, respectively. The Constitutional Court tends to play a bigger role. Constitutional accountability of the top state officials is not fully implemented – instead, they mostly bear political accountability – and thus in practice, the Tribunal of State does not play any constitutional role.

As was explained in Chapter 1, the Constitutional Court was established during the transition from the falling Communist state to the emerging democracy. The Constitutional Court was shaped according to a Kelsenian model of constitutional judiciary, with its main function being the constitutional review of laws in various forms. In addition, the Constitutional Court exercises ancillary functions such as supervision of political parties, adjudicating competence conflicts and determining whether there exists an impediment to the exercise of the office by the President.

In 2015, the Constitutional Court celebrated 30 years of its functioning. However, the anniversary was overshadowed by the attack of the governing majority on the Constitutional Court.

II. THE CONSTITUTIONAL COURT

A. A Kelsenian Court with Ancillary Functions

The Constitution of 1997 endows the Constitutional Court with competences typical of a Kelsenian model constitutional court: it reviews compliance of the law with the Constitution. In addition to this central function, the Constitutional Court exercises some ancillary functions – not excluded from the Kelsenian model – and also present to different extents in other constitutional courts.[1] Those functions, exercised rather infrequently, include the settlement of disputes of competence between central state organs, the review of aims and functioning of a political party, and determining whether there exists an impediment to the exercise of the office by the head of state.[2] This section first discusses the competences of the Constitutional Court concerning the review of the constitutionality of laws, followed by an analysis of its ancillary competences.

i. Constitutional Review of Laws

The 1997 Constitution remains the basic benchmark of constitutional review. The Constitutional Court reviews the compatibility of statutes and international agreements with the Constitution. It also checks the compliance of statutes with ratified international agreements.[3] Finally, it reviews the compliance of legal provisions issued by central organs of state administration with the Constitution, ratified international treaties and statutes.[4] However, acts of local law-making bodies – organs of local self-government or of government administration – do not undergo constitutional review. Instead, their review remains within the competence of the administrative courts.[5]

The Constitutional Court controls normative acts that are in force, including international agreements (either ratified or not ratified). However, a characteristic element of the Court's jurisdiction is that it can also control provisions that are no longer legally binding when the protection of constitutional rights and freedoms is at stake.

[1] A Harding, P Leyland, and T Groppi, 'Constitutional Courts: Forms, Functions and Practice in Comparative Perspective' (2008) 3 *Journal of Comparative Law* 1, 6.

[2] Articles 189, 188(4) and 131(1) of the Constitution, respectively.

[3] See ch 2.

[4] Article 188 of the Constitution.

[5] See ch 7.

Accordingly, the Constitutional Court has reviewed the constitutionality of important laws, which at the moment of their review were no longer legally binding, yet whose assessment was crucial from the perspective of human rights protection in Poland.[6] Such was the case concerning the review of the martial law decrees of 12 December 1981, which had a concrete legal meaning.[7] The martial law decrees issued to stop the democratic change started by the Solidarity movement were formally repealed in 2002, yet were still applied in practice to individuals. Until the decrees were declared unconstitutional, the victims of martial law could not claim their rights. The law on the Constitutional Court of 2016 has limited the review of provisions that are no longer in force, which is now possible only in the form of a constitutional complaint when the protection of constitutional freedoms and rights is at stake. This constraint on the Court's competence raises doubts. Possibly, in this way the legislature attempts to exclude from constitutional review 'remedy laws' issued between 2015 and 2016 on the request of eligible applicants. This presents a clear regression in the competences of the Constitutional Court when compared to its position between 1997 and 2015. In addition, the approach of the legislature cannot be sustained from the perspective that the Constitution is the supreme law of the state. Accordingly, the law system cannot contain loopholes that are excluded from review for compliance with the Constitution.

Another element of the Constitutional Court's jurisdiction is the material understanding of a legal act. To qualify as such, an act must provide a legal norm – a general and abstract norm. The way in which an act is officially named does not matter. For this reason, the Court is able to control pronouncements of central organs of administration, be they resolutions or instructions. Similarly, it may review acts issued by social organisations or trade unions, as long they contain legal norms. For instance, the Court reviewed the code of medical ethics issued by the National Council of Medical Doctors.[8] In contrast, it does not review acts of an individual and concrete character. For instance, notwithstanding the further discussed controversies surrounding the election of judges, the Court refused to check the resolution the Chamber of Deputies concerning the election of new judges of the Constitutional Court for the seats that had already been occupied.[9]

[6] This review was based on art 39(3) of the Law on Constitutional Court of 1997, JL 1997 No 102 Pos 643 with changes.

[7] Constitutional Court, judgment of 16 February 2011, K 35/08, OTK ZU 2A/2011, poz 11.

[8] Constitutional Court, decision of 7 October 1992, U 1/92, OTK ZU 1992, poz 38.

[9] Constitutional Court, decision of 7 January 2016, U 8/15, OTK ZU A/2016, poz 1.

Within the constitutional review of normative acts, the Constitutional Court explores both the content of the act (material conformity) as well as the competence to issue the act and compliance with procedural requirements (formal conformity). While the former implies a hierarchical comparison of legal norms, formal conformity includes a factual analysis of the procedural steps toward the adoption of the act in question. The review of formal conformity can sometimes lead to a derogation of an invalidly adopted statute as a whole rather than only of a specific provision. For example, the Court found the 'remedy law' of 22 December 2015 to be unconstitutional as a whole.[10] This act contained a number of provisions with the aim of blocking the functioning of the Court. For instance, the Court was obliged to consider cases in the order of their registration on the docket. Crucially, in this case, when adopting that statute, the Chamber of Deputies decided that it should enter into force with immediate effect, intentionally removing *vacatio legis*. The parliament's intention was to block constitutional review of the act in question. This law was supposed to be both the subject of the constitutional review as well as the legal basis for that review. In such a situation, the Court would only be able to find that the 'remedy law' complied with the Constitution. On logical grounds, finding the act in question to be unconstitutional would be excluded. In the end, the Court declared the 'remedy law' to be unconstitutional as a whole. In its review, it applied the provisions of the Constitution directly, leaving aside the majority of the provisions of the act in question.

The Constitutional Court, as is the case for any classic constitutional court, does not assess the fitness, effectiveness or rationality of acts of parliament. For example, when considering the 2010 Act on the rationalisation of employment in some of the state organs, the Court indicated that it does not evaluate the expediency and necessity of workforce reduction in government administration.[11] Similarly, it does not consider the legislature's interests or views that were the basis for the act at stake, leaving such assessments to the electorate. Moreover, it is not competent to decide on cases where the Constitution or another act obliged the law-maker to issue a specific provision, but the law-maker failed to do so (legislative failure, *zaniechanie ustawodawcze*). For example, the Court found that the law regulating payments from social insurance funds in cases of illness and maternity leave lacked a provision indicating the

[10] See Constitutional Court, judgment of 9 March 2016, K 47/15.

[11] Constitutional Court, judgment of 14 June 2011, Kp 1/11, OTK ZU 5A/2011, poz 41.

minimal amount of that benefit in the case of inability to work.[12] The Court decided to discontinue the proceedings. It is rightly argued that the Court has no legitimacy to relieve the legislature in this respect or, in other words, to act as a 'positive legislator'.[13] A different situation distinguished in the Court's case law, one where the Court does step in, is when the legislature omitted part of a legal norm which is demanded by the constitutional benchmark (legislative omission, *pominięcie ustawodawcze*).[14] For instance, the Court found that a statute which offered teachers a reduced fare on public transportation excluded from that benefit – in violation of the Constitution – kindergarten teachers.[15] In practice, such cases tend to concern a lack of procedures allowing citizens to claim a certain right.

The Constitutional Court reviews the compliance of law with the Constitution on request by two types of applicants with either general or limited eligibility. General eligibility permits the review of any legal act that falls within the Court's jurisdiction. The group accorded general eligibility includes the most important organs of state, such as the President, the Prime Minister or the presidents of the highest courts.[16] In practice, most frequently, the Ombudsman and a group of 50 deputies petition the Constitutional Court.[17] The applicants who have limited access to the Court, including, for example, churches and religious organisations, can request review only if an act concerns matters relevant to the scope of their activity. Finally, the National Council of the Judiciary can demand review only to the extent to which the provision concerns the independence of courts and judges.[18]

Beyond those instances of abstract constitutional review, the Constitutional Court conducts concrete control in the procedural form of legal questions and constitutional complaints, which will be discussed in turn. A legal question is available exclusively to courts when

[12] Constitutional Court, decision of 8 February 2017, P 44/15, OTK ZU A/2017, poz 3.

[13] L Bosek and M Wild, *Kontrola konstytucyjności prawa. Zagadnienia ustrojowe, procesowe i materialnoprawne* (Warsaw, CH Beck, 2011) 83–85.

[14] See Constitutional Court, judgment of 20 November 2007, SK 57/05, OTK ZU 10A/2007, poz 125; judgment of 6 May 1998 K 37/97, OTK ZU 3/1998, poz 33; judgment of 9 October 2001, SK 8/00, OTK ZU 7/2001, poz 211. See also Venice Commission, Special Bulletin on Legislative Omission (Council of Europe, 2008).

[15] Constitutional Court, judgment of 16 November 2010, K 2/10, OTK ZU 9A/2010, poz 102.

[16] For full list of eligible applicants, see art 191(1), point 1 of the Constitution.

[17] See Constitutional Court, *Informacja o istotnych problemach wynikających z działalności i orzecznictwa Trybunału Konstytucyjnego* (Warsaw, 2017), 71.

[18] For full list of applicants, see art 191(1), points 2–5 of the Constitution.

deciding a case and must concern a provision whose compliance with the benchmark of review, be it the Constitution or ratified international agreement, would influence the outcome of the case of the requesting court. The requesting court must demonstrate a functional link, namely that the Constitutional Court's reply is meaningful for deciding the case before the requesting court. In reply, the Constitutional Court, after a public hearing of the case, issues a judgment addressed to the requesting court. Sometimes such a judgment can trigger the need for action by the parliament. In practice, between 1998 and 2016, the number of legal questions has been steadily growing, and the Constitutional Court decided an average of around 48 legal questions per year, originating predominantly from the ordinary courts.[19] A well-known case initiated by a legal question concerned a provision of the criminal code regulating responsibility for publicly offending the President – punishable by up to three years' imprisonment. The regional court in Gdańsk enquired whether the law in question complied with the constitutionally guaranteed freedom of speech. Ultimately, the Constitutional Court found the provision to be compatible with the Constitution.[20]

Constitutional complaint, the second form of concrete review, is the essential legal remedy available to everyone (individuals and other eligible applicants). This type of review concerns constitutional freedoms and rights (subjective rights). As such, constitutional complaint is one of the crucial novelties brought into the Polish system of fundamental rights protection by the Constitution of 1997. Known in the Constitutions of Germany, Austria or Spain, since the 1990s, it has also been present in the legal systems of Central and Eastern European states such as the Czech Republic and Slovakia.[21] However, in contrast to the well-known German constitutional complaint system, the Polish model is designed narrowly, as it does not take into account the application of law.[22] Specifically, within this procedure, the Constitutional Court does not review ordinary court judgments and administrative decisions in the manner of its German counterpart. A remarkable example of a case initiated by a constitutional complaint concerned the system of ordinary courts. An individual, who was temporarily detained, questioned the

[19] Authors' own calculation based on Constitutional Court (n 17) 72.

[20] Constitutional Court, judgment of 6 July 2011, P 12/09, OTK ZU 6A/2011, poz 51.

[21] See M de Visser, *Constitutional Review in Europe: A Comparative Analysis* (Oxford, Hart Publishing, 2015) 142.

[22] W Heun, *The Constitution of Germany* (Oxford, Hart Publishing, 2011) 174.

staffing of the judicial bench adjudicating his case. The judge deciding his case was an assessor: a person who had the status of a judge in terms of adjudicating, but was not granted the immunities available to judges and was appointed by the Justice Minister without the involvement of the National Council of the Judiciary. The judgments of assessors were supervised by assigned judges. Surprisingly, in proceedings launched by a constitutional complaint, the Constitutional Court declared the legal provisions concerning the assessors to be unconstitutional as they violated the right of access to the court, part of which requires the correct staffing of the bench.[23]

Within the constitutional complaint procedure, the Constitutional Court reviews the conformity with the Constitution of a statute or another normative act that was the basis of a court or organ of public administration's final decision concerning the applicant's constitutional freedoms or rights or on obligations.[24] Thus, the legal basis of the final decision and not the decision itself is the subject of the constitutional complaint. Beyond the constitutional prerequisite of finality of decision in one's case, other material requirements to launch a constitutional complaint have a statutory basis. The applicant must indicate which of his or her constitutional freedoms or rights were violated, and how. The violation must be present at the moment of lodging the constitutional complaint. The constitutional complaint has no *actio popularis* character, as the applicant must act to protect his or her right, and not that of a third party. Moreover, the constitutional complaint has a subsidiary character: all possible legal remedies in courts or within the administrative procedure must be exhausted before launching a constitutional complaint. However, this does not require a previous application for a cassation complaint (for civil cases) or cassation (for criminal cases) before the Supreme Court. The Constitutional Court would halt its own proceedings and wait for the decision of the Supreme Court in such cases. Finally, the constitutional complaint has an incidental character: the court or administrative decision must affect the applicant.

The constitutional complaint, which is free from any fees, must fulfil a few procedural requirements, such as being drafted in the form of a pleading (*pismo procesowe*) by a legal professional (an advocate or an attorney), unless the applicant himself or herself exercises one

[23] Constitutional Court, decision of 24 October 2007, SK 7/06, OTK ZU 9A/2007, poz 108.

[24] Article 79(1) of the Constitution.

of the legal professions.[25] The aim is to eliminate evident cases where a constitutional complaint will not be available, such as an applicant's dissatisfaction with a court's judgment as such. The complaint must be launched within three months of the delivery of the final judgment or decision.

The Constitution makes the constitutional complaint available to anyone whose freedoms or rights have been infringed, except for foreigners who were declined the right to asylum.[26] In addition, the Constitutional Court allows constitutional complaints from applicants other than a natural person, such as political parties, associations, trade unions or economic organisations, to the extent that they can be a subject of freedoms and rights under the Constitution.[27] These cases usually concern freedom of association, freedom of economic activity, and the right to protect private property. A crucial issue here is the extent to which these rights are connected with the protection of human dignity.[28] Finally, the lack of legal personality is not an obstacle to being a subject of constitutional rights and, as a consequence, to eligibility. However, thus far, the Constitutional Court has denied communes and other organs of local self-government the eligibility to launch a constitutional complaint, as they exercise state authority and are eligible to initiate abstract constitutional review.

Further limitations developed in the case law concern the subject of the constitutional complaint. For example, a constitutional complaint cannot use as a benchmark for review programme principles of the Constitution,[29] or constitutional principles such as equality or the democratic state ruled by law;[30] they can only be an additional, and not a self-standing, basis for constitutional review. A constitutional complaint cannot question the compliance of a provision of a statute (or another normative act) with an international treaty or a provision of international law. However, a constitutional complaint can concern an act of EU secondary law, such as a regulation. In such a case, the constitutional

[25] See Law of 30 November 2016 on the Organisation and Proceedings before the Constitutional Court.

[26] Articles 79(2) and 56(1) of the Constitution.

[27] For a case in which the Constitutional Court declined eligibility to political parties under some circumstances, see Constitutional Court, judgment of 15 September 2012, Ts 256/09, OTK ZU 5B/2011, poz 359.

[28] Article 30 of the Constitution. See Constitutional Court, K 19/00 of 7 May 2001, OTK ZU 4/2001, poz 82; decision of 12 October 2004, Ts 35/04 of, OTK ZU 1B/2005, 1B, poz 25. See also ch 7.

[29] See ch 9.

[30] Articles 32 and 2 of the Constitution, respectively. See ch 2.

complaint should 'make probable' that the act in question substantially lowers the protection of fundamental rights in comparison to the standard guaranteed by the Constitution of 1997.[31]

As a consequence of a successful constitutional complaint, the unconstitutional legal provision is eliminated from the legal system with an *erga omnes* effect. Yet, the judgments or decisions that were issued on the basis of the unconstitutional provision in question are not eliminated or invalidated, although the applicant can, on the basis of the Constitutional Court's judgment, request resumption of proceedings. All types of legal procedures (civil, criminal and administrative) contain mechanisms enabling such a resumption. In cases where the unconstitutional provision does not lose its binding force immediately, the Constitutional Court can still endow the applicant with a right to request resumption of proceedings.[32]

As a procedural filter, the constitutional complaint undergoes a preliminary screening by the Court sitting as a lone judge. In case of inadmissibility, the applicant can lodge a complaint, to be decided by the Court sitting as a bench of three judges. Between 1997 and 2016, only 18 per cent of all constitutional complaints received were admissible.[33] As a consequence, on average, the Constitutional Court decides around 50 constitutional complaints per year.[34] In sum, after its introduction in 1997, the constitutional complaint turned out to be a successful tool in the protection of fundamental rights, and although some ideas to widen its scope were discussed, these were decided against.[35]

ii. Aims and Functioning of Political Parties

One of the ancillary competences of the Constitutional Court, although exercised sporadically, concerns political parties.[36] The review of the aims of a political party can take place before the party's registration by the regional court in Warsaw or when the party is already functioning in the political life of the state. For instance, the Court checked the

[31] Constitutional Court, judgment of 16 November 2011, SK 45/09, OTK ZU 9A/2011, poz 97.

[32] See Constitutional Court, judgment of 18 May 2004, SK 38/03, OTK ZU 5A/2004, poz 45.

[33] Constitutional Court (n 17) 87.

[34] Authors' own calculation for the years 1998–2016 based on Constitutional Court (n 17) 72.

[35] On various models of constitutional complaint, see J Trzciński (ed), *Skarga konstytucyjna* (Warsaw, Wydawnictwo Sejmowe, 2000) 33.

[36] See ch 3.

constitutionality of the aims of the far-right Polish National Revival party. The party introduced as symbols in its statute a logo that expressed a prohibition of homosexual propaganda and a Celtic cross. The regional court in Warsaw had doubts as to whether the aims of the party expressed by those symbols were admissible. However, the Constitutional Court dismissed the case, delegating the assessment of these symbols to the regional court.[37] Beyond reviewing of the aims of a political party, the Court can review its actual functioning. For example, it sought to assess the activities of an agrarian party which included that party blocking roads,[38] or forcing a candidate in parliamentary elections to sign a bill of exchange guaranteeing that the person would remain in the party after elections.[39]

A characteristic element of the review of the functioning of a political party is, first, that the applicant must prove that the functioning of the party infringes the Constitution and, second, that the Constitutional Court can request the Public Prosecutor to conduct a necessary fact-finding inquiry. This was the case, for instance, with regard to bills of exchange mentioned earlier. The Constitutional Court itself is not competent to declare a political party to be illegal. If it finds the aims or functioning of the party to be in violation of the Constitution, this creates a basis for the Warsaw regional court to declare the party to be illegal by striking it off the registry of political parties. However, the reasons for illegality are restricted to those indicated in the Constitution, which prohibits, inter alia, political parties the programmes of which are based upon totalitarian methods and the modes of activity of Nazism, fascism or Communism.[40] Over the years, the Constitutional Court has reviewed only a handful of requests concerning political parties. In particular, no party has ever been declared illegal.

iii. Competence Disputes

Another function of the Constitutional Court is the resolution of competence disputes between central constitutional organs.[41] Those cases concern situations where two or more organs declare themselves competent to decide an issue, but also those where none of the organs declares

[37] Constitutional Court, decision of 6 April 2011, Pp 1/10, OTK ZU 3A/2011, poz 27.

[38] Constitutional Court, decision of 16 July 2003, Pp 1/02, OTK ZU 6A/2003, poz 71.

[39] Constitutional Court, decision of 17 December 2007, Pp 1/07, OTK ZU 11A/2007, poz 165.

[40] Article 13 of the Constitution.

[41] ibid art 192.

itself competent (positive and negative conflicts). Vertical disputes – for instance, between the Prime Minister and a minister, or between a minister and a voivode – do not fall within the competence of the Court. Such disputes are resolved through a political rather than a legal process. Similarly, the Court does not delve into the controversies between local organs or between non-constitutional organs. The controversies need to be real in character – not potential or hypothetical – and must concern the existence of a competence or its lack thereof, and its legal shape, as well as conflicting competences. The Court has exercised this competence only occasionally. Between 1997 and 2018, there have only been three requests in this matter. The first of the disputes, between the National Council of the Judiciary and the President, concerned the lack of appointment of judges by the latter.[42] The second case concerned the constitutional organ eligible to represent Poland in the European Council.[43] In the third case, the Marshal of the Chamber of Deputies called upon the Constitutional Court to settle a competence 'conflict' between the President and the Supreme Court with regard to the presidential exercise of the power of pardon. This issue has thus far not been decided, but does not have the character of a real competence dispute.[44]

iv. Impediment

The final competence of the Constitutional Court concerns the office of the head of state. First, the Court determines whether there exists an impediment to the exercise of the office by the President. Second, if such an obstacle exists, the Court endows the Marshal of the Chamber of Deputies with the power of exercising the office of the head of state. Thus far, the Constitutional Court has not been called upon to exercise this function.

B. Election of the Justices and Structure of the Constitutional Court

The Court consists of 15 judges elected individually by the Chamber of Deputies for a nine-year term.[45] The individual character of the election

[42] The case was discontinued. Constitutional Court, decision of 23 June 2008, Kpt 1/08 OTK ZU 5A/2008, poz 97. See ch 4.

[43] Constitutional Court, decision of 20 May 2009, Kpt 2/08, OTK ZU 5A/2009, poz 78. See ch 4.

[44] Constitutional Court, Kpt 1/17 (pending). See especially the arguments of the First President of the Supreme Court and of the Ombudsman.

[45] Article 194(1) of the Constitution.

process of a judge implies that the parliament votes on each of the candidates separately and that each of the candidates serves his or her own term for a defined period of time. The judges cannot be re-elected. Both the size of the court and the terms of the judges are typical of constitutional courts elsewhere.[46]

The candidates for justices are chosen from amongst 'persons distinguished by their knowledge of the law',[47] who fulfil the requirements necessary to become a judge of the Supreme Court.[48] The candidacies for justices are put forward by the Presidency of the Chamber of Deputies or at least 50 MPs. The Chamber of Deputies elects the judges with an absolute majority in the presence of at least half of the MPs. The introduction of a qualified majority vote could potentially increase the legitimacy of the judges. Still, the argument that the current absolute majority requirement is too political can be rejected relatively easily. The election of judges takes place within the system of parliamentary government and the judges receive their mandates directly from the nation. The political dimension of the election process is always present in a system of representation, regardless of the necessary majorities or participating organs. Although the Chamber of Deputies elects the members of the Constitutional Court, according to the Constitution, the Court is a power that is distinct and separate from the legislative power. Since November 2016, the Rules of Procedure of the Chamber of Deputies, rather than a statute, as had previously been the case, regulate the required vote threshold of the election process.[49] This change weakens the prominence of the election procedure, possibly expressing the idea that the composition of the Constitutional Court remains within the legislature's competence.

The President is obliged to accept the oath of office immediately after the Chamber of Deputies elects a new judge. The head of state has no freedom of decision in this respect. The President's role in the selection of judges is merely a ceremonial rubber stamp of the competence of the Chamber of Deputies within this procedure. If it were otherwise, the President would become an additional organ, next to the Chamber of Deputies, co-deciding on the staffing of the Court.[50] The term of office

[46] See de Visser (n 21) 224.

[47] Article 194(1) of the Constitution.

[48] Article 3 of Law of 30 November 2016 on the Status of Judges of the Constitutional Court.

[49] Article 30 of the Rules of Procedure of the Chamber of Deputies, MP 2018 Pos 729.

[50] See Constitutional Court, judgment of 3 December 2015, K 34/15, OTK ZU 11A/2015, poz 185; and of 9 December 2015, K 35/15, OTK ZU 11A/2015, poz 186.

of the judge starts not on the day of judges' swearing in before the President, but instead on the day indicated in the resolution of the Chamber of Deputies, or on the day when the term of office of the judge who previously occupied the office in question expires.[51]

The selection of justices in Poland by just one institution – the Chamber of Deputies – is relatively simple compared to the mechanisms in place in other, more mature democracies. For instance, in France, Italy and Germany, the right to elect a judge to the constitutional court is distributed among several public institutions and, at the same time, the entry requirements for the candidates are more liberal, as is the case, for example, in France, where a person with no legal qualification can become a judge.[52] Nonetheless, the political culture, the mutual trust of the main political parliamentary forces and the long legal tradition enable a smoothly functioning nomination process in these countries. In other words, although the judicial appointment in such countries relies much less on legal rules than in Poland, they tend to result in the selection of judges whose position is not put into question.

Judges of the Constitutional Court are independent and subject only to the Constitution in the exercise of their office.[53] They cannot be removed from office. Their mandate can expire before the end of term only in the cases foreseen in the statute and this must be confirmed by the Assembly General of the Judges.[54] Moreover, judges of the Constitutional Court cannot be a member of a political party or a trade union, or perform public activities that are incompatible with the principles of the independence of the courts and judges.[55] This restriction continues to apply after a judge has retired. Finally, the judges cannot be held criminally responsible or deprived of liberty without the prior consent of the Constitutional Court.[56] They cannot be detained or arrested, unless they are apprehended in the commission of an offence and when such detention is necessary for securing the proper course of proceedings. However, the President of the Constitutional Court may order an immediate release of the detained.

In organisational terms, the Constitutional Court consists of the General Assembly of the Judges and the President and Deputy President

[51] See Constitutional Court, K 35/15.
[52] For a comparison, see de Visser (n 21) 224.
[53] Article 195(1) of the Constitution.
[54] See art 18 of the Law on the Status of the Judges of the Constitutional Court of 2016.
[55] Article 195(3) of the Constitution.
[56] ibid art 196.

of the Constitutional Court. The head of state appoints the President of the Constitutional Court and his or her deputy from amongst a list of candidates put forward by the General Assembly of the Judges. The President of the Constitutional Court is chosen for a six-year term,[57] represents the institution and has a number of functions indicated in statute and the rules of procedure. The General Assembly of the Judges of the Constitutional Court, which consists of all the judges of the Constitutional Court, besides proposing the candidates for the President of the Constitutional Court and his or her deputy, adopts the rules of procedure of the Court, and discusses the activities of the Court and issues arising from its case law.

C. The 2015 Crisis in Judicial Appointments

The model of selection of judges by the Chamber of Deputies which has been in force since the beginning of the Court's existence – over 30 years ago – allowed for the uninterrupted election of new justices and the filling of vacant seats. This system transpired not to promote the selection of politicians for the judges of the Constitutional Court; instead, the Chamber of Deputies perceived the Court as a court of law and usually elected university professors and legal professionals (advocates, judges etc).

In 2015, a conflict over vacant seats in the Constitutional Court erupted at the intersection of the outgoing 7th Chamber of Deputies (2011–15) led by the Civic Platform party and the incoming 8th Chamber of Deputies (2015–present) controlled by the Law and Justice party. The departing 7th Chamber of Deputies introduced a provision into the Law of 25 June 2015 that enabled it to put forward candidates for judges for all seats becoming vacant in 2015. As a consequence, on 8 October 2015, the 7th Chamber of Deputies elected five judges. Three of the seats in question became vacant during the term of office of that parliament, while the two other seats would become vacant only in December 2015, and therefore after the parliamentary elections scheduled for 25 October 2015. President Andrzej Duda, formerly affiliated with the Law and Justice party, did not accept the oath of office of any of the five judges elected by the 7th Chamber of Deputies. Following the parliamentary elections, the incoming 8th Chamber of Deputies, now under the control of the Law and Justice party, passed five resolutions depriving all

[57] Before 2016, the President's term was not defined in the statute, but the nomination was made for the entirety of that judge's term at the Court.

five resolutions of 8 October 2015 of legal force on electing five Constitutional Court judges adopted by the 7th Chamber of Deputies.[58] Soon afterwards, in December 2015, the new governing majority elected five new judges for the vacant seats and the President immediately swore them in that same night.

In the meantime, the Constitutional Court examined the statutory basis for the election of judges.[59] It held the provision of the Law on Constitutional Court of June 2015, which formed the statutory basis for the election of judges, to be compliant with the Constitution with regard to the three judges elected by the 7th Chamber of Deputies for seats that were vacant before the parliamentary elections. The Constitutional Court declared their election valid and there was no obstacle for these three incoming judges to take an oath before the President. However, the Constitutional Court found the same statutory basis to be incompatible with the Constitution to the extent to which it was the basis for the election of judges for the two seats that became vacant only after the parliamentary elections, implying that their appointment procedure should be halted and closed.[60] Despite some delay, the Prime Minister published the Constitutional Court's judgment, thereby making it binding. Nonetheless, as of July 2019, the three justices chosen by the 7th Chamber of Deputies have yet to be, de jure, sworn in by the President. Instead, the head of state has accepted the oath of office from all the five justices elected by the Chamber of Deputies during its 8th term.

This serious and painful conflict remains unresolved. However, from the perspective of the constitutional system of the state, even more pertinent is the lack of publication of the Constitutional Court's judgments resulting from the dispute. Specifically at stake are three judgments of the Constitutional Court that concerned the constitutionality of the 'remedy laws'.[61] According to the Prime Minister, the Constitutional Court issued these judgments in violation of the Law on the Constitutional Court, as it did not include the three judges elected by the 8th Chamber of Deputies in December 2015. In June 2018, under pressure from the European Commission, the government decided to publish the

[58] See MP 2015 poz 1131–35. The Constitutional Court discontinued the proceedings on the compliance of the resolutions of the parliament with the Constitution. See Constitutional Court, decision of 7 January 2016, U 8/15, OTK ZU A/2016, poz 1.

[59] See Constitutional Court, K 34/15.

[60] ibid.

[61] Constitutional Court, K 47/15; judgment of 11 August 2016, K 39/16; and judgment of 7 November 2016, K 44/16.

judgments in question.[62] However, the publication of these judgments did not follow the constitutional procedure that demands immediate publication by the Prime Minister in the official journal.[63] The requirement was bypassed by issuing a special statute publishing the judgments in question. In addition, these judgments were labelled 'decisions' (*rozstrzygnięcia*) instead of 'judgments' (*wyroki*) in order to diminish their legal value. By not publishing the judgments of the Constitutional Court, the executive branch questioned their finality, undermining the position of the Court in the system of powers.

D. The Institutional Design of Constitutional Adjudication

Above all, constitutional review in Poland is a posteriori (or *ex post*) in character. The Constitutional Court assesses provisions of acts that have already been adopted and are legally binding, or are in the process of *vacatio legis*, the period between the promulgation of a law and the moment it takes legal effect. The posterior review is often perceived as the most appropriate, as the lack of compliance with the Constitution is usually best exposed when a provision is applied in the legal system.[64] This type of constitutional review, present in principle in all constitutional courts, can be launched on the basis of a motion of eligible state organs, through a constitutional complaint, and by courts in the form of a legal question.

The Polish constitutional system also foresees the opposite of a posteriori constitutional review in the form of a preventive review (or a priori review) which takes place before the entry into force of a legal act. Specifically, the President requests the Constitutional Court to check whether a statute adopted by the parliament complies with the Constitution before signing it, and if the statute is constitutional, the head of state cannot refuse the signature.[65] In addition, the President can request the constitutional review of international agreements and, it is assumed that in the case of a negative judgment, he or she should decline the ratification of the agreement at stake.[66] The preventive review is sometimes questioned as an undue involvement of the Constitutional Court in the legislative process, the domain of the parliament, and as representing

[62] See ch 9.
[63] Article 190(2) of the Constitution.
[64] B Banaszak, *Prawo konstytucyjne* (Warsaw, CH Beck, 2008) 109.
[65] Article 122(3) of the Constitution. On the practice, see ch 3.
[66] Article 133(2) of the Constitution.

a form of 'government of judges' (*gouvernement des juges*) leading to judicial activism.[67] Nonetheless, the preventive review averts unconstitutional provisions from entering the legal system and offers some legal certainty for legal affairs, as it does not demand cumbersome procedures to eliminate an unconstitutional provision. A provision that was subject to a preventive review can subsequently also be questioned within a posteriori review.

Another division within the constitutional review in Poland is between abstract and concrete review. The abstract review takes place when a legal provision is questioned based on a general conviction that it is not compatible with the Constitution. This type of review concerns statutes before they are signed into law by the President, international agreements before their ratification by the President, and statutes when requested by the applicants indicated in Article 191(1) of the Constitution. In contrast, concrete review of an act takes place in the context of a specific case before an ordinary court. The legal question or constitutional complaint exemplify concrete review.

Figure 6.1 The number of cases received by the Constitutional Court in 2015

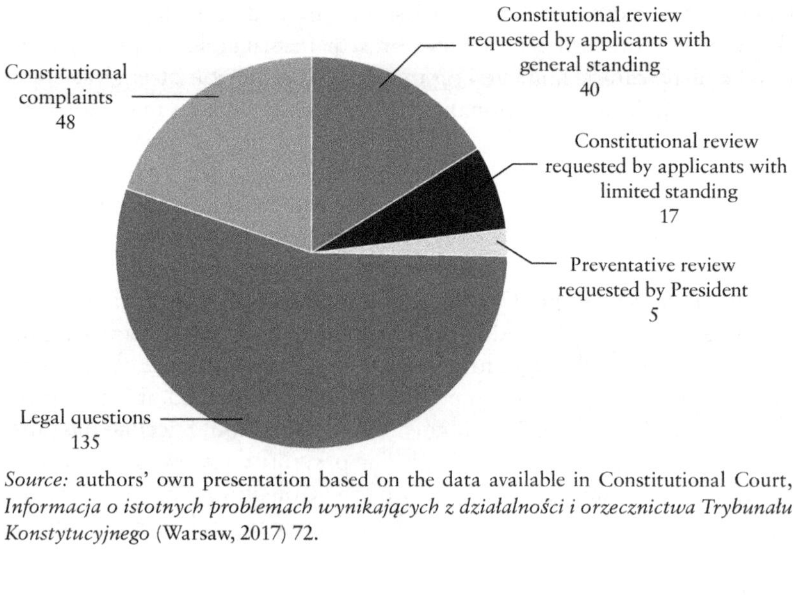

Source: authors' own presentation based on the data available in Constitutional Court, *Informacja o istotnych problemach wynikających z działalności i orzecznictwa Trybunału Konstytucyjnego* (Warsaw, 2017) 72.

[67] E Lambert, *Le Gouvernement des juges et la lutte contre la législation sociale aux États-Unis. L'expérience américaine du contrôle judiciaire de la constitutionnalité des lois* (Paris, Marcel Giard & Cie., 1921).

Against this overview of the Constitutional Court's competences, Figure 6.1 shows the distribution of the case load of the Constitutional Court in 2015, the year preceding the constitutional crisis. The largest share, over half of the 245 cases in total, is accounted for by exercising constitutional review upon a legal question by a court. The second most frequent type of case received relates to constitutional complaints. Constitutional review requested by applicants with general standing and limited standing represent 40 and 17 cases, respectively. Finally, there were five requests for preventive review made by the President. There were no instances of cases involving the investigation of political parties or a conflict of competences that year, both of which, as was pointed out earlier, are launched rather infrequently.

E. Judgments and Their Legal Effect

The Court's judgments are made by a majority of votes of the judges.[68] Since 2016, the text of the judgment indicates whether it was adopted unanimously or by a majority of votes of the judges. Judges may issue both dissenting and concurring opinions. Regarding the merits, in its early days the Constitutional Court issued mostly so-called simple judgments on a provision's compliance (positive judgment) or non-compliance with the Constitution (negative judgment), in addition to the judgments declaring the benchmark of review as inadequate (irrelevant) vis-a-vis the challenged measure (*wyrok o nieadekwatności*). Since the 1990s, however, simple judgments, despite maintaining the original Kelsenian spirit, have been revealed to be too coarse to express the complexity of constitutional adjudication, which often takes place not at the level of the provision itself, but rather at the level of its interpretation. As a consequence, the Court developed new types of judgments, namely interpretative (*wyroki interpretacyjne*) and spatial (*wyroki zakresowe*) judgments. These new types of judgments clearly exceed the limits of a Kelsenian model of constitutional courts. In the Kelsenian model, a judge was a reviewer of the correctness of issued laws; a judge was reminiscent of a sorter whose role was only to reject invalid provisions. However, in the model functioning in Poland, a judge takes it upon himself or herself to interpret the Constitution and the provisions of the controlled act.

In its interpretative judgments, the Constitutional Court searches for an understanding of a provision that is closest to the constitutional

[68] Article 190(5) of the Constitution.

benchmark involved. In such a judgment, the Court includes a precise understanding of the provision under review. The provision in question does not lose its legal force; rather, the Court repeals a specific understanding of that provision that does not comply with the Constitution. In spatial judgments, the Court decides whether an understanding of a provision is compliant (or non-compliant) with the Constitution in a particular set of circumstances (eg, a particular timeframe). For example, the Court found the withdrawal of a driver's licence in case of speeding to be compliant with the Constitution; however, the retention by the state of the driver's licence is unconstitutional to the extent that the speeding occurs due to force majeure.[69] A special type of judgment is application judgments (*wyroki aplikacyjne*), where the Court indicates the effect of the judgment on the legal system. A well-known example is the judgment where the Court found that a parking fee paid in Warsaw on the basis of an unconstitutional provision would not be reimbursed.[70]

The development of interpretative and spatial judgments is a direct consequence of the complexity of the Constitution as a normative act. Constitutional norms often demand complex methods of adjudication. These new types of judgments play a role as part of the Constitution's safeguards and enable the maintenance of legal consistency. As such, the interpretative and spatial judgments do not lead to a derogation of a provision, but rather give it a meaning that is compatible with the Constitution or eliminate the unconstitutional meaning of a certain provision. The Constitutional Court is often criticised, especially by the Supreme Court, for its interpretative judgments, which are perceived as exceeding the Constitutional Court's competences as indicated in the Constitution. According to the Supreme Court, the judgments of the Constitutional Court that declare a specific interpretation of a normative act to be contrary to the Constitution, but do not lead to a loss of the legally binding effect of that provision, cannot constitute a basis for reopening civil court proceedings.[71]

According to the Constitution, the judgments of the Constitutional Court are universally binding and final.[72] All judgments of the Court demand immediate publication in the official journal (*Journal of Laws*

[69] Constitutional Court, judgment of 11 October 2016, K 24/15, OTK ZU A/2016, poz 77.

[70] Constitutional Court, judgment of 10 December 2002, P 6/02, OTK ZU 7A/2002, poz 91.

[71] Supreme Court, resolution of 17 December 2009, III PZP 2/09.

[72] Article 190(1) of the Constitution.

of the Republic of Poland), or in the Official Gazette of the Republic of Poland, *Monitor Polski*. A judgment declaring a provision to be unconstitutional, be it published or not yet published in the official journal, calls into question the presumption of constitutionality of the law at stake. However, its publication is necessary in order for the change in the law to occur.[73] In principle, the judgments of the Constitutional Court enter into force on the day of their publication in the official journal.[74] Exceptionally, the Court can indicate a date other than the publication date of the judgment for the end of the binding force of the act. However, such a time period cannot exceed 18 months in the case of a statute or 12 months in relation to any other normative act. In the case of judgments with financial consequences not provided for in the budget, the Court specifies the date for the end of the binding force of the normative act concerned, after seeking the opinion of the Council of Ministers. Postponement of the derogation of an unconstitutional provision usually has some rational aim, such as preventing legal gaps, or other unforeseen consequences, such as sudden budgetary expenses. However, the Constitutional Court tends to be reluctant to set a date different from that of the judgment's publication date to end the binding force of a legal provision. One of the reasons for this is that the postponement is problematic for the courts. In the legal system, even an unconstitutional provision must be applied until the moment of its derogation. In practice, this is often interpreted as implying that courts are not unconditionally bound to apply the unconstitutional provision in question, deciding on a case-by-case basis while considering the protected values at stake.[75]

The Constitutional Court's judgments declaring a provision under review to be compliant with the Constitution do not affect the validity of that provision. Any proceedings questioning the same provision against the same constitutional benchmark and making identical claims will be discontinued (*ne bis in idem*). However, a negative judgment does have a derogative effect. The provision at stake is no longer valid and applicable. It is removed from the legal system not only in the formal sense, but also in the substantial sense, so that the provision does not affect the practice of law. Therefore, these judgments affect the sphere of existence and application of law. The Court describes such a change as the

[73] See Constitutional Court, K 35/15.

[74] Article 190(3) of the Constitution.

[75] See W Płowiec, *Orzeczenia Trybunału Konstytucyjnego z terminem utraty mocy obowiązującej niekonstytucyjnej regulacji* (Poznań, Wydawnictwo Naukowe Uniwersytetu im Adama Mickiewicza, 2017) 229–89.

'absolute, unconditional, and direct elimination of legal provisions' indicated in the judgment.[76] These provisions are eliminated independently from the actions of state organs in this regard. In this sense, the Constitutional Court is sometimes labelled in Kelsenian terms as a so-called 'negative legislator'.[77] Yet, this notion is inadequate to describe the Polish Constitutional Court, as it does not act in any form typical of the legislature. The Constitutional Court has argued that loss of the validity of a legal provision as a consequence of a judgment differs from the repeal of a provision as a consequence of the legislature's action.[78] Lastly, if a final judgment of a court or an administrative decision was issued on the basis of a provision declared unconstitutional, this presents a basis for reopening the relevant proceedings or for challenging the decision.[79]

F. Compliance with and the Implementation of Judgments

The Court has no power over the implementation of its judgments, which corresponds to the Kelsenian model. The judgments on the unconstitutionality of provisions demand action on the part of the relevant state organ, most frequently the legislature. In practice, the Senate and the Government Centre for Legislation (*Rządowe Centrum Legislacji*) monitor the judgments of the Constitutional Court. Up to the end of 2018, the Senate had adopted a total of 162 legislative initiatives that aim at adjusting law to the Court's jurisprudence.[80] The implementation of judgments may encounter certain obstacles as the parliament, for various reasons, may ignore judgments that are inconvenient or hard to implement. This is the case especially with regard to judgments that imply financial costs for the state, for example, an increase of the tax-free amount of personal income.[81] Obviously, the Court has no impact on the execution of its judgments by the parliament. Although the Court and the parliament represent different branches of state power, they need to cooperate.

[76] See Constitutional Court, decision of 21 March 2000, K 4/99, OTK ZU 2/2000, poz 65.

[77] H Kelsen, *General Theory of Law and State* (Cambridge, MA, Harvard University Press, 1945) 269.

[78] Constitutional Court, judgment of 16 February 2010, P 16/09, OTK ZU 2A/2010, poz 12.

[79] Article 190(4) of the Constitution.

[80] Chancellery of the Senate, 'Liczbowe zestawienie inicjatyw ustawodawczych Senatu w latach 1989–2018', available at: http://www.senat.gov.pl/gfx/senat/userfiles/_public/k8/statystyki/podstawowe_dane_9/08_inicjatywy_1-9.pdf.

[81] Constitutional Court, judgment of 28 October 2015, K 21/14, OTK ZU 9A/2015, poz 152.

Such an obligation, for the good of Polish citizens, is expressed in the Constitution's preamble. The judgments of the Constitutional Court are issued 'in the name of the Republic of Poland' and their non-implementation consequently undermines the rule of law.

A particular competence of the Polish Constitutional Court that has existed since the 1980s are 'signalisations'.[82] These decisions of the Court indicate to the parliament and other organs issuing legislative acts the existence of legal gaps and other deficiencies of law that need to be eliminated in order to ensure the integrity of the law system. Signalisations are generally issued after the Court has declared a provision incompatible with the Constitution. Despite their lack of binding force on the addressee, the President of the Constitutional Court can request information on the implementation of a signalisation. The Court only issues a few signalisations per year; between 1998 and 2016, it issued a total of 50 signalisations.[83] In principle, the addressees tend to follow the signalisations, which is arguably a sign of the respect for the authority of the Court and which is beneficial for the quality of the legal system.

G. The Power of Constitutional Interpretation

Over the years, the Constitutional Court achieved a significant position within the constitutional system of Poland thanks to its constitutional competences and the development of its own jurisprudence. For example, the Court interpreted the right of access to court expressed in Article 45 of the Constitution in a way that is broader than the guarantees of its counterpart, Article 6 of the European Convention on Human Rights (ECHR). Similarly, the Constitutional Court interpreted the eligibility to file a constitutional complaint in an extensive manner, also encompassing some public economic operators.[84] In doing so, it was motivated by the protection of citizens' rights.

A significant example of Constitutional Court's reading of constitutional principles concerns the principle of a 'democratic state ruled by law' expressed in Article 2 of the Constitution. Over the years, the

[82] Article 35 of Law of 30 November 2016 on Organisation and Procedure before the Constitutional Court.

[83] See Constitutional Court (n 17) 76.

[84] See Constitutional Court, decision of 18 December 2013, Ts 13/12, OTK ZU IIB/2014, poz 833. For exclusions, see Constitutional Court, decision of 20 December 2007, SK 67/05, OTK ZU 11A/2007, poz 168; decision of 6 April 2011, SK 21/07, OTK ZU 3A/2011, poz 28.

Court 'unpacked' this principle, making the vague and open principles of law more precise. In this way, the Court has served the Constitution through its interpretation. This process was criticised by the scholarship at the time. However, it was unclear if the issue called into question was the specific principles derived from Article 2 of the Constitution or, more probably, the manner in which the Court proceeded. In addition, the Solidarity movement and the importance of human rights played a significant role in the Court's understanding of the principle of the democratic state ruled by law.

There are three crucial interpretations of Article 2 of the Constitution that the Constitutional Court has developed through its comprehensive approach.[85] Some of those principles, which had previously been seen as derived from the principle of democratic state ruled by law, were explicitly introduced into the new Constitution's text – for instance, *nullum crimen sine lege* (Article 42).

Classical methods of interpretation in constitutional law such as textual, systematic and teleological methods are applied in the Constitutional Court. In the application of these methods, priority is offered to dynamic interpretation over static, textual interpretation. One type of dynamic interpretation, and a basic tool of the Constitutional Court's toolbox, is constitution-conform interpretation (*prokonstytucyjna wykładania*), which searches for the meaning of the provision under review that would render it compliant with the Constitution. Specifically, from among the many potential meanings of a legal norm, the interpretation that is the closest to the Constitution should prevail. Only if a constitution-conform interpretation of that provision fails can the provision at stake be declared unconstitutional and removed from the legal system. Therefore, both the Constitutional Court and other courts seek an interpretation of a provision that would be compatible with the Constitution, but only the Constitutional Court can eliminate a legal norm from the legal system. The constitution-conform interpretation is limited, to the extent that it cannot reach a stage where the interpretation would lead to the creation of a new legal norm.

The Constitutional Court is not vested with a separate competence to interpret the Constitution, as is the case, for example, in Hungary.[86] In other words, the Constitutional Court cannot interpret the

[85] See ch 2.
[86] K Lach and W Sadurski, 'Constitutional Courts of Central and Eastern Europe: Between Adolescence and Maturity' (2008) 3 *Journal of Comparative Law* 212, 221.

Constitution *ex officio*. However, it does interpret the Constitution in the process of reviewing the constitutionality of legal provisions (*wykładnia operatywna*). The Court's interpretation of the Constitution has a number of characteristic elements. First, when interpreting constitutional norms, the Court refers to values, therefore reaching out to an order of values. It uncovers relationships between legal norms and values, which indirectly influence the hierarchy of legal principles. For instance, it has granted a high rank to the legal protection of the life of every human being.[87] The high rank of this principle, in the view of the Court, stems from the fact that this principle protects a value of extreme importance – that of a human life.[88] Second, the Court's systematic interpretation is in a way orthodox, as it refers to its own previous decisions. This interpretational loop is justified by the Court's idea of safeguarding stability in the interpretation of the Constitution. For instance, in the judgments concerning the conditions for European integration, it has referred to its own earlier judgment on the EU Accession Treaty.[89]

H. The Constitutional Court in the System of European Law

The system of law in Poland has a multi-faceted character, encompassing laws enacted by the Polish legislature, as well as acts of European law and international law.[90] These laws co-exist in a cooperative manner in accordance with the principle of 'mutually friendly interpretation'.[91] The CJEU ensures uniform application and interpretation of EU law, while the Constitutional Court remains the guardian of the Polish Constitution.

The key to understanding the position of the Polish Constitutional Court in this system is the role it ascribes to the Constitution. The Constitutional Court's case law underlines the Constitution as of supreme legal force (*najwyższe prawo Rzeczypospolitej Polskiej*).[92] In its judgment on the Lisbon Treaty, the Constitutional Court underscored that the Constitution expresses the sovereign will of the nation and

[87] Article 38 of the Constitution.

[88] Constitutional Court, judgment of 28 May 1997, K 26/96, OTK ZU 2/1997, poz 19.

[89] Constitutional Court, judgment of 24 November 2010, K 32/09, OTK ZU 9A/2010, poz 108; judgment of 16 November 2011, SK 45/09,OTK ZU 9A/2011, poz 97.

[90] K 32/09 of 24 November 2010, point III 2.3.

[91] ibid.

[92] Constitutional Court, judgment of 11 May 2005, K 18/04, OTK ZU 5A/2005, poz 49, point III 2.1.

that maintaining the primacy of the Constitution within the process of European integration is equal to maintaining state sovereignty.[93] In an earlier judgment concerning Poland's accession to the EU, the Court indicated that the Constitution enjoys precedence of binding force and precedence of application within the territory of Poland.[94] This enables the primacy of application of EU law over national law, yet it does not imply the supremacy of EU law over the Constitution.

The Constitutional Court remains the final arbiter with regard to the Polish Constitution, but this setting considers the different roles of the Constitutional Court and of the CJEU, which should not be positioned as competing courts.[95] Accordingly, the Constitutional Court maintains a cooperative approach by applying a constitutional interpretation that is favourable to EU law. Such an interpretation of national law is possible, unless it results in contradicting the explicit wording of constitutional norms or is irreconcilable with the minimum guarantee functions realised by the Constitution, especially in the field of individual rights and freedoms. In case of an irreconcilable inconsistency between a constitutional and a European legal norm, a constitutional amendment might be necessary, or Poland should take action at EU level aiming to change the European provision at stake.[96] Ultimately, Poland may withdraw from the EU.[97]

Finally, the Constitutional Court also participates in the judicial dialogue with its EU counterpart. In 2015, the Court called on the CJEU for the first time with a preliminary reference in a case concerning the compliance of a national statute implementing an EU tax directive with the Polish Constitution, initiated by the Ombudsman. The question concerned the validity and compliance of the directive in question with the principle of tax neutrality, as the tax rates applicable to e-books were higher than those for traditional publications.[98] The CJEU declared the relevant EU provision to be valid and, after the relevant motion was withdrawn by the Ombudsman, the Constitutional Court discontinued the proceedings. This example of the Constitutional Court's reference, together with the references of other Polish courts discussed in

[93] Constitutional Court, K 32/09, point III 1.3.
[94] Constitutional Court, K 18/04, point III 4.2.
[95] Constitutional Court, SK 45/09, point III 2.4.
[96] Constitutional Court, K 18/04, point III 6.4.
[97] ibid.
[98] Constitutional Court, decision of 7 July 2016, K 61/13, OTK ZU 7A/2015, poz 103 and the CJEU's reply: Case C-390/15 *RPO*, EU:C:2017:174.

Chapter 5, highlights the role of Polish judges as European judges and their contribution to the European system of judicial cooperation.

III. CONSTITUTIONAL ACCOUNTABILITY (TRIBUNAL OF STATE)

Constitutional accountability is a relatively new concept for the Polish legal system. It is driven by the idea that officials serving the country should be penalised for acts that are socially harmful and illegal, even if they do not always imply criminal responsibility.[99] The Tribunal of State was introduced in Poland in March 1982 following a period under martial law (1981–82), yet the perpetrators of martial law have never been held accountable in any form. Today, the Tribunal of State is solidly anchored in the Constitution of 1997 with further regulation in the 1982 Law on the Tribunal of State.

The Tribunal of State is a permanent court. At the beginning of its term of office, the Chamber of Deputies elects 19 judges of the Tribunal of State, with an individual vote for each candidate elected (since 2011, previously *en bloc*) for a four-year term. MPs and senators are excluded from being judges. The chairperson of the Tribunal of State is *ex officio* the First President of the Supreme Court. Article 199(1) of the Constitution requires that the deputy chairpersons and at least one half of the members have the qualifications necessary to hold the office of judge. This requirement aims to balance the professional and social dimensions of the Tribunal of State. The judges of the Tribunal of State remain independent and subject only to the Constitution and the statutes. They cannot be recalled or removed from office.

The Tribunal of State deals with constitutional delicts that are violations of the Constitution or statutes, committed knowingly or unknowingly, by the highest state officials in connection with their office or within its scope. Constitutional accountability is individual in character. Specifically, the President, the Prime Minister, the members of the Council of Ministers, and heads and members of other most important constitutional organs, as well as in certain cases MPs and senators,[100] may be held individually constitutionally accountable.[101] Moreover, in

[99] See Constitutional Court, judgment of 21 February 2001, P 12/00, OTK ZU 3/2001, poz 47.

[100] See ch 3.

[101] Article 198(1) and (2) of the Constitution.

comparison to other organs, the accountability of the head of state before the Tribunal of State is complete (covering all types of crimes committed by the President) and exclusive (the President can be held accountable only before the Tribunal of State).[102] Finally, in some circumstances, the constitutional accountability of the Prime Minister and of the ministers can be combined with criminal accountability before the Tribunal of State.

Holding a person constitutionally accountable is a two-step procedure starting with proceedings in the Chamber of Deputies, or before the National Assembly in the case of the President. After an indictment by parliament, the Tribunal of State decides on the constitutional accountability of the accused. The Tribunal of State does not have its own rules of procedure and, in principle, applies the code of criminal procedure. The penalties imposed by the Tribunal of State have a specific character, such as the loss of voting rights or the prohibition of holding managerial positions in state organs, and mostly aim at damaging the honour of the official in question. In cases combining criminal and constitutional accountability, the Tribunal of State can also impose criminal sanctions, such as imprisonment.

The experience to date shows that in practice accountability before the Tribunal of State – be it constitutional or criminal – does not function. This concerns all the types of subjects that can be held responsible before the Tribunal of State. This is because political accountability in fact 'consumes' constitutional accountability. The only case thus far, concerning a former government minister, has been ongoing for more than 10 years without any end in sight. One of the problems is the perception that constitutional accountability has a preventive character. As such, constitutional accountability demands reforms through the political process to create an effective accountability instrument.

IV. CONCLUSION

Although the Constitutional Court was established in the 1980s, its case law really started developing in the following decade. The blossoming of the Court was connected with the protection it offered to the Constitution as the supreme law of the state. Despite the relatively short experience of the Constitutional Court, its case law was appreciated early on and

[102] See P 12/00. See also ch 4.

its position was widely respected. The legality of Constitutional Court's judgments was not questioned, and in particular the governing political powers always respected its pronouncements, despite not always agreeing with them. This situation changed with the parliamentary elections of 2015.

As a consequence of the negative changes concerning the Constitutional Court introduced by the governing majority, its position and impact in exercising its judicial power, including its role in guaranteeing the freedom and rights of the citizens, has been diminished. In part, this has been reflected in a 42 per cent decrease in the number of cases received by the Court in 2016.[103] This is the lowest number of cases since 2004, which is particularly noteworthy as previously the number of cases in the Court's docket had been increasing every year. The numbers for 2016 are partially vindicated by the fact that citizens actively continued to lodge constitutional complaints (they amounted to 74 per cent of all cases brought to the Constitutional Court). In contrast, the significant decrease in legal questions and requests for constitutional review by applicants with limited eligibility points to a loss of authority of the Court from their perspective. As a consequence, the Court itself was less active – it issued 43 per cent fewer judgments than in 2015 – and it was also more divided than before, with dissenting opinions attached to 44 per cent of judgments, as compared to 25 per cent in 2015 and even fewer in previous years. This appears to be an expression of the opposition among some of the current justices towards the participation in the adjudication of cases of the judges that were illegally elected to the Court.[104] In sum, the ongoing constitutional crisis has deeply affected the external perception of the Court as well as its effectiveness.

FURTHER READING

Bugarič, B and Ginsburg, T, 'The Assault on Postcommunist Courts' (2016) 27 *Journal of Democracy* 69–82.

Garlicki, L, 'The Experience of the Polish Constitutional Court' in W Sadurski (ed), *Constitutional Justice, East and West: Democratic Legitimacy and Constitutional Courts in Post-Communist Europe in a Comparative Perspective* (The Hague, Kluwer International, 2003) 265–82.

[103] Constitutional Court (n 17) 69 and 73, 80.

[104] See, eg, the dissenting opinion in Constitutional Court, judgment of 20 April 2017, K 10/15, OTK ZU A/2017, poz 31, or in judgment of 4 April 2017, P 56/14, OTK ZU A/2017, poz 25.

Koncewicz, TT, 'Of Institutions, Democracy, Constitutional Self-Defence and the Rule of Law: The Judgments of the Polish Constitutional Tribunal in Cases K 34/15, K 35/15 and beyond' (2016) 53 *Common Market Law Review* 1753–92.

Koncewicz, TT et al, 'Poland' in R Albert, D Landau, P Faraguna and Š Drugda, *The I·CONnect-Clough Center 2016 Global Review of Constitutional Law* (Clough Center for the Study of Constitutional Democracy, 2017) 165–69.

Kustra, A, 'Reading the Tea Leaves: The Polish Constitutional Tribunal and the Preliminary Ruling Procedure' (2015) 16 *German Law Journal* 1543–68.

Safjan, M, 'Poland: The Constitutional Court as a Positive Legislator' in A Brewer-Carias (ed), *Constitutional Courts as Positive Legislators: A Comparative Law Study* (Cambridge, Cambridge University Press, 2011) 701–20.

Sadurski, W, *Rights before Courts: A Study of Constitutional Courts in Postcommunist States of Central and Eastern Europe* (Springer, Dordrecht, 2014).

——. '"Solange, Chapter 3": Constitutional Courts in Central Europe – Democracy – European Union' (2008) 14 *European Law Journal* 1–35.

7

Local Governance

Civil Society – Territorial Division – Local Self-Government – Commune – County – Voivodeship – Local Elections – Local Referendum – Government Administration – Oversight – European Integration – Subsidiarity

I. BETWEEN A CIVIL SOCIETY AND A POLITICAL STATE

THE ESTABLISHMENT AND development of local self-government in Poland have been of unquestioned success in the process of transformation into a democratic state. In surveying the domain of local self-government, it is important to assess both the kind of factors that played a decisive role in this achievement and the role of the 1997 Constitution. This chapter deals with the elements that have contributed to the success of local self-government. These are mostly connected to its design. The focus here will be on its construction, the main institutional bodies themselves and the tasks they perform, and the role played by oversight mechanisms.

Poland is a unitary state.[1] This principle of state structure has been present since 1918, when Poland regained its independence after the First World War. The unitary character of the state is broadly accepted by political powers and legal scholarship today.[2] In the past, Poland has had some experience of federalism. Prior to the partitions of Poland – the last in 1795, which put an end to the existence of Poland for 123 years – the state consisted of a number of territories, or provinces, under the name of Commonwealth (*Rzeczpolspolita*), meaning a community of people residing on its territory.[3]

[1] Article 3 of the Constitution.

[2] P Sarnecki, 'Komentarz do Art 3' in L Garlicki (ed), *Konstytucja Rzeczypospolitej Polskiej. Komentarz Tom V* (Warsaw, Wydawnictwo Sejmowe, 2007) 1–2; M Safjan and L Bosek, *Konstytucja RP, Tom I* (Warsaw, Wydawnictwo CH Beck, 2016) 254.

[3] See ch 1.

Over the centuries, the division of the whole territory of Poland consisted of a number of levels, the most important being communes (*gminy*), placed at the lowest tier, the counties (*powiaty*) and voivodeships (*województwa*).[4] The first counties and voivodeships were established at the end of the fourteenth century. Voivodeships, counties and communes are the units of the territorial division of the state. In this respect, the territorial division is similar to France, for example, which consists of regions, departments and communes.[5] In Poland, the voivodeships are created and abolished via statute. The current form of the voivodeships (16) has been a source of political and social controversy. The government initially proposed the creation of only 12 voivodeships that would cover larger territories.[6] In the end, a final agreement on 16 voivodeships – a compromise between political forces and local societies – was reached. Politicians as well as local communities were accustomed to a large number of small voivodeships because between 1975 and 1999, the territory of Poland was divided into 49 voivodeships. In turn, each voivodeship is subdivided into counties. For instance, the Masovian voivodeship consists of 37 counties. Thus, a county encompasses a part of the territory of a voivodeship. In turn, a commune encompasses a part of the territory of a county. Usually a county consists of a small number of communes. In the Masovian voivodeship there are 314 communes. Figure 7.1 shows the units and subunits of the Masovian voivodeship.

Figure 7.1 The territorial division of Poland: the example of the Masovian voivodeship

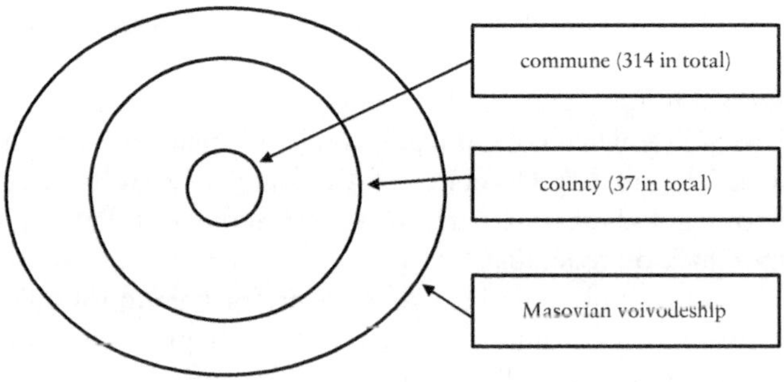

Source: authors' own compilation based on information from Statistics Poland[7]

[4] J Bardach, B Leśnodorski and M Pietrzak, *Historia ustroju i prawa polskiego* (Warsaw, PWN, 1996) 130–31.

[5] S Boyron, *The Constitution of France: A Contextual Analysis* (Oxford, Hart Publishing, 2013) 208–17.

[6] Government proposal No 230 of 13 March 1998.

[7] See http://eteryt.stat.gov.pl/eteryt/raporty/WebRaportZestawienie.aspx.

The Council of Ministers creates and abolishes counties and communes through regulations. When delineating the borders of these territorial units, the government should aim to encompass territories that are unitary with regard to social and economic links.

The current territorial division of Poland is as follows. As of 1 January 2018, there are 2,478 communes, 66 cities with the status of counties, 314 counties and 16 voivodeships.[8] Poland is inhibited by 38 million people, 60 per cent of whom live in cities and 40 per cent in rural areas.[9]

The Constitution requires that the territorial division of the state takes into account existing social, economic and cultural ties, and that it allows the territorial units to perform their public duties.[10] This provision turned out to be very significant in practice. In fact, the Constitutional Court has dealt with a number of conflicts between the government shaping the borders of communes and counties, on the one hand, and the local communities, the interests of which were affected by that change, on the other hand.[11] The involvement of the Constitutional Court in this matter has been crucial, as the regulations issued by the Council of Ministers cannot be controlled for their legality by the administrative courts due to their legal form. The territorial division of the state and the issues arising from it are therefore not indifferent or abstract from the perspective of both the citizens and the state power.

The territorial division of the state described above has to be distinguished from the exercise of power at the local level. In Poland, the territorial division of the state provides the basis for the establishment of bodies exercising authority in the units of territorial division of the state. The main way in which power is exercised is through local self-government (*samorząd terytorialny*). Compared to other Eastern European states, Poland's local self-government system is positioned among the 'champions of decentralisation' due to the wide scope of functions granted to local self-government, sharing some affinity with other forms of local government in Northern Europe.[12] Polish local self-government functions at each of the tiers of the basic territorial division

[8] Statistics Poland, *Area and Population in the Territorial Profile in 2018* (Warsaw, 2018) 8. According to the authors' own calculation, of the 2,478 communes, around 12 per cent are urban, 63 per cent are rural and 25 per cent are of mixed character.

[9] Authors' own calculation based on Statistics Poland, *Statistical Yearbook of the Republic of Poland* (Warsaw, 2018) 206.

[10] Article 15(2) of the Constitution.

[11] See Constitutional Court, judgment of 8 April 2009, K 37/06, OTK ZU 4A/2009, poz 47.

[12] P Swianiewicz, 'An Empirical Typology of Local Government Systems in Eastern Europe' (2014) 40 *Local Government Studies* 292, 303.

of the state. The units of local self-government consist of legislative (councils or assemblies) and executive bodies. This construction of local governance therefore creates a certain paradox. Each unit of local self-government – commune, county and voivodeship – functions at a different tier of the territorial division of the state, namely commune, county and voivodeship, respectively. Despite this structure, all of these local self-government entities are equal in status. The competences of the units of local self-government differ among each other and do not overlap; in other words, there is no lower or higher tier of local self-government. The Constitution establishes the commune as the basic unit of local self-government, but it does not imply any hierarchy between the units of local self-government. Moreover, local self-government does not exhaust the notion of local governance, as the government administration also operates locally.

The establishment of local self-government in Poland has always been connected to building civil citizenry. This is understood as a collective of free people, citizens who are aware of their rights and freedoms. Local self-government, as a structure independent from the political influence of state power, equipped with property and legal personality, though overseen by the state for the legality of its actions, was and has been perceived as the right form of organisation of civil society. Certainly, this does not exhaust the notion of civil society in Poland, and narrowing it down to local self-government would be a mistake. Civil society also involves other forms and institutions, such as non-governmental organisations (NGOs), trade unions and engaged public opinion. Their functioning is supported by a number of laws that are generally favourable to civil society.[13] Nonetheless, between 2016 and 2017, the governing Law and Justice majority party introduced some legal changes negatively affecting the constitutional freedom of peaceful assembly and participation in such assemblies.[14]

The development of civil society in Poland should be seen against the backdrop of the pre-1989 situation. The relevant starting point in time is that of Poland in the interbellum. The March Constitution (1921) created a legal basis for local self-government that functioned until the Second World War. During the Communist period, local self-government was destroyed: in 1950, national councils (*rady narodowe*) took over local

[13] Law of 24 April 2003 on activities of public benefit and voluntary work, JL 2018 Pos 450, 650, 723, 1365; Law of 27 June 1997 on political parties, JL 2018 Pos 580; Law of 23 May 1991, JL 2015 Pos 1881, JL 2018 Pos 1608.

[14] Law of 13 December 2016 amending the Law on Assemblies, JL 2017 Pos 579.

power. Despite the similarity in name, national councils significantly differed from the present bodies of local self-government. They were a bureaucratic unit that was not democratically elected or accountable to the citizens, but to the Communist Party, and was organisationally tied to it. As in other Eastern European states, the Communist Party – through the national councils – controlled local societies. The Communist Party in power at the time saw local government as an aspiration of an independent society. Thus, during that time, society was perceived as 'the inert social structure' (*martwa struktura*), people were dependent on the state's power and civil society was repressed.[15] In the 1980s, circumstances began to change with the Solidarity movement, which, amongst other goals, postulated the rebuilding of a genuine system of local self-government.[16]

After the fall of Communism in 1989, Poland gradually began reconstructing local self-government.[17] This process took into account, among other things, the legal concepts of the Constitution of 1921. First, local self-government was created in communes, including small towns and cities, in March 1990. Soon afterwards, in May 1990, the first free elections to commune (and city) councils since the Second World War took place. This was a historic moment, since these elections were the first free elections in Poland after the fall of Communism, preceding the parliamentary elections. Next, local self-government was created at the county and voivodeship level in 1999.

As a consequence, a system of local governance with directly and universally elected councils of all local authorities and mayors in communes and cities, and indirectly elected county and voivodeship boards (with their chairpersons) was established.[18] This construction of local self-government enabled the actual decentralisation of public power in the state.

II. CITIZENS AS THE BENEFICIARIES OF LOCAL SELF-GOVERNMENT

Local self-government has garnered appreciation among the citizens and in general is effective in dealing with local problems. For instance,

[15] J Staniszkis, *Ontologia Socjalizmu* (Kraków, Ośrodek Myśli Politycznej, 2006).
[16] Z Pelczynski, 'Solidarity and the "Rebirth of Civil Society" in Poland, 1976–81' in J Keane (ed), *Civil Society and the State: New European Perspectives* (London, Verso, 1988).
[17] See M Kulesza, 'Niektóre zagadnienia prawne definicji samorządu terytorialnego' (1990) *Państwo i Prawo* 16.
[18] See further section III below.

saving the educational system after the central government's reform of 2017 – the abolition of the middle school system – was possible chiefly thanks to the efforts of local self-government.[19] Another example of the impact of local self-government on the quality of citizens' lives concerns sport infrastructure. Many towns and cities host impressive sports facilities such as stadiums or swimming pools.[20] Local self-government also provides childcare facilities such as kindergartens or playgrounds.[21] Responding to the needs of young people, local authorities organise concerts and festivals.[22] The expansion of free wireless networks in public places – around 5,623 hotspots operating in 2017 – indicates that local government follows new trends.[23] Finally, the functioning of the municipal police, which complements the work of national police forces, ensures the security of citizens. Nonetheless, some conflicts between the municipal police and the national police may arise in practice. One such example concerns a lack of willingness on the part of the national police to cooperate with the municipal police, no common patrols and the reduction in the number of policemen patrolling city districts accompanied by the expectation of additional funds from the city.[24] Such political conflicts can be resolved by improved efforts to achieve mutual understanding.

Local self-government has also made efforts to reduce negative impacts on the environment. This includes limiting the number of vehicles that can enter cities, operating city bikes stations and expanding bike lanes, and introducing electric buses and electric vehicle charging stations.[25] Cities offer financial support to exchange home coal-heating devices for environmentally friendly ones in an attempt to fight the smog.[26]

Thanks to the efforts of local self-government, the aesthetics of Polish cities and towns has improved. The greyness, typical of the

[19] See also European Commission, Education and Training Monitor 2017. Poland (2017) 7.

[20] 'Aquaparki w Polsce to duże inwestycje i wielkie koszty dla samorządów' *Rzeczpospolita* (15 February 2018).

[21] 'Coraz więcej samorządów finansuje opiekę w przedszkolach' *Rzeczpospolita* (6 December 2017).

[22] See http://samorzad.pap.pl/depesze/redakcyjne.kultura/184403/Miasta-festiwali--Samorzady-przescigaja-sie-w-przygotowaniu-ciekawej-oferty-imprez-.

[23] See https://www.portalsamorzadowy.pl/spoleczenstwo-informacyjne/szybszy-internet-w-gminach-samorzady-jeszcze-poczekaja-na-darmowe-hotspoty,110939.html.

[24] 'Sopot: Straż Miejska skarży się na policję. Policja – nie ma sporu ze strażą' *Dziennik Łódzki* (11 November 2009).

[25] See, eg, https://www.portalsamorzadowy.pl/gospodarka-komunalna/autobusy-elektryczne-polska-liderem-ale-wciaz-wiele-do-zrobienia,106167.html.

[26] For an overview, see https://www.bankier.pl/wiadomosc/Dofinansowanie-wymiany-pieca-weglowego-co-oferuja-miasta-7557731.html.

Polish People's Republic period, has been left behind in favour of more colourful streets and well-maintained greenery. The units of local self-government, in contrast to the national councils of the Communist period which served the government, are closely linked to citizens and respond to their needs.

Nonetheless, the level of public services provided by local self-government can differ across the country. First, the provision of local self-government in bigger cities is of a higher level as there are greater financial and organisational possibilities compared to smaller communes. This is evident in the purchase of new buses or the construction of modern bus stops.[27] Nonetheless, the level of services, for instance, with regard to public transportation, remains much higher as compared to the period of the Polish People's Republic. Second, the level of public services – for example, with regard to education – is safeguarded by the government administration. Local authorities manage schools and other educational units – at varying educational levels – but the Central Examination Committee, an unit of government administration, carries out major exams such as the final high school exam. Such an approach cultivates a higher quality of education. Third, the most diverse level of public services concerns the public health system. Hospitals are managed by units of local self-government (eg, voivodeship hospitals), medical schools (clinics), the military (military hospitals) or private operators (private hospitals). As a consequence, it is hard to compare the quality of health services. Nonetheless, access to medical services remains problematic, especially when long waiting times to see a physician are taken into account.

The contribution of local authorities to the well-being of the citizens comes at a price. This is evident in the debt of many of the units of local self-government.[28] In this context, the development of public-private partnership (PPP) is used predominantly by the units of local self-government (around 91 per cent of all contracts), rather than government administration, to provide services for which it does not have sufficient resources.[29] Poland established a legal framework for the PPP in 2008.[30]

[27] 'Miasta finansują floty ekologicznych autobusów' *Rzeczpospolita* (4 February 2019).

[28] See http://samorzad.pap.pl/depesze/redakcyjne.praca.akty/179872/Zadluzenie-na-mieszkanca-wg-danych-ze-sprawozdan-z-wykonania-budzetow-JST-po-3-kw--2017-r-.

[29] K Szymański, B Korbus and D Zalewski, 'Analiza rynku ppp za okres od 2009 r. do grudnia 2017 r.', available at: www.ppp.gov.pl/Aktualnosci/Documents/2018_03_18_analiza_rynku_PPP_2017.pdf.

[30] Law of 19 December 2008 on public-private partnership, JL 2017 Pos 1834, JL 2018 Pos 1639.

Despite its potential, some limitations – such as the effectiveness of the proceedings of private partner selection – hinder the successful operation of PPP.[31] Between 2009 and 2017, public (mostly communes) and private parties concluded 117 contracts, which represented only around one-quarter of all commenced proceedings.[32] The main factor hindering PPP agreements seems to be a lack of interest on the part of private parties in the projects designed by local self-government.[33] In successful cases, PPP dominated in sectors such as sports and tourism, transportation infrastructure, energy efficiency or telecommunications.[34]

Unsurprisingly in the light of the contribution of the local authorities to the quality of life of citizens, social research indicates that around three-quarters of society positively assess the work of local self-government.[35] Moreover, over the last 10 years, public opinion has seen local elections as being the most important of all national elections.[36] As of January 2018, 78 per cent of respondents to a national poll declared their interest in the decisions of commune bodies, while the levels of interest in the decisions of county and voivodeship bodies are lower, namely 65 per cent and 40 per cent respectively.[37] In that context, this chapter aims to show that the functioning of local self-government should not be viewed uncritically. Its structure and functioning display some flaws; in particular, the low turnouts in the local elections and referendums raise questions about the development of public life in a pluralist and civil society.

III. SELF-GOVERNMENT AND GOVERNMENT ADMINISTRATION AT THE LOCAL LEVEL

Local self-government has been the main form of organisation of society and this is reflected in the principles underlying the Constitution of 1997. Among the relevant constitutional principles are the decentralisation

[31] M Słodowa-Hełpa, 'Zagraniczne doświadczenia w zakresie partnerstwa publiczno-prywatnego – inspiracje i rekomendacje dla Polski' (2014) 39 *Studia BAS* 17.

[32] Szymański, Korbus and Zalewski (n 29) 11.

[33] ibid 23.

[34] ibid 12. For examples of PPP contracts, see www.ppp.gov.pl/Aktualnosci/Documents/Fiszki_umow_PPP_19032018.pdf.

[35] CBOS, Komunikat z Badań Nr 21/2018, 'Opinie o działalności parlamentu, prezydenta, władz samorządowych i IPN', Luty 2018, 4.

[36] CBOS, Komunikat z Badań Nr 23/2018, 'Wybory samorządowe – znaczenie, gotowość uczestnictwa oraz zainteresowanie decyzjami władz różnych szczebli', Luty 2018, 2.

[37] ibid 6.

of public powers,[38] self-government[39] and subsidiarity, expressed in the Constitution's preamble.[40] The latter principle concerns the relationship between the state and local self-government, demanding that public tasks should be exercised by the governmental unit closest to the citizen. Only if that local unit is unable or ill-equipped to act, does another, 'higher' unit of local self-government, or the state, step in. Therefore, the subsidiarity principle has two aspects: public tasks should not be taken away from a unit able to achieve them on its own and, simultaneously, that unit should not be assigned public tasks exceeding what it is able to achieve on its own. In other words, each unit of local self-government should perform public tasks that are suitable for it.[41]

These basic constitutional principles – decentralisation of public power, self-government and subsidiarity – offer a foundation for further regulation of local self-government. The Constitution prescribes that local self-government performs all public tasks not reserved by the Constitution or statute to other units of public authority.[42] Thereby, the Constitution expresses a presumption of competence for local self-government, and not the government administration functioning at the local level or other bodies. The Constitution designates the commune as the basic unit of local self-government.[43] Commune membership is obligatory and the membership status is acquired *ex lege* as a consequence of residing in a specific territory. As such, an individual cannot reject being a member of this self-governing community, but can remain passive, and at the same time the local self-government cannot exclude a person from membership. An expression of the self-governing character of the commune is that it decides on its own internal system by adopting a statute.

Communes exercise all tasks of local self-government not reserved for counties and voivodeships.[44] The communes perform these tasks in their own name and under their own responsibility to fulfil the needs of their residents. For this purpose, communes are also equipped with legal personality, their own financial resources and their own property. They cooperate with the government administration in exercising some

[38] Article 15(1) of the Constitution.

[39] ibid art 16.

[40] See P Sarnecki (ed), *Samorząd terytorialny. Zasady ustrojowe i praktyka* (Warsaw, Wydawnictwo Sejmowe, 2005).

[41] Constitutional Court, judgment of 26 May 2015, Kp 2/13, OTK ZU 5A/2015, poz 65.

[42] Article 163 of the Constitution.

[43] ibid art 164(1).

[44] ibid art 164(3).

of their own tasks. In addition, communes can, if foreseen by statute, exercise the tasks of government administration, and receive funding for that purpose. Some examples of such tasks are conducting elections or referendums, issuing identity documents or maintaining population records. Finally, communes enter into intracommunal relationships with other communes to exercise public tasks together, for example, to establish an enterprise to manage waste serving a group of communes.

State power cannot interfere in the activities of the commune, unless this is foreseen by a statute. An expression of this independence of the commune is the possibility for it to enter into legal relationships as equal legal subjects with state bodies. For instance, the commune's office can sign a contract with the voivode regarding financial support for road renovation in a town. As such, the commune's exercise of public tasks is limited only by the oversight tools indicated in the applicable laws and discussed in section IV below. Apart from this constraint, the commune decides independently – without influence from the state power and its bodies – about its own tasks and their implementation. The independence of the communes is also visible in their lack of hierarchical subordination to other units of local self-government.

Each commune is equipped with its own bodies: an elected council and a mayor. The commune council fulfils a legislative and controlling function. It decides on all local issues which statutes do not reserve for a referendum or reserve to another entity. The commune council, an elected and representative body consists of deputies (*radni*). The typical deputy of a commune council is male, between 40 and 60 years old and has completed at least secondary education.[45]

The main source of funding for local self-government is grants from the state budget.[46] The aims of these grants may vary, but in principle they aim to support the exercise of the tasks of the local self-government. Such tasks may include, for instance, investments in schools, roads infrastructure or building electric car charging stations. Grants from the state budget may also be used as disaster relief (eg, flooding) or to commemorate places related to history of Poland.

The commune council sets the priorities for the functioning of the commune and controls its spending. The revenue of communes is

[45] Authors' own calculation based on Statistics Poland, *Mały Rocznik Statystyczny Polski 2018* (Warsaw, 2018), 56.

[46] Law of 13 November 2003 on the income of the units of local self-government, JL 2018 Pos 1530.

generated from local taxes and fees.[47] These include property taxes, agricultural and forest taxes, or transportation tax (applicable to trucks and buses). Moreover, communes may charge local fees such as market fees, advertisement fees or tourist tax. In practice, the latter fee has raised some controversies. Since 2008, the commune of Zakopane – the 'winter capital city of Poland' – has charged a tourist tax of 2 PLN (around €0.50) per day, generating an income of 3 million PLN per year.[48] Nonetheless, due to the air pollution in Zakopane, many tourists declined to pay the tax. In 2017, the Voivodeship Administrative Court in Kraków, adjudicating a complaint made by one such tourist concerning the resolution of the Zakopane City Council regarding the tourist tax, decided that due to the air pollution, the city cannot charge the aforementioned fee.[49] In 2018, the Supreme Administrative Court in Warsaw confirmed the invalidity of Zakopane's resolution.[50] As a consequence, any tourist who was charged the tourist tax in Zakopane can apply for its reimbursement.

The executive arm of the commune is the mayor, known either as *wójt* (village mayor), *burmistrz* (mayor) or *prezydent miasta* (president of a city) depending on the type and size of a commune. The mayor represents the commune and executes the resolutions of the commune council. In the exercise of these tasks, he or she is assisted by the communal office (*urząd gminy*). A characteristic element for the Polish system of local governance is that a mayor can be removed before the end of the term of his or her office exclusively via a local referendum. Such an approach is generally unheard of elsewhere in Europe, with the exception of Austria.[51]

All major cities, such as Kraków or Poznań, are communes with a special – city – status and they exercise the tasks of a county. This means that their tasks and competences are wider in scope when compared to communes. In addition, Warsaw has a particular status as the capital city. The particular position of the largest Polish cities, including Warsaw, does not call into question their self-governing character.

[47] Law of 12 January 1991 on local taxes and fees, JL 2018 Pos 1445, 1588, 1669, 1693 and 1722, 2073.

[48] 'Zakopane nielegalnie pobierało opłatę miejscową – wyrok NSA' *Rzeczpospolita* (15 March 2018).

[49] Voivodeship Administrative Court in Cracow, judgment of 10 July 2017, III SA/Kr 535/15.

[50] Supreme Administrative Court, judgment of 15 March 2018, II FSK 3579/17.

[51] C Panara, 'Conclusion: The Contribution of Local Self-Government to Constitutionalism in the Member States and in the EU Multilayered System of Governance' in C Panara and M Varney (eds), *Local Government in Europe* (Abingdon, Routledge, 2013) 403.

The special position of Warsaw as the capital city is evident in a number of ways. First, Warsaw's legal status is regulated in a dedicated statute.[52] Second, Warsaw performs tasks that are larger in comparison to other communes. In particular, this concerns the necessity to provide conditions for the functioning of central state bodies, headquarters of international organisations and diplomatic representations of other states. Third, as a unit of local self-government, Warsaw is divided into 18 supporting units – boroughs. Each borough has its own legislative and executive arms, council and board, respectively. In Warsaw, tasks of the local self-government are decentralised – delegated to boroughs – which is accompanied by the transfer of financial means.[53] Fourth, the elections of the mayor of Warsaw are closely followed by citizens and have an important political significance. The intensity of the political campaign is comparable to that of a mayor of London or New York City. The outcome of the elections in Warsaw is usually indicative of the levels of support enjoyed by political parties before the next parliamentary elections. In 2017, the Law and Justice party put forward a proposal that would amend the system through which Warsaw was organised as a unit of local self-government.[54] This project aimed to create a large metropolitan unit encompassing Warsaw and 32 bordering communes. However, the proposal was withdrawn after a number of local referendums in the communes – which were to be included in the metropole – signalled a lack of support for the project.[55]

Counties – as units of local self-government – are designed in a uniform manner, taking into account the existing social and economic links between neighbouring communes. The Council of Ministers sets the borders between the counties after seeking the opinion of interested residents. In turn, voivodeships are units of local self-government and, at the same time, a unit of state power at the local level, as the government administration is strongly present there. As a consequence, voivodeships are often described as being dual in character.

The systems of local self-government in counties and voivodeships are organised in a similar manner to the communes, yet with some presence of government administration. Specifically, their bodies include a

[52] Law of 15 March 2002 on the system of the capital city Warsaw, JL 2018 Pos 1817.

[53] H Gronkiewicz-Waltz and B Jakacka, 'O ustroju samorządu miasta stołecznego Warszawy' (2015) LXXVII *Ruch Prawniczy, Ekonomiczny i Socjologiczny* 147, 151.

[54] Chamber of Deputies, Print No 1259, Poselski projekt ustawy o ustroju miasta stołecznego Warszawy, available at: www.sejm.gov.pl/Sejm8.nsf/druk.xsp?nr=1259.

[55] 'Powiększenie Warszawy. Legionowo w referendum odrzuciło PiS-owską ustawę metropolitalną' *Gazeta Wyborcza* (27 March 2017).

council (*rada powiatu*) and executive board (*zarząd powiatu*) headed by a chairperson (*starosta*) in the county, and an assembly (*sejmik województwa*) and executive board (*zarząd województwa*) headed by a chairperson (*marszałek*) in the voivodeship. The legislative bodies issue local laws, control the budget, and elect and recall the members of the board. The board, which is accountable before the council (or assembly), executes its resolutions and dispenses the budget.

Each of the units of the local self-government – commune, county or voivodeship – has its own financial policy, its own budgets and its property rights. The units are also vested with individual tasks, which guarantee them legal subjectivity, allowing for their full participation in legal transactions. Tasks of the communes include obligatory tasks with a statutory basis and facultative tasks which the commune undertakes on its own volition. The commune's mandatory responsibilities can be roughly grouped into those concerning technical infrastructure (roads, transportation), social infrastructure (health, education), public order and safety (fire protection) or spatial order and the environment (land management). Communes also exercise tasks of government administration imposed by statutes that are obligatory in character or based on an agreement with the government administration. The main difference between the commune's own and its commissioned tasks is that the exercise of the former is financed from the commune's own budget and implies the commune's own responsibility for their execution. In contrast, whenever the government commissions a task, it provides funds and takes responsibility for their execution. In turn, the elected local authority in counties exercises tasks that have a supplementary character to the tasks of the commune. These include, inter alia, addressing alcohol and drug addiction, running hospitals, flood protection or the protection of cultural heritage. The exercise of these tasks by the county cannot interfere with the tasks already executed by communes. Moreover, upon the justified request of a commune, counties hand their tasks to communes under conditions specified in an agreement between these entities. Finally, the tasks of voivodeship self-government supplement those of the county self-government. The local self-government of a voivodeship deals with public affairs of a regional character, such as unemployment, general development strategy for the region, or cooperation with EU regions. The voivodeship self-government also exercises tasks commissioned by the government administration, for example, relating to geodesy and land maps.

The central government administration functioning at the local level complements the role played by local self-government. This concerns only some tasks, especially those that are supra-local in character. The current design of government administration at the local level stems from the 1995–96 reform, which aimed at rendering that administration more flexible and able to absorb the social and economic change occurring in the state. At the local level, there is therefore an integrated administration (*zespolona*) and a specialised administration (*niezespolona*). The former is headed by the voivode (*wojewoda*). Voivodes are local politicians nominated and removed by, and politically accountable to the Prime Minister. Their role is to represent the Council of Ministers in the voivodeship. Voivodes fulfil that task with the assistance of their own executive arm, the voivodeship office (*urząd wojewódzki*). In turn, the specialised administration consists of a number of bodies subordinate not to the voivode, but to the central units of administration in Warsaw. Those include, for example, financial administration (subordinate to the Finance Minister), administration responsible for statistics (subordinate to the Interior Minister) or administration dealing with state forests (subordinate to the Agriculture Minister).

Political tensions are unavoidable between the chairperson of the voivodeship self-government, on the one hand, and the voivode, on the other, who at times represent different political forces – the opposition and the governing majority, respectively. For instance, the local authorities advocate the development of regional airports, while the government focuses on expanding one, centrally located airport. This concerns the conflict around the Central Communication Port advocated by the government administration, while the local self-government of the Masovian voivodeship seeks to further develop its own airport in Modlin located near Warsaw.[56] Similar conflicts between the government administration (voivode) and local authorities concern the layout and the course of roads. Although local residents may appreciate new roads, they often oppose their location when these are too close to their homes, which in turns causes delays to the construction process. Only administrative courts are competent to review local law and the conflicts between the different bodies of local self-government, as well as between the government administration and local self-government. The Constitutional Court does not review the constitutionality of local laws or their application, and therefore remains outside of such conflicts between central and regional government.

[56] 'Modlin i Warszawa na kolizyjnym kursie' *Rzeczpospolita* (17 April 2018).

A. The Electoral System

The Constitution articulates the general principles governing elections to councils of local self-government.[57] As in all other national elections, each Polish citizen who has reached 18 years of age has the active right to choose representatives for local government. The usual restrictions to the active right to vote apply.[58] The passive right to vote – that is, the right to be elected – is afforded to all citizens of 18 years of age who possess active voting rights and have not been sentenced for an intentional crime. Since 2006, the first elections after EU accession, all EU citizens have the right to vote and be elected to communal councils if they have been registered to vote at least a year before the election takes place.

The deputies to the councils of small communes (those of up to 20,000 residents) are elected in single-member districts via a first-past-the-post system. In the case of commune councils with more than 20,000 residents, councils of cities with a county status, county councils and voivodeship assemblies, the elections are proportional; seats are allocated to parties in proportion to the overall number of valid votes awarded to candidates. In addition, there is a five per cent minimum vote threshold that a party list must gain in order to take part in the proportional allocation of seats.

Only electoral committees – created by political parties, associations, social organisations and voters – can put forward candidates for the local self-government elections at all levels. The electoral committees present lists of candidates supported by a minimum number of voters, depending on the type of election, ranging from 25 for commune council lists to 300 in the case of voivodeship assemblies. The election districts are created on the basis of resolutions of councils at each level and remain under the scrutiny of the administrative courts.[59] In some cases, seats are filled without a vote occurring if the number of candidates equals the number of vacancies. The regional courts confirm the validity of the local self-government elections. Since 2002, the electoral law incorporates restrictive rules concerning the financing of the electoral campaign for local self-government elections, similar to those in parliamentary and presidential elections.[60] Their aim was to afford more transparency during electoral campaigning.

[57] Article 169(2) of the Constitution.
[58] See ch 3.
[59] Constitutional Court, judgment of 6 April 2016, P 5/14, OTK ZU A/2016, poz 15.
[60] See ch 3.

Other rules apply to executive bodies. The county and voivodeship's boards (and their chairpersons) are elected indirectly by the legislative bodies of local self-government (councils and assemblies). In contrast, mayors – the executive bodies of commune self-government – are universally and directly elected by the local electorate. Previously, between 1990 and 2001, mayors were elected by commune councils. Direct election of mayors brought a revolutionary change to the local political system, leading to a revival of political life in communes. In addition, especially in small towns, the election of a mayor by the people has had a positive impact, shielding the electoral process from the influence of local cliques. The election of the mayors takes place at the same time as the election of deputies to commune councils. The candidates for the mayor's office need to be Polish citizens of 25 years of age with active voting rights. They are not obliged to reside in the commune in which they are candidates. The elections are majoritarian and resemble presidential elections (with two rounds of voting). The term of office of the mayor is the same as that of the commune council. A number of incompatibilities are foreseen, such as that mayors cannot be simultaneously employed in government administration, be MPs or engage in certain economic activities connected to the functioning of the local self-government, such as being shareholders of the waste management company.

In practice, in the 2014 local self-government elections for all types of elected representatives, the turnout was around 47 per cent and has been similar in past elections of this type.[61] This is only slightly less than in the parliamentary and presidential elections held in 2015 (around 51 and 55 per cent, respectively). As such, the candidates in commune self-government elections are usually residents engaged in the community's life.[62] In fact, a growing trend of reluctance towards partisanship has been observed. Just before the 2014 local elections, around two-thirds of voters declared a preference to vote for a candidate not connected to any political party.[63] However, for the higher tiers of local government, especially for the voivodeship assembly, candidates are usually local members of political parties or local businessmen. These candidates are relatively less well known to the residents, who, as a consequence, are more likely

[61] See http://samorzad2014.pkw.gov.pl/356_Frekwencja.

[62] The first-past-the-post system in the commune council elections seems to benefit especially independent candidates. See A Gendźwiłł and T Żółtak 'How Single-Member Districts are Reinforcing Local Independents and Strengthening Mayors: On the Electoral Reform in Polish Local Government' (2017) 43 *Local Government Studies* 110.

[63] CBOS, Komunikat z Badań CBOS Nr 124/2014, Warsaw, Wrzesień 2014, 6.

to follow their political party preferences.[64] In political terms, the local authority elections (2006–14) have thus far taken place one year before the parliamentary elections and have generally reflected the tendency that the party that garnered the most votes won the following parliamentary elections at the national level. For this reason, local elections play an important role for political parties.

B. Female Representation in Local Self-Government

Since 2011, the Electoral Code has required that candidate lists in all local elections that follow the proportionality method of vote allocation – to commune councils with more than 20,000 residents, councils of cities with a county status, county councils and voivodeship assemblies – must contain no less than 35 per cent female and no less than 35 per cent male candidates.[65] In practice, in the first elections to which this requirement was applicable (in 2014), the share of female candidates was 38 per cent.[66] This outcome indicates a slight improvement compared to the 2010 elections, in which female candidates comprised 31 per cent of the total.[67] As a consequence of the gender quota, after the 2014 local elections, the share of female deputies was as follows: 27 per cent in commune councils; 28 per cent in councils of cities with a county status; 19 per cent in county councils; and 23 per cent in voivodeship assemblies.[68] Compared to the 2010 elections, which did not require a gender quota, the outcome of the 2014 vote indicates only a 1–2 per cent point increase in the share of female deputies across all councils and assemblies.[69] Across the local councils, female deputies are generally highly educated, with more than 80 per cent of those on councils of cities with county status, county councils and voivodeship councils having a tertiary education.[70] However, this share is significantly lower in commune

[64] ibid 10.

[65] Article 425 §3 of the Law of 5 January 2011 (Electoral Code), JL 2018 Pos 754, 1000, 1349.

[66] Statistical data on elections to councils and elections of mayors of 16 November 2014, available at http://samorzad2014.pkw.gov.pl/aktualnosci/0/109_Informacje_statystyczne_na_temat_wyborow.

[67] See http://wybory2010.pkw.gov.pl/geo/pl/000000.html#tabs-2.

[68] Authors' own calculation based on Statistics Poland (n 45) 56.

[69] Authors' own calculation based on Statistics Poland, *Mały Rocznik Statystyczny Polski 2012* (Warsaw, 2012) 72.

[70] Authors' own calculation based on Statistics Poland (n 45) 56.

councils, where fewer than half of female deputies have a tertiary education. A similar picture emerges for the professions of female deputies. On the larger city, county and voivodeship councils, more than three-quarters of female deputies are managers or professionals, whereas of those on the commune councils, this figure is only around one-third.[71] Instead, the commune councils tend to have significantly larger shares of female deputies who are technicians, clerical and services or sales workers and skilled workers in the agriculture, forestry and fisheries sectors.

The data show that although some improvement can be observed, especially in the number of female candidates, the share of council and assembly seats occupied by women is growing very slowly and is still far from parity with the share held by male representatives. Some reasons may include the traditional social roles that are assigned to women or female stereotypes.[72] Moreover, women tend to choose commune over county or voivodeship bodies, as local activities may be easier to combine with other obligations and are more socially acceptable.[73]

Another issue is that the gender quota does not apply to the majoritarian elections of mayors. The share of female candidates in these elections, as compared to the elections to councils and assemblies, was much lower – 14 per cent in 2010 and 16 per cent in 2014.[74] The low participation of women in mayoral elections resulted in a relatively low number of women holding this office. Accordingly, after the 2014 elections, only around 11 per cent of mayors are women in communes and in cities with a county status, while the share of female leaders of Warsaw's boroughs is slightly higher (16.7 per cent).[75] With regard to other executive arms, in the indirectly elected county and voivodeship boards, the share of female members was 16.2 per cent and 21.3 per cent, respectively.[76] In sum, one may conclude that the share of women exercising executive offices in local authorities is similar to the rather low number of women in the national legislature. The very low share of female mayors is even more disappointing.

[71] ibid 57.

[72] A Łukasik-Turecka, 'Kobiety w jednostkach samorządu terytorialnego w dobie debaty nad parytetami i kwotami' (2013) 41 *Roczniki Nauk Społecznych* 73, 74.

[73] ibid 75.

[74] See http://wybory2010.pkw.gov.pl/geo/pl/000000.html#tabs-2 and http://samorzad2014.pkw.gov.pl/aktualnosci/0/109_Informacje_statystyczne_na_temat_wyborow.

[75] As of 31 December 2017. See Statistics Poland (n 45) 57.

[76] ibid.

C. Recent Trends in Local Self-Government Elections

In 2018, the governing majority, the Law and Justice party, conducted a significant reform of electoral law for local authorities.[77] The formal aim (as indicated in the name of that law) is to increase public participation in the process of electing, functioning and controlling councils and mayors. At the same time, this new law changes the organisational model of elections. The National Electoral Commission, which is the most important electoral watchdog body in Poland, will now predominantly consist of officials elected by the Chamber of Deputies instead of judges, as was previously the case.[78] This reform expresses the continuing distrust of the governing majority towards the judiciary.[79]

The terms of office of both the legislative as well as the executive institutions of local self-government have been extended from four to five years. At the same time, the previously unlimited number of terms that a mayor can serve has been restricted to two. This seeks to limit the existing practice where some mayors have been in office since 2002. This particular reform was fully enforced in the local government elections in the autumn of 2018, but did not apply to mayors elected previously. Moreover, as was indicated earlier, the majoritarian system applicable in communes will be limited to those that have fewer than 20,000 residents, while the more populated communes will adopt a proportional system.

Other changes are procedural in character. Instead of one electoral commission, in the 2018 local elections, two electoral commissions were involved, each dealing with a different task: the first responsible for conducting the elections and the second for counting votes. However, by 2019, a system with just one electoral commission was reinstituted. Even before the 2018 elections, the governing majority retracted the proposal that communes provide internet transmission from the polling station, including the vote count.[80] As it transpired, this idea proved to be undeliverable due its costly implementation.

The governing majority has justified these demanding electoral experiments[81] by reference to 'unprecedented' irregularities in the local

[77] Law of 11 January 2018 amending some of the laws to increase the participation of citizens in the process of electing, functioning, and controlling of some of the public organs, JL 2018 Pos 130, 1349.

[78] See ch 3.

[79] See chs 5 and 6.

[80] Law of 15 June 2018 on the amendment of the law–Electoral Code and of other laws, JL 2018 Pos 1349.

[81] 'Komisje z wakatami, urzędnicy wyborczy dopiero na starcie. A do wyborów samorządowych miesiąc' *Dziennik Gazeta Prawna* (21 September 2018).

elections of 2014.[82] In practice, these allegations were confirmed only to a small extent. The ordinary courts confirmed irregularities affecting the outcome of elections in 62 cases, and, as a consequence, in 54 cases the relevant mandate was terminated and the respective elections were repeated.[83] Although the reform might add some transparency, its negative aspects are significant, especially with regard to the re-organisation of the National Electoral Committee.[84]

D. Direct Democracy

One of the crucial tools enabling civil society to exercise their rights is local referendums.[85] These can take place at any of the various units of local self-government outlined above and can be either obligatory or non-obligatory in character. A referendum is necessary to recall a council (or assembly) or a mayor; and when residents of a commune wish to self-impose a tax for a public aim included in the competences of the commune. Crucially, a non-obligatory referendum may concern any matter that is important to the local community,[86] therefore extending beyond issues within the competence of the elected local authority.[87] A local referendum can be launched by a local council (assembly) and on the request of a proportion of eligible residents: 10 per cent in commune and county and five per cent in voivodeships. In general, a local referendum is valid when at least 30 per cent of eligible voters have participated. In situations in which the referendum concerns the recall of a directly elected body, such as the mayor, the applicable threshold is the participation of at least three-fifths of the number of voters who elected the mayor in the first place. Furthermore, a local referendum is binding only if one of the proposed solutions gained more than half of the valid votes, or more than two-thirds of the valid votes if the referendum concerned self-imposed taxation. A binding outcome demands the execution of the

[82] See Chamber of Deputies, Print No 2001, 10 November 2017, 81–82.

[83] In 2010, local elections were declared illegal in 23 cases. See Fundacja Batorego, Co się stało 16 listopada? Wybory samorządowe 2014 (Warsaw, 2015) 63, available at: www.batory.org.pl/upload/files/Programy%20operacyjne/Masz%20Glos/Co%20sie%20stalo%2016%20listopada.pdf.

[84] See ch 3.

[85] Law of 15 September 2000 on the local referendum, JL 2016 Pos 400, JL 2017 Pos 850, 1349, JL 2018 Pos 1579.

[86] Article 170 of the Constitution.

[87] Constitutional Court, judgment of 26 February 2003, K 30/02, OTK ZU 2A/2003, poz 16.

decision of the residents by the council (assembly). If the referendum at stake aimed at the recalling of a local authority, a binding outcome *ex lege* ends the term of that body. The actual practice of local referendums is discussed below.

Amongst all types of local referendums, those regarding the recall of a mayor tend to be of the greatest importance. This is understandable, as the actions of the mayor – a single-person body – gather more attention on the part of the residents and are easier to relate to when compared to a commune council with between 15 and 45 deputies. Thus, frequently, the residents develop views on the mayor's activities, and the referendum can represent something approaching a mere popularity check. The commune council must order a referendum to remove a mayor who was not discharged at the end of the budgetary year, but can also launch a referendum to recall the mayor on any other ground. In addition, the residents themselves can initiate a referendum to recall a mayor. Beyond the local referendum, the Prime Minister recalls a mayor in cases of repeated violations of the Constitution or statutes. However, this competence has not been exercised in practice. Beyond these possibilities to recall a mayor, since 2006, mayors can be suspended. This has represented a response to the rather rare circumstances where mayors were trying to exercise their function from behind bars.

Practice shows that the removal of a mayor remains problematic, as local referendums easily miss the turnout thresholds necessary for their validity. However, the insufficient turnout is pertinent to all local referendums regarding the recall of bodies of local self-government. Between 2001 and June 2016, 377 local referendums concerned the recall of a commune council (111), a mayor (193), both a commune council and a mayor (66) or a county council (7).[88] Nonetheless, only 13 per cent of local referendums were valid, while the remaining share failed due to a low turnout. Such poor participation in local referendums is hard to explain. Some reasons might include disbelief that a referendum will improve the situation of the community or indifference to local affairs. Still, there have been some successful cases of the removal of a mayor in a local referendum. These instances generally concerned persons who were compromised due to moral reasons or economic abuses. For instance, the mayor of Trzebiatów, who faced allegations of negligence and a lack of appreciation for the development of the commune, was removed from office following a successful referendum.[89] Finally, despite the low

[88] Information received from the Office of the National Electoral Commission.

[89] 'Burmistrz Trzebiatowa odwołany przez mieszkańców. Udane referendum' *Gazeta Wyborcza Szczecin* (29 February 2016).

turnout, social research indicates a general feeling among the majority of respondents that local referendums are not frequent enough and not sufficiently used to allow for co-decision in local matters.[90] Thus, local referendums continue to serve as a valuable tool of direct democracy.

IV. DIFFICULTIES IN OVERSIGHT OF LOCAL SELF-GOVERNMENT

The Constitution guarantees to local self-government the exercise of a substantial part of public duties.[91] This principle is safeguarded by the requirement of statutory allocation of these tasks. As has already been mentioned, local self-government exercises these tasks in its own name and under its own responsibility. This means that neither the state nor the government administration in Warsaw, but rather the bodies of self-government take responsibility for these tasks. At the same time, to ensure the legality of the actions of local self-government, the Constitution provides for state oversight over the functioning of the former.[92] Only with regard to the communes' tasks commissioned by the state, such as issuing passports, is the oversight exercised taking into account the appropriateness, reliability and economic prudence of local self-government. The oversight bodies are the office of the Prime Minister, the voivode and – in the case of financial affairs – the Regional Audit Chambers. Again, the oversight is exercised by state bodies exclusively within the limits set by the law. In contrast, there is no oversight within local self-government as such, meaning that a county does not oversee a commune and a voivodeship does not oversee a county. Such oversight mechanisms between the units of local self-government do not exist, as all of them are equal.

The oversight tools at the disposal of watchdog bodies are either controlling or correcting in character. Accordingly, as a controlling mechanism, the watchdog bodies can request information on the organisation and functioning of the local government. Moreover, each mayor and chairperson of the executive board presents every resolution of the executive arm of the local self-government to the voivode shortly after its adoption. The same concerns resolutions on financial matters, which

[90] CBOS, Komunikat z Badań Nr 97/2017, 'O czym Polacy chcieliby się wypowiedzieć w referendum?', Lipiec 2017, 2–4.

[91] Article 16(2) of the Constitution.

[92] ibid art 171(1). See B Dolnicki, *Samorząd Terytorialny* (Warsaw, Wolters Kluwer, 2016) 387.

must be submitted to Regional Audit Chambers. The oversight body controls the legality of those resolutions. In turn, the correcting tools include the right of the Prime Minister to suspend a body of local self-government and introduce a receivership (*zarząd komisaryczny*) for up to two years. The correcting tools available to the voivodes are the replacing regulations (*zarządzenia zastepcze*), which are discussed in more detail below. The units of local self-government can challenge all decisions of the oversight bodies before the administrative courts. Beyond the correcting means available to the government administration, a last resort is the Chamber of Deputies, on the request of the Prime Minister, dissolving a council (or assembly) in cases of repeated breaches of the Constitution and statutes.[93] This 'repressive and disciplinary instrument' cannot be challenged before the administrative courts.[94] However, since 1990, this competence has never been exercised; moreover, the rules of procedure of the Chamber of Deputies do not even regulate this matter, suggesting that it might never be put into practice. However, this does not call into question the functioning of the oversight as such. The dissolution of a council (or an assembly) would be an extraordinary and final measure.

A telling example of the oversight of the voivode over the functioning of local authorities is the problem of 'decommunisation of the public sphere', which concerns the change of street names that refer to persons, organisations or events that symbolise the Communist system in Poland. Specifically, in 2016, a new law was introduced demanding that commune councils remove such street names within a certain period of time.[95] However, some of the commune councils did not follow this edict, or lingered, indicating that they needed to consult the residents. In practice, this has led to open conflicts between the voivodes and councils, whereby the latter wanted to maintain a specific street name, pointing to, for instance, residents' habits. Therefore, since September 2017, the voivodes, issuing replacing regulations, themselves began to change the street names in question. For instance, the Masovian voivode issued a total of 103 replacing regulations, 50 of which concerned the streets of Warsaw.[96] Nonetheless, in 2018, the Supreme Administrative Court decided that 44 of these replacing regulations violated relevant laws, and

[93] Article 171(3) of the Constitution.

[94] Constitutional Court, judgment of 5 October 1994, W 1/94, OTK ZU 1994, poz 47.

[95] Law of 1 April 2016 on a prohibition on propagating communism or other totalitarian system by names of buildings, facilities and public utility facilities, JL 2018 Pos 1103.

[96] 'Warszawa: Nie będzie al. Lecha Kaczyńskiego. Jest decyzja NSA' *Rzeczpospolita* (7 December 2018).

the opinion of the Institute of National Remembrance – which was the basis of the voivode's acts – was inadequate.[97]

Beyond this example, in addition, voivodes issue replacing regulations in individual cases. This concerns cases where, for instance, the commune council fails to remove a deputy who exercises a forbidden economic activity, such as renting a commercial space from the commune on preferential conditions to run a shop. In such a case, the replacing regulation terminates the deputies' mandate. However, the deputies can challenge these regulations before the administrative courts.[98]

The review of legality of the actions of bodies of local self-government at all levels also remains in the interests of citizens. An individual complaint is available to anyone whose legal interest was infringed by a resolution of an elected local authority, after a frustrated request to rectify that violation. This legal means, which naturally differs from the state oversight discussed earlier, provide residents – members of a self-governing community – with a possibility to shield themselves from their own potentially illegal acts.

Each year, increasing funding is channelled from the state budget to local self-government. In 2016, the units of local self-government received PLN 36.9 billion, which amounted to 17 per cent of all their income.[99] As has already been mentioned, this funding takes the form of various grants to implement specific public tasks. The management of these resources is controlled by the Regional Audit Chambers. In 2017, the Regional Audit Chambers reported that 98 per cent of the audited budget and other financial resolutions of local authorities were made in accordance with the relevant laws.[100] This indicates that local authorities largely spend their budgets legitimately. Yet this oversight certainly has its own limits, especially when it comes to sanctioning problematic actions by local authorities. For instance, the Ostrowice commune did not follow the recommendations of the Regional Audit Chamber and has since fallen into insolvency.[101] In 2019, the Council of Ministers decided

[97] See, eg, Supreme Administrative Court, judgment of 7 December 2018, II OSK 2642/18.

[98] Constitutional Court, judgment of 17 July 2007, P 19/04, OTK ZU 7A/2007, poz 78.

[99] Supreme Chamber of Control, 'Dotowanie zadań zleconych jednostkom samorządu terytorialnego z zakresu administracji rządowej i innych zadań zleconych ustawami', 15 September 2017 available at: https://www.nik.gov.pl/kontrole/P/16/009.

[100] See L Budner-Iwanicka, 'Działalność regionalnych izb obrachunkowych w 2017 r. Omówienie Sprawozdania Krajowej Rady Regionalnych Izb Obrachunkowych złożonego do Sejmu i Senatu Rzeczypospolitej Polskiej' (2018) *Miesięcznik Regionalnych Izb Obrachunkowych* 122.

[101] 'Gminy coraz bogatsze, ale ciągle im mało' *Dziennik Gazeta Prawna* (4 February 2019).

to dissolve the commune and the state treasury took over its debts, the first time that such a step has been taken.[102]

V. LOCAL SELF-GOVERNMENT IN THE EU

The prospect of EU accession (2004) played a part in the reform of local self-government in Poland, as well as in other candidate countries from Central and Eastern Europe.[103] The reform was motivated by the need to improve institutional structures, enabling the receipt of structural funds from the EU.[104] As a consequence, the establishment of local self-government in voivodeships (1999) allowed for the management and implementation of funds expected at the time by the country. Poland as a candidate state was the major beneficiary of PHARE (Poland and Hungary Assistance for the Restructuring of the Economy), the EU's financial instrument helping Central and Eastern European states to strengthen public administration and invest in economic development of the region. Local self-governments could also apply for financial support from ISPA (Instrument for Structural Policies for Pre-Accession) and SAPARD (Special Accession Programme for Agricultural and Rural Development) for investments in infrastructure, environment protection and agriculture with the aim to enhance social and economic cohesion of the EU newcomers. Nowadays, amongst all EU Member States, Poland is the largest beneficiary of the European Structural and Investment Funds for 2014–20, an €86 billion budget translated into a range of national and regional programmes.[105] The executive boards of voivodeship self-government manage EU regional programmes, which comprise around 40 per cent of the aforementioned budget.[106] Funds are made available to businesses, educational entities or NGOs, but also to the elected local authority. Local authorities can apply for EU funding to invest in a range of local policies such as waste management (eg, waste segregation),

[102] 'Gmina Ostrowiec zlikwidowana od 1 stycznia 2019' *Rzeczpospolita* (31 December 2018).

[103] M Baun, 'EU Regional Policy and the Candidate States: Poland and the Czech Republic' (2002) 24 *Journal of European Integration* 261, 272; M Ferry, 'The EU and Recent Regional Reform in Poland' (2003) 55 *Europe-Asia Studies*, 1097, 1101.

[104] European Commission, 'Agenda 2000 – Commission Opinion on Poland's Application for Membership of the European Union', DOC/97/16, 15 July 1997, 89.

[105] European Commission, European Structural and Investment Funds, 'Country Factsheet: Poland', available at: http://ec.europa.eu/regional_policy/sources/policy/what/investment-policy/esif-country-factsheet/esi_funds_country_factsheet_pl_en.pdf.

[106] Ministry of Development, Fundusze Europejskie, Biuletyn Informacyjny nr 44, Czerwiec 2017, 8.

transportation (eg, building new roads or purchasing low-carbon footprint buses) and cultural heritage (e.g, renovation of monuments).

Another dimension of the EU's impact on local government concerns subsidiarity, the exercise of competences shared between the EU and the Member States as close as possible to the citizen. The principle of subsidiarity expresses the idea that the EU level should act only when the objectives of the proposed policy cannot be sufficiently achieved by the Member States and, by reason of its scale or effects, the EU can better pursue that action.[107] Since the Lisbon Treaty (2009), the subsidiarity principle distinguishes between the different levels of Member State action – central, regional and local – in contrast to referring to the Member States only in general terms. By introducing this region-friendly reference, the Lisbon Treaty acknowledged the competence of smaller units to set and achieve governance tasks.[108] One of the guardians of the EU subsidiarity principle is the Committee of the Regions, which gathers elected or politically accountable representatives of regional and local bodies across the EU. It is estimated that about 70 per cent of EU legislation directly affects the regional and local levels.[109] Therefore, the Committee of the Regions enables its members to offer input concerning the development of EU laws in the form of opinions or resolutions. The Polish representation to the Committee of the Regions (21 members) contributes in both ways: to promote the interests of the Committee of the Regions in Poland and at the EU level; and to inform the EU decision-making process about issues crucial to the Polish regional and local authorities. In addition, some of the Polish local authorities are partners of the Subsidiarity Monitoring Network, run by the Committee of the Regions, reviewing EU legislative proposals for their compliance with the subsidiarity principle.[110]

Beyond the role of the Council of the Regions concerning the promotion and attention offered to local matters, all Polish voivodeships, and some of the cities, maintain a representative office in Brussels. The aim is to keep their residents informed about EU laws and policies that may affect the region, as well as to feed local interests into the EU policy process. The representations also serve as promotional points of reference for tourism or cultural events.

[107] Article 5(3) TEU.

[108] K Granat, *The Principle of Subsidiarity and its Enforcement in the EU Legal Order* (Oxford, Hart Publishing, 2018).

[109] See http://cor.europa.eu/en/about/Pages/key-facts.aspx.

[110] Committee of the Regions, Subsidiarity Annual Report 2016, 19 April 2017.

VI. CONCLUSION

The wholesale reform of 1990 abandoned the centralised model of government typical of Communist systems, thereby facilitating a rebuilding of civil society. The key stage in this long-term process was the Constitution of 1997 and the adoption of the principles of decentralisation of power, self-government and subsidiarity, allowing the citizens to fully exercise power at the local level. The commune became the basic unit of local self-government, independent from the two other – counties and voivodeships – larger units of local self-government. All of these entities have directly elected local authorities, their own budgets and specific competences. In addition to the representation of their interests by the local self-government, the residents participate in the local decision-making process via local referendums. Local self-government has been granted relative freedom in the exercise of public tasks, as its actions are controlled only for their legality. To this extent, the Constitution assigns oversight to the Prime Minister and the voivodes, whose decisions can be challenged before administrative courts.

The current shape of local governance seems appropriately designed for the tasks faced by local communities. Crucially, the establishment of local self-government has helped to overcome the social apathy which characterised the socialist state. Over the longer term, it has enabled the blossoming of localism and citizen engagement in the public life of their communities. At the same time, the adopted model of a strong local democracy still allows the state to administer the issues that fall within the scope of its interests, such as protection of forests or road construction. Additionally, Poland's EU accession offered a crucial stimulus for subnational government, both in institutional and financial terms. In short, Poland seems to have found its own successful model of local governance.

At the same time, the system of local governance present in Poland for what now amounts to over 30 years shows some flaws. This is especially visible in the relatively low participation of citizens in local elections and referendums. The residents seem to take local self-government and its institutions for granted, and are becoming uninterested in their functioning. Another issue – seen from the perspective of a pluralist society with self-government structures – is the attempts of political parties to influence the running of local self-government, as envisaged in the 2018 electoral reforms. Nonetheless, the positive aspects of local self-government continue to prevail over these shortcomings.

FURTHER READING

Banaszak, B, 'Poland – Local Government in Poland: Towards Consolidation?' in C Panara and M Varney (eds), *Local Government in Europe* (Abingdon, Routledge, 2013) 255–76.

Brusis, M, 'Between EU Requirements, Competitive Politics, and National Traditions: Re-creating Regions in the Accession Countries of Central and Eastern Europe' (2002) 15 *Governance: An International Journal of Policy, Administration, and Institutions* 531–59.

Dawson, AH, 'The Transformation of Polish Local Government' (1999) 77 *Public Administration*, 897–902.

Kulesza, M, 'Options for Administrative Reform in Poland' (1993) 71 *Public Administration* 33–40.

Łętowski, J, 'Polish Public Administration between Crisis and Renewal' (1993) 71 *Public Administration* 1–11.

Nowacka, E, 'Local Government in Poland after the Reforms of 1990' (1996) 2 *European Public Law* 393–400.

Swianiewicz, P, 'Poland: Europeanization of Sub-national Governments' in J Loughlin, F Hendriks and A Lidström (eds), *The Oxford Handbook of Local and Regional Democracy in Europe* (Oxford, Oxford University Press, 2010) 481–504.

8

Constitutional Freedoms and Rights

Human Rights – Human Dignity – Freedom of the Person – Equality – Judicial Protection – Proportionality – Ombudsman – State Liability – Access to the Court – Charter of Fundamental Rights of the European Union – European Convention on Human Rights

I. INTRODUCTION

THE PROTECTION OF human rights in law and in practice provides a litmus test for every system of government, including that of Poland. One of the characteristics of the Polish Constitution is the creation of a robust system of protection of human rights.[1] The legal framework of this system is based on three elements. The first of these is the Constitution itself and the principles established in its Chapter II, which are further discussed in section III below. The 1997 Constitution opened up the Polish legal system to international human rights law.[2] The best example thereof is the European Convention on Human Rights (ECHR), which establishes a European system of human rights protection. As a consequence of its ratification in January 1993 on the basis of Article 91(1) of the Constitution, the ECHR became a part of binding Polish law and is directly applicable.[3] Moreover, the ECHR enjoys precedence over statutes if they cannot be reconciled with its provisions.[4] The International Covenant on Civil and Political Rights and of the International Covenant on Economic, Social and Cultural

[1] For a historical perspective, see ch 1.
[2] Article 9 of the Constitution. See ch 2.
[3] See https://www.coe.int/en/web/conventions/full-list/-/conventions/treaty/005/signatures.
[4] Article 91(2) of the Constitution.

Rights, ratified in 1977, enjoy similarly strong positions under the Polish Constitution.

EU law presents another source of human rights introduced by the 1997 Constitution. For the relationship between constitutional law and EU law – discussed in detail in Chapter 2 – the crucial aspect is that the latter is directly applicable and has precedence in the event of conflict with national statutes.[5] Poland as an EU Member State is bound by, most prominently, the EU Charter of Fundamental Rights.

Thus, the system of protection of human rights in Poland consists of a number of elements – the Constitution, international law and European law – that complement each other. The jurisprudence of the Constitutional Court and national courts (led by the Supreme Court and Supreme Administrative Court), on the one hand, and the case law of the European Court of Human Rights (ECtHR) in Strasbourg and the Court of Justice of the European Union in Luxembourg (CJEU), on the other hand, delineate the precise relationship between these sources of human rights.

This chapter focuses on the understanding of constitutional freedoms and rights, and their protection. The main idea is to highlight the meaning of the jurisprudence of the Constitutional Court and other courts for the functioning of human rights under the Constitution of 1997. No other part of the Constitution is determined by the case law of the Court more than that concerning individual freedoms and rights.

II. THREE BILLS OF RIGHTS

As mentioned above, there are three main systems of fundamental rights protection that apply to Poland today – the Constitution of 1997, the ECHR and the EU Charter. In addition, international covenants have played an important role as they were applied by the Constitutional Court in its early jurisprudence.[6]

Poland has been party to the Council of Europe since 1993. Polish citizens often perceive the Strasbourg Court as their 'last resort' when their rights have been violated. This is even more the case as, in principle, a prior referral of the case to the Constitutional Court is

[5] ibid art 91(3).

[6] M Łabor-Soroka, W Łączkowski, 'Orzecznictwo Trybunału Konstytucyjnego a ochrona praw człowieka' (1994) 12–13 *Roczniki Nauk Społecznych* 87.

not required.[7] In 2017, the ECtHR dealt with 2,466 applications concerning Poland (2.5 per cent of all applications received by the Court that year), but only a few (20) of them were found to be admissible.[8] Between Poland's accession to the ECHR and the end of 2017, the ECtHR issued a total of 1,145 judgments concerning Poland and in 84 per cent of cases, it found at least one violation of the ECHR.[9] This inglorious share of ECHR violations ranks Poland immediately after the five states with the highest total number of violations confirmed by the Strasbourg Court (Turkey, the Russian Federation, Italy, Romania and Ukraine).[10] The largest number of violations by Poland concerns Article 5 ECHR (the right to liberty and security) and Article 6 ECHR (length of proceedings).[11] In 2017, the Council of Ministers of the Council of Europe was supervising the implementation of 124 judgments concerning Poland, a significant decrease compared to 2011, with 924 judgments.[12] Although Poland is undertaking actions to execute the ECtHR's judgments, in some cases legislative amendments as well as changes in the practice of national organs are still demanded, especially concerning the excessive length of court proceedings.[13] So far, a parliamentary subcommittee, supported by the Ombudsman and by human rights organisations, tasked with dealing with the implementation of ECtHR judgments and thereby exercising a review function over the executive, has not yet been established.[14]

A number of Polish cases before the ECtHR were covered by the pilot judgment procedure which identifies systemic problems underlying repetitive cases and obliges states to address the problem.[15] This procedure enabled a number of difficult and crucial Polish cases to be settled. The first ever pilot judgment procedure launched by the Strasbourg Court concerned Poland's failure to compensate persons repatriated from the 'territories beyond the Bug River' after the Second World War who were

[7] For the conditions on when the applicant is required to exhaust the remedy of constitutional complaint before addressing the Strasbourg Court, see ECtHR, *Szott-Medyńska v Poland* (Application No 47414/99), 9 October 2003.

[8] https://www.echr.coe.int/Documents/Facts_Figures_2017_ENG.pdf.

[9] Authors' own calculation based on the ECtHR's data available at https://www.echr.coe.int/Documents/Stats_violation_1959_2017_ENG.pdf.

[10] ibid.

[11] ibid.

[12] Ministry of Foreign Affairs, Raport z wykonywania wyroków Europejskiego Trybunału Praw Człowieka przez Polskę za 2017 r, 26 March 2018, 35.

[13] ibid 36–37.

[14] See https://www.rpo.gov.pl/pl/content/25-rocznica-ratyfikowania-przez-polskę-europejskiej-konwencji-praw-człowieka.

[15] See ECtHR, *Hutten-Czapska v Poland* [GC] (Application No 35014/97) (protection of property); and *Rutkowski and Others v Poland* (lengthy court proceedings) (Application

forced to abandon their property on those territories, therefore constituting a violation of the right of property under the ECHR.[16] The case had a far-reaching scope as it affected a whole class of individuals who brought their cases before the ECtHR. As a consequence, Poland introduced an effective compensation scheme meeting the requirement posed by the ECHR and the pilot judgment procedure was concluded.[17]

Finally, three of the ECtHR's judgments concerning Poland or Polish citizens have raised particular interest and have reflected the important role that the Strasbourg Court plays in the eyes of the society. These concern different dimensions of human rights protection. The case of *Tysiąc v Poland* underscored the problem of regulation and access to abortion in Poland.[18] The ECtHR found Poland to be in breach of the applicant's right to respect for private life. According to the Court, Polish law did not provide any effective mechanism to determine whether the conditions for obtaining a lawful abortion had been met.[19] In turn, the cases *Al Nashiri v Poland* and *Husayn v Poland* concerned the secret detention at a CIA 'black site' in Poland of two men suspected of terrorist acts.[20] The ECtHR held that Poland cooperated in the preparation and execution of the CIA operations on its own territory, subjecting the applicants to treatment in violation of the Convention. Poland infringed, inter alia, the right to life and the prohibition of torture and inhuman or degrading behaviour, which represent drastic violations of human rights. Finally, the case *Janowiec and Others v Russia* was brought by a group of Polish nationals, relatives of victims of the Katyń massacre conducted by Soviet secret police in 1940, arguing that the Russian authorities failed to conduct an effective investigation into the death of their relatives.[21] However, the Strasbourg Court declared that it had no temporal jurisdiction to deal with the adequacy of the Russian investigation. The outcome of the case was disappointing for Polish society, taking into account the importance of the Katyń massacre in the national memory.

Beyond those high-profile cases that have been followed in Poland with great attention, the ECtHR issued a number of judgments concerning

Nos 72287/10, 13927/11 and 46187/11). After Poland's implementation of the judgments, the procedures were concluded. See ECtHR, press release of February 2018, available at: https://www.echr.coe.int/Documents/FS_Pilot_judgments_ENG.pdf.

[16] ECtHR, *Broniowski v Poland* [GC] (Application No 31443/96), ECHR 2004-V.

[17] ECtHR, 'Bug River Cases Resolved', press release of 12 December 2007.

[18] ECtHR, *Tysiąc v Poland* (Application No 5410/03).

[19] ibid para 124.

[20] ECtHR, *Al Nashiri v Poland* (Application No 28761/11) and *Husayn (Abu Zubaydah) v Poland* (Application No 7511/13).

[21] ECtHR, *Janowiec and Others v Russia* (Application Nos 55508/07 and 29520/09).

the length of proceedings before Polish courts. Specifically, in the *Kudła v Poland* case of 2000, it found Poland to be in violation of the Convention because the national proceedings against the applicant in question exceeded nine years and no effective remedy against this excessive length was provided to the applicant.[22] As a consequence, Poland introduced the possibility of lodging complaints in cases where proceedings were of excessive length.[23] Nonetheless, the Strasbourg Court was still receiving repetitive Polish cases concerning unreasonably long court proceedings and the constraints involved in the complaint procedure, including insufficient compensation. As a result, the pilot judgment procedure was launched in 2015 against Poland.[24] In the following years, Poland has satisfactorily implemented the ECtHR judgment, amended the existing law to eliminate its systemic dysfunctions, and the pilot judgment procedure was concluded in 2017.[25]

The final group of ECtHR cases is nestled between the high-profile judgments and those concerning the Polish judicial system. These decisions concern the Polish lustration process that aims to expose persons exercising public functions who had worked for or collaborated with the state's security services during the Communist period. One such case is the *Matyjek v Poland* judgment, which concerned an MP who was deprived of his parliamentary mandate by a court and was banned from running for a seat or holding public office for 10 years as a consequence of lying in his lustration declaration.[26] The issue at stake was the fairness of the lustration procedure, its secret nature and unequal character, as the Commissioner of the Public Interest had broad access to all relevant documentation, in contrast to the applicant. The ECtHR found that the proceedings against the applicant were unfair, did not respect the principle of equality of arms and were thus in breach of the Convention. This judgment of the Strasbourg Court improved the position of other persons subject to this procedure. The legislative changes introduced

[22] ECtHR, *Kudła v Poland* (Application No 30210/96).

[23] Law of 17 June 2004 on the complaint concerning violation of the right of a party to hear her case in court without unreasonable delay, OJ 2018 Pos 75.

[24] *Rutkowski and Others v Poland* (n 15).

[25] See https://www.echr.coe.int/Documents/FS_Pilot_judgments_ENG.pdf. For an assessment of the legal changes in national law, see Helsińska Fundacja Praw Człowieka, 'Wykonanie wyroku Europejskiego Trybunału Praw Człowieka w sprawie Rutkowski i inni przeciwko Polsce', available at: http://www.hfhr.pl/wp-content/uploads/2017/12/Rutkowski-analiza-KM-PL.pdf.

[26] ECtHR, *Matyjek v Poland* (Application No 38184/03).

over time largely responded to ECtHR jurisprudence on the fairness of the investigative procedure.[27]

Beyond the ECHR, the EU Charter presents an additional source of fundamental rights protection. With the entry into force of the Lisbon Treaty, the EU Charter gained binding legal force in 2009 and constitutes part of the primary norms of EU law. It is addressed to EU institutions and to the Member States 'only when they are implementing EU law'.[28] Poland, like any other EU Member State, is bound by the EU Charter 'in all situations governed by European Union law, but not outside such situations'.[29] In other words, 'even national provisions adopted without any connection (direct or indirect) with EU law have to observe the Charter standards if they are to serve as national instruments in implementing European law'.[30]

Prior to the entry into force of the Lisbon Treaty, Poland and the UK negotiated a protocol which intended to limit the impact of the Charter in those Member States.[31] The possible reason for Poland to join the protocol was the fear that the Charter would limit its freedom to regulate issues such as abortion, euthanasia and same-sex marriage.[32] Still, the protocol does not exempt Poland (or the UK) from the obligation to comply with the provisions of the Charter and it does not prevent courts from ensuring the compliance of national provisions with the EU Charter.[33] In other words, the protocol does not offer a general 'opt-out' from the Charter.

In addition to the Charter, other acts of EU law can also have a direct impact on the application of the constitutional freedoms and rights. A case in point concerns the constitutional prohibition of extradition of Polish citizens.[34] As an EU Member State, Poland was obliged to

[27] A Mężykowska, 'Wykonywanie przez Polskę wyroków Europejskiego Trybunału Praw Człowieka dotyczących postępowań lustracyjnych' (2012) *Ius Novum* 153.

[28] Article 51(1) of the EU Charter.

[29] CJEU, Case C-617/10, *Åkerberg Fransson*, EU:C:2013:105, para 19.

[30] M Safjan, 'Fields of Application of the Charter of Fundamental Rights and Constitutional Dialogues in the European Union', CJC DL 2014/02, 6, available at: http://cadmus.eui.eu/bitstream/handle/1814/32372/CJC_DL_2014_02.pdf?sequence=3&isAllowed=y.

[31] Protocol No 30 to the Lisbon Treaty. See also Declarations 61 and 62.

[32] A Arnull, 'Protocol (No 30) on the Application of the Charter of Fundamental Rights of the European Union to Poland and the United Kingdom', in S Peers et al (eds), *The EU Charter of Fundamental Rights: A Commentary* (Oxford, Bloomsbury Publishing, 2014) 1608 ff.

[33] CJEU, Cases C-411 and 493/10, *NS and ME v Minister for Justice*, EU:C:2011:865, paras 119–20.

[34] Article 55 of the Constitution.

implement the 2002 EU framework decision on the European Arrest Warrant (EAW), which establishes a simplified cross-border judicial surrender procedure for the purpose of prosecuting or executing a custodial sentence or detention order.[35] Accordingly, Poland amended the criminal code to allow for such a surrender of a Polish citizen. However, the Constitutional Court found the provision in question to be contrary to the prohibition of extradition of a Polish citizen expressed in the Constitution.[36] Still, the Constitutional Court indicated that the EAW plays an important role for the functioning of the EU justice system, and represents a form of advanced cooperation between the EU Member States to fight against crime and improve security. Thus, according to the Constitutional Court, implementation of the EAW required a change in the national law, including a possible amendment of the Constitution. Indeed, following the judgment, the Constitution was changed to allow for the extradition of Polish citizens based on a ratified international treaty or a statute implementing EU law.[37] This necessity to ascertain compliance of the Constitution with EU law led to its first amendment since 1997. In short, to allow extradition, the criminal act should be committed outside the territory of Poland and should constitute an offence under Polish law.

Nonetheless, since the Polish government has been conducting major changes in its judicial system that endanger the rule of law, the execution of the EAW vis-a-vis Poland has raised some concerns.[38] In particular, the Irish High Court referred a case to the CJEU concerning an application of the EAW that would involve the extradition of a Polish citizen to stand trial in Poland.[39] The Irish High Court claimed that it was impossible to maintain mutual trust between the EU Member States and execute the EAW when the independence of the courts in Poland was in jeopardy. In reply, the Luxembourg Court indicated that only in exceptional circumstances may the executing judicial authority refrain from giving effect to the EAW. To this extent, the Irish judicial authorities should follow a two-step test reviewing: (1) whether there is a real risk of a violation of the fundamental right to a fair trial; and (2) whether there are

[35] Council Framework Decision of 13 June 2002 on the European arrest warrant and the surrender procedures between Member States [2002] OJ L190, 18 July, 1–20.

[36] Constitutional Court, judgment of 27 April 2005, P 1/05, OTK ZU 4A/2005, poz 42. See D Leczykiewicz, '*Trybunal Konstytucyjny* (Polish Constitutional Tribunal), Judgment of 27 April 2005, No. P 1/05' (2006) 43 *Common Market Law Review* 1181.

[37] See art 55(2) and (3) of the Constitution.

[38] See chs 5 and 6.

[39] CJEU, Case C-216/18 PPU, *LM*, EU:C:2018:586. See M Krajewski, 'Who is Afraid of the European Council? The Court of Justice's Cautious Approach to the Independence

substantial grounds to believe that the person involved will run that risk when surrendered to the Member State.[40] Implementing the CJEU's judgment, the Irish High Court confirmed a violation of the first prong by referring to the Commission's reasoned opinion in the Article 7 of the Treaty on European Union (TEU) proceedings. With regard to the second prong of the CJEU's test, the Irish High Court requested additional information from the Polish judicial authorities.[41] The CJEU's decision also led other courts – in Spain and the Netherlands – to halt the surrender of Polish citizens and request more information on the state of judicial independence in Poland.[42] In the end, the Irish High Court maintained that there are systemic deficiencies of the judiciary in Poland, yet in the specific case they did not reach the threshold of a real risk to the fair trial of the person in question, and ordered him to be surrendered to Polish authorities.[43]

National judges play an important role in upholding fundamental rights in the EU and the Council of Europe systems. The referrals of Polish courts to the EU Charter are 'at times substantial, sometimes more ornamental', which is typical of other EU Member State courts.[44] In turn, Polish courts invoke the ECHR more often, which is understandable as it has been in force since 1993.[45] The frequent referencing of the ECHR possibly stems from the status of the Convention as a ratified international treaty that has primacy before statutes. The ECHR holds an established position in the Polish legal system. The EU Charter as a source of EU law also enjoys primacy before national statutes, yet it applies to the Member States 'only when they are implementing EU law'.

The Constitutional Court often relies on European and international human rights sources.[46] Looking specifically at the position of

of Domestic Judges: ECJ 25 July 2018, Case C-216/18 PPU, *The Minister for Justice and Equality v LM*' (2018) 14 *European Constitutional Law Review* 792.

[40] *LM* (n 39) paras 73–78.

[41] Irish High Court, *Minister for Justice and Equality v Celmer (No 4)* [2018] IEHC 484. For the rather conflicting replies received from Polish judges, see Irish High Court, *Minister for Justice and Equality v Celmer (No 5)* [2018] IEHC 639, paras 85–91.

[42] 'Hiszpański sąd pyta o niezawisłość sędziowską w Polsce' *Rzeczpospolita* (1 October 2018); 'Ekstradycja trzech Polaków wstrzymana przez holenderski sąd' *Rzeczpospolita* (4 October 2018).

[43] *Minister for Justice and Equality v Celmer (No 5)* (n 41). See C Bracken, 'Episode 5 of the Celmer Saga – The Irish High Court Holds Back' *Verfassungsblog* (28 November 2018).

[44] Fundamental Rights Agency, Fundamental Rights Report 2017, 41.

[45] K Kowalik-Bańczyk and M Wróblewski, 'Application of the Charter of Fundamental Rights by Polish Courts and the Jurisprudence of the Polish Constitutional Tribunal' (2015) 18 *Yearbook of Polish European Studies* 239, 240.

[46] See A Syryt, 'Wpływ Europejskiej Konwencji Praw Człowieka na działalność orzeczniczą polskiego Trybunału Konstytucyjnego' in E Karska (ed), *Wpływ Europejskiej Konwencji*

those two bills of rights – the ECHR and the EU Charter – in its case law, one can observe that especially the former plays an important role in proceedings before the Constitutional Court. This includes both the procedure of abstract constitutional review as well as the legal questions addressed to the Constitutional Court. An exception is the constitutional complaint procedure, as only freedoms and rights expressed exclusively in Chapter II of the Constitution can be used as a benchmark in reviewing of a constitutional complaint.[47] In turn, the Constitutional Court invokes the EU Charter to strengthen its own arguments, yet without basing its judgments on any of the EU Charter provisions.[48] In addition, the Constitutional Court has thus far not indicated whether the EU Charter can act as a benchmark for constitutional review at all.[49]

The following section turns to the 1997 Constitution and discusses its basic principles of human rights protection. The three systems of human right protection discussed in this Chapter – the ECHR, the EU Charter and the 1997 Constitution – are related as they share common core values.

III. GENERAL PRINCIPLES OF HUMAN RIGHTS IN POLAND

The constitutional regulation of freedoms and rights of persons and citizens is based on the principles of human dignity, freedom and equality. Human rights, according to the Polish Constitution, stem from those particular principles – dignity, freedom and equality. The courts apply and interpret concrete freedoms and rights in the context of these principles.

A. Human Dignity

Human dignity is the cornerstone of the Polish system of human rights. The Constitution of 1997 declares human dignity to be 'inherent and inalienable' and 'the source of freedoms and rights of persons and

Praw Człowieka na systemy ochrony praw człowieka oraz międzynarodowe prawo karne i humanitarne (Warsaw, Katedra Ochrony Praw Człowieka i Prawa Międzynarodowego Humanitarnego Uniwersytetu Kardynała Stefana Wyszyńskiego, 2013); M Wróblewski, 'Karta Praw Podstawowych UE w orzecznictwie Trybunału Konstytucyjnego – stan obecny i perspektywy' (2015) 10 *Europejski Przegląd Sądowy* 19.

[47] Article 79(1) of the Constitution. See also ch 5.

[48] Kowalik-Bańczyk and Wróblewski (n 45) 249.

[49] ibid 262.

citizens'.[50] In its case law, the Constitutional Court does not clarify human dignity by applying any specific doctrine or concept. It does not explain it by referring to Kant, Alexy, Waldron or Barak. Instead, it shows the meaning and importance of human dignity in concrete cases, as will be discussed below.

Before moving on to a discussion of these cases, it is worth pointing out that the notion of human dignity embodied in the Constitution is one of the deepest expressions of human dignity in contemporary constitutionalism. In this regard, the Polish Constitution exceeds the standard of the ECHR or the EU Charter, or the expression of human dignity in the constitutions of other states, such as Italy, Hungary and Lithuania,[51] as it defines both the content (inherent, inalienable and inviolable) and the function (as the source of freedoms and rights) of human dignity. The strong anchoring of the legal and human rights system on human dignity is understandable from the point of view of Poland's unique history of oppression – both in the atrocities of the Second World War and the subsequent suppression of the individual under Communism, as was discussed earlier.[52]

i. Human Dignity before the Constitutional Court

Human dignity functions in the case law both as a subjective right and as a constitutional value.[53] The question of the infringement of human dignity before the Constitutional Court is mostly incidental to a violation of a specific right or freedom. In this dimension, human dignity is easier to capture in comparison to its expression as a value.

In the first understanding, human dignity as a subjective right is a type of respect due to every single person,[54] independent of his or her physical or psychological state or actual life situation.[55] For example, based on, inter alia, an infringement of human dignity, the Constitutional Court declared unconstitutional provisions enabling eviction without

[50] Article 30 of the Constitution.

[51] Articles 3 and 41 of the Constitution of the Italian Republic of 1947; art II of the Fundamental Law of Hungary of 2011; art 21 of the Constitution of the Republic of Lithuania of 1992.

[52] See ch 1.

[53] A Barak, *Human Dignity: The Constitutional Value and the Constitutional Right* (Cambridge, Cambridge University Press, 2015) 111.

[54] See Constitutional Court, judgment of 9 July 2009, SK 48/05, OTK ZU 7A/2009, poz 108.

[55] See Constitutional Court, judgment of 30 September 2008, K 44/07, OTK ZU 7A/2008, poz 126.

providing another housing opportunity.[56] The Constitutional Court stated that the legislature cannot create 'legal or factual situations which would take away the sense of dignity from an individual'.[57] The evicted families could not afford the rent and often neither food nor clothing. The eviction not only made them homeless but also deprived them of the chance of a 'normal and dignified life'.[58]

In cases of conflict with other constitutional principles, human dignity as a subjective right always 'wins' when competing with them. The Constitutional Court does not conduct a proportionality test with regard to human dignity, as doing so would imply employing a norm to 'measure' human dignity. Human dignity is excluded from any such balancing against other freedoms and rights. For this reason, in the eviction case, the Constitutional Court had no choice but to declare the provisions in question as unconstitutional because human dignity can be argued to protect the evicted persons.[59]

At the same time, human dignity as a subjective right is separate from any concrete expression of freedoms or rights. For instance, the Constitutional Court declared the limitations imposed on a driver's freedom (the obligation to wear a seat belt) to be constitutional and did not find therein an infringement of human dignity, as had been argued in the constitutional complaint.[60] Freedom of a person as well as other constitutional freedoms and rights are anchored in human dignity, yet the violation of any specific freedom or right should not automatically be identified as a violation of dignity.

ii. Human Dignity as the Cornerstone of the Legal System

In the second understanding, human dignity as a constitutional value is the 'basis and prerequisite of the whole constitutional order'.[61] The Constitutional Court describes it as a transcendental value, which would imply that it derives authority from outside of the legal order. It is a primary value that does not need to be acquired. It is universal and serves everyone (ie, is not selective).[62] Thus, dignity influences human rights, but itself remains outside or beyond law.

[56] See Constitutional Court, judgment of 4 April 2001, K 11/00, OTK ZU 3/2001, poz 54.
[57] ibid.
[58] ibid.
[59] ibid.
[60] Constitutional Court, SK 48/05.
[61] ibid.
[62] See ibid and judgment of 5 March 2003, K 7/01, OTK ZU 3A/2003, poz 19.

In the case law of the Constitutional Court, human dignity as a value plays the role of a 'measure' for human rights. For instance, in the case concerning the obligation to wear a seat belt in a car, in which freedom was understood as the liberty to decide about oneself, the Constitutional Court decided on the constitutionality of provisions in the traffic code, invoking human dignity for this purpose.[63] Freedom of a person without a reference to human dignity would probably have lost its meaning.

Moreover, human dignity constitutes a point of reference for other constitutional rights. It enables the creation of a hierarchy of rights in any specific case. For example, the Constitutional Court offered a privileged position to freedom of religion over an infringement of public morality due to the suffering of animals in the ritual slaughter case because freedom of religion is closer to human dignity.[64] Ritual slaughter of animals, per the Constitutional Court, takes place only for the purpose of a specific religion and is otherwise illegal. Another example concerns the case of a physician's conscience clause: the Constitutional Court favoured the freedom of conscience of a physician over the patient's right to access medical treatment (abortion).[65] A physician can refuse to conduct a medical treatment, or even to inform the patient where such a procedure could be conducted. In both cases, human dignity was key to supporting the hierarchy of freedoms and rights involved.

In the case law, human dignity as a value enters into relationships with other values. In most cases, this other value is the principle of the common good.[66] This is because sometimes human dignity is insufficient to decide a case. One such case concerns the shooting down of an abducted civilian plane with passengers on board in the event of a terrorist attack.[67] The Aviation Law of 2002 enabled the shooting down of a passenger plane in the event of a threat to the security of the state, and where the plane in question had been used for unlawful acts, in particular as a means for carrying out a terrorist attack. The Constitutional Court was unable to decide on the constitutionality of the relevant provision of aviation law on the basis of human dignity alone. The value of human life was on both sides of the conflict of values – the passengers and the

[63] Constitutional Court, SK 48/05.

[64] Constitutional Court, judgment of 10 December 2014, K 52/13, OTK ZU 11A/2014, poz 118.

[65] Constitutional Court, judgment of 7 October 2015, K 12/14, OTK ZU 9A/2015, poz 143.

[66] Article 1 of the Constitution.

[67] Constitutional Court, judgment of 30 September 2008, K 44/07, OTK ZU 7A/2008, poz 126.

residents of the city to be struck by the falling plane, leading to a 'life for life' dilemma or the question of 'whose life is more important'. Human dignity does not divide people into 'guilty' (the plane with them can be shot down) or 'not guilty' (they can survive on the basis of the decision), especially as the Court underlined the symmetry between the 'saved' and 'sacrificed' good (it was impossible to indicate which one is which). Thus, the Constitutional Court applied, next to human dignity as an individual value connected to the lives of concrete people, the principle of the common good. In the case in question, the common good required that the legislature respects every life, as each life is connected to human dignity. Violation of the principle that one cannot shoot innocent people in any case (even a small number thereof) would destroy the value of the common good. The common good in that case meant that one could not sacrifice the life of a minority for the sake of saving a majority.

This judgment, which was similar to a decision issued by the German Constitutional Court on this matter, indicated that a right articulating the principle of the common good cannot at the same time violate human dignity.[68] Usually, the protection of the common good also implies care for human dignity. In the case concerning the shooting down of a civil plane, the Constitutional Court obliged the legislature to respect every life – both those of the passengers and those of the city's residents – because these lives are anchored in both human dignity and common good. These two principles prevented the legislature from adopting an 'economic' approach to life or considering the life of a minority vis-a-vis the life of a majority.

iii. Cautious Application of Human Dignity in the Court's Case Law

In sum, moving on from the more theoretical discussion of human dignity as a subjective right and a constitutional value, the practice of constitutional review shows that human dignity remains a rare standalone benchmark of control. It usually acts as a normative background for other benchmarks. In fact, human dignity is present in many situations of life and could be easily attached to numerous cases brought before the Constitutional Court. However, the Court exercises judicial restraint with regard to human dignity.[69] Specifically, in its judgments, human dignity is present primarily in cases of a violation of the

[68] German Constitutional Court, judgment of the First Senate of 15 February 2006, 1 BvR 357/05.

[69] See Constitutional Court, SK 48/05.

fundaments of the state system, as for example in the case concerning the application of martial law decrees of 1981.[70] The Constitutional Court limits its own pronouncements on human dignity to the minimum extent necessary to issue a judgment because it is aware of the immense value of human dignity, which should also not be overused.

As mentioned earlier, human dignity as an unconditional and inviolable value, and the highest value in the Constitution, presents a suitable fundament for the system of law and human rights. According to the Constitution, human dignity is the source of freedoms and rights of persons and citizens. This implies that human rights do not have their origin in positive law, but arise as a consequence of human dignity. The Constitution suggests here a certain primordiality of dignity vis-a-vis other freedoms and rights. These freedoms and rights stem from human dignity, but are separate from it (and have their own status).

B. Freedom

The Constitution does not define the content of freedom of the person. The Constitution only indicates that the freedom of the person is legally protected.[71] Thus, the law does not create freedom, but only guarantees it. This primordiality of freedom is visible in the Constitutional Court's judgment concerning the status of an incapacitated person.[72] The Court declared as unconstitutional the prohibition of an incapacitated person to independently apply for the lifting of his or her incapacity status. This prohibition interfered with the 'right to freedom' of the incapacitated person. It is a 'self-standing, subjective right to freedom of a person', which means that a person directs his or her behaviour, and decides about oneself on his or her own.

The courts, predominantly the Constitutional Court, step in to establish the content of a given freedom. For instance, the Constitutional Court found that freedom of religion is one of expressions of freedom of the person.[73] In that context, it declared the provisions allowing for ritual slaughter of animals to be constitutional, as the law must respect freedom of religion, which itself is a form of freedom of the person.[74]

[70] See Constitutional Court, judgment of 16 February 2011, K 35/08, OTK ZU 2A/2011, poz 11. See ch 5.

[71] Article 31(1) of the Constitution.

[72] Constitutional Court, judgment of 7 March 2007, K 28/05, OTK ZU 3A/2007, poz 24.

[73] Article 53 of the Constitution.

[74] Constitutional Court, K 52/13, point III 6.1.

In most cases, the Constitutional Court adjudicates conflicts between freedom of the person and other 'competing' freedoms. In so doing, it applies the proportionality test to solve conflicts between different constitutional principles regulating human rights. This approach is well known in the case law of other European constitutional and international courts.[75] The proportionality test in Poland consists of three steps: necessity (*niezbędność*), suitability (*adekwatność*) and proportionality *stricto sensu* (*proporcjonalność sensu stricto*).[76] The order of the two first steps may vary.[77] Any limitations to the exercise of freedom of the person (as well as other freedoms and human rights) can be introduced only on the basis of a statute, and when necessary in the democratic state. The Constitution lists the values on the basis of which the legislator can limit the exercise of freedoms and rights: to protect security or public order, the natural environment, health or public morals, or the freedoms and rights of other persons.[78] Even if these conditions are present, the limitations cannot violate the essence of these freedoms and rights. Again, similar concepts are known in the case law of constitutional courts of other European states.[79]

One case illustrating the application of the proportionality test concerns the constitutionality of the law concerning so-called 'beasts' ('bestie'). This term is commonly used to refer to a person who has served time in prison for particularly violent crimes and is deemed to remain a danger for other people even after his or her release from prison. In such cases with a very high probability of committing a future crime, the law foresees that a 'beast' is compulsorily restricted to a closed facility, even for life.[80] In 2018, there were 47 'beasts' in such a facility, including a number of individuals who were previously condemned to the death penalty, but who were not executed because of its abolition in the 1990s

[75] A Stone Sweet and J Mathews, 'Proportionality Balancing and Global Constitutionalism' (2008) 47 *Columbia Journal of Transnational Law* 68.

[76] See, eg, Constitutional Court, judgment of 23 November 2016, K 6/14, OTK ZU A/2016, poz 98, point III 4.1. See further K Wojtyczek, *Granice ingerencji ustawodawczej w sferę praw człowieka w Konstytucji RP* (Kraków, Wolters Kluwer, 1999).

[77] Constitutional Court, K 6/14, dissenting opinion of Judge Andrzej Wróbel. On the order of steps in proportionality review, see Stone Sweet and Mathews (n 75).

[78] Article 31(3) of the Constitution.

[79] See, eg, K Möller, 'Proportionality: Challenging the Critics' (2012) 10 *International Journal of Constitutional Law* 709.

[80] Law of 22 November 2013 on treatment of persons with mental disorders that pose a threat to the life, health or sexual freedom of others, JL 2014 Pos 24, JL 2015 Pos 369, JL 2016 Pos 2205.

in Poland.[81] The defenders of human rights before the Constitutional Court argued that this isolation following their release from prison had the character of a double penalty for the same act.[82] It was argued that this is evidently not compliant with the constitutional standard of freedom of the person, as well as ECHR standards, and was in violation of other constitutional principles, for example, *lex retro non agit*. The Constitutional Court concluded that the statute proportionally limited the freedom of the person. 'Beasts' are incapable of exercising the freedom of the person and, as a consequence, they have to be isolated from other people. The application of the principle of proportionality indicated that the isolation of 'beasts' is a suitable and necessary means of last resort. The Constitutional Court gave priority to the security, health and life of other people before the freedom of the persons called 'beasts'. It highlighted that the isolation is imposed by a court and only when preventive supervision over the 'beast' after the release from prison would be insufficient.

The major discussion about the understanding of the freedom of the person concerns the access to abortion. In Poland, this conflict was not as prominent as in other countries. Since the 1990s, the so-called 'abortion compromise' has been in force: abortion is not available on demand and a legal termination of pregnancy is possible only in three specific cases as set out in a 1993 law: (1) a threat to the life or health of the pregnant woman; (2) up to viability, if there is a high probability of severe and irreversible foetal defect or incurable illness endangering the life of the foetus; and (3) up to the twelfth week of pregnancy, where the pregnancy is the result of an unlawful act.[83] Therefore, in comparison to other EU Member States, the access to abortion in Poland is available to a very limited extent.[84] Although discussions have been ongoing and are often accompanied by public demonstrations, thus far no new laws to either liberalise or tighten these restrictions have been adopted.[85] The most advanced attempt at liberalisation in 1996 that sought to permit abortion due to social grounds – 'difficult living conditions or a

[81] 'Ośrodek dla niebezpiecznych przestępców pęka w szwach' *Rzeczpospolita* (12 April 2018).

[82] Constitutional Court, K 6/14.

[83] Article 4a of Law of 7 January 1993 on family planning, protection of the foetus, and admissibility of pregnancy termination, JL 1993 No 17 Pos 78, JL 1995 No 66 Pos 334, JL 1996 No 139, Pos 646, JL 1997 No 141 Pos 943, No 157 Pos 1040, JL 1999 No 5 Pos 32, JL 2001 No 154 Pos 1792.

[84] Compare at http://srhr.org/abortion-policies.

[85] See 'Poland's Conservatives are Pushing One of Europe's Toughest Abortion Laws' *The Economist* (5 April 2018).

difficult personal situation of a woman' – was ultimately unsuccessful. In that case, the Constitutional Court did not review the admissibility of abortion as such.[86] Still, it was the only case in which the Court issued a judgment on this matter, with the conclusion that the legal protection of life is one of the fundamental tenets of the principle of a state ruled by law. In the balancing of values conducted by the Court, the freedom of a woman to seek an abortion gave way to the legal protection of human life.

The constitutional provisions at the time were silent on the legal protection of life, but the Constitutional Court interpreted the right to life in the light of the principle of a democratic state ruled by law. It argued that a state ruled by law is a community of people and the characteristic feature of a human being is their life. According to the Court, a state ruled by law must therefore respect the value of human life from the beginning of its existence. The Court argued that the value of the constitutional good of human life, including its prenatal phase, could not be differentiated depending on the phase of development of human life. It further argued that there are no precise criteria allowing the legislature to differentiate between the phases of human life and to legally protect them to different extents.

The Constitutional Court inferred the argument against the admissibility of abortion based on the freedom of a woman from the state's obligation to protect motherhood and the family. The protection of motherhood, in the view of the Court, does not imply the protection of the interests of the pregnant woman only, as it extends to 'the life of the foetus without which the motherhood relationship would break'.[87] The foetus and its development are an equal subject of this safeguard. The Court made a similar statement with regard to the notion of family: its 'basic, procreational function' implies that 'the life of a conceived child must be protected … The same degree of protection of the relationship of fatherhood or motherhood vis-à-vis already born children has to apply to that relationship vis-à-vis children in the prenatal phase of their life'.[88]

In the view of the Constitutional Court, the legalisation of abortion due to the living conditions of a woman or personal hardship presents a disproportional interference with constitutional values. According to the Court, the legal good protected here cannot be a subjective perception

[86] Constitutional Court, judgment of 28 May 1997, K 26/96, OTK ZU 2/1997, poz 19.
[87] ibid point 3.
[88] ibid.

of a woman of a possible threat to her financial status or threat to the possibility to realise her own needs. As a consequence of the constitutional principle of freedom of the person, a pregnant woman has a right not to worsen her financial status. However, the protection of that right cannot violate the good of human life. In such a relationship, as seen by the Court, the living conditions of the mother have a secondary character. A difficult situation of the mother (or parents) could also occur after the child's birth. Thus, if the living conditions would be an admissible prerequisite for conducting an abortion, 'it must necessarily mean that the legislature differently assesses the value of life of a conceived child and of a child already born'.[89] In the light of the Court's balancing of constitutional values, the legislature could not grant priority or equality to freedom of the mother over human life, including during the prenatal phase. The Court indicated that the legislature could not suspend in a statute the validity of a constitutional norm concerning the state ruled by law. It condemned the law-maker who ascribed to itself the right to decide whether and to what extent the life of a foetus could be legally protected.

The Constitution of 1997, which was in preparation at that time, in some measure 'consumed' the judgment of the Constitutional Court. Accordingly, its Article 38 provides that the state 'ensures the legal protection of the life of every human being'. However, the drafters of the Constitution did not specify when life begins. In 2006, attempts to make this constitutional regulation more precise – arguing that life begins in the moment of conception – failed and even led to tensions within the governing party.

The abortion case and the other case law of the Constitutional Court discussed earlier point to three aspects of the understanding of the principle of freedom of the person before the Court. First, the Court protects freedom of the person that the person already has. Freedom of the person under the Constitution of 1997 has the character of a natural law.

Second, a statute which limits the exercise of freedom must be well balanced. The Constitutional Court's case law shows that freedom is usually on both sides of the equation. For instance, in the ritual slaughter of animals case, freedom serves both the followers of a religion as well as those who argue that certain cruel religious rites violate public morality.[90] The Court does not balance freedom and its limits according to the principle that the more freedom, the better. The application of the

[89] ibid point 4.3.
[90] Constitutional Court, K 52/13.

proportionality test shows that freedom of the person cannot function according to such a rule. The case law indicates that it can also work to the contrary – that is, that an unlimited freedom of the person can pose a danger both to the person involved and to society as a whole. For instance, the obligation to wear a seat belt in a car or the obligatory treatment of an addicted person indicates that the exercise of freedom can be limited and that this is not contrary to the freedom of the person expressed in the Constitution.[91]

Third, according in the Constitutional Court's understanding of freedom, its limitations are an integral part to understanding that freedom. The jurisprudence suggests that it is not possible to separate the essence of freedom from its exercise. Freedom of the person does not function separately from its exercise. If the law-maker could separate freedom of the person from its exercise, it would enable the manipulation of freedom. Such an approach to freedom of the person is reminiscent of the understanding of 'freedom' during Communism. At that time, the Communist authorities underlined that the citizens are free to travel abroad, but need a passport. However, that same authority arbitrarily decided who could acquire a passport. In the same vein, it cannot be the case that the Constitution guarantees freedom of religion, but the Constitutional Court restricts the exercise of that freedom, as would be the case if it forbade ritual slaughter and the consumption of that type of meat.

The Constitutional Court's decision in the 'ritual slaughter' case, confirming the constitutionality of the provisions allowing that type of slaughter of animals, has faced strong critical reaction from animal rights defenders and environmentalists,[92] but also from legal scholars.[93] This response highlights the emotions among legal academia and society surrounding the Court's judgments that fall at the intersection of law and morality. Thus, some of the other decisions of the Court falling within the area discussed in this chapter – on abortion or the shooting of a civil aircraft – have also faced some criticism, mostly with regard to the reasoning of the Court.[94]

[91] Constitutional Court, judgment of 9 July 2009, SK 48/05, OTK ZU 7A/2009, poz 108; judgment of 4 November 2014, SK 55/13, OTK ZU 10/2014, poz 111.

[92] 'Ubój rytualny dopuszczalny. Organizacje ochrony zwierząt załamane' *Gazeta Wyborcza* (12 December 2014).

[93] M Grochowski, E Łętkowska and A Wiewiórska-Domagalska, 'Wiąże, ale nie przekonuje (wyrok Trybunału Konstytucyjnego w sprawie K 52/13 o uboju rytualnym)' (2015) *Państwo i Prawo* 53, 64.

[94] J Woleński, 'Glosa do orzeczenia TK z dnia 28 maja 1997 r., K 26/96' (1998) *Państwo i Prawo* 88, 89–91; W Lang, 'Glosa do orzeczenia TK z dnia 28 maja 1997 r., K 26/96' (1997)

C. Equality

The Constitution expresses the equality principle in a positive manner: 'all persons shall be equal before the law'.[95] Following the classic definition, this principle can be explained as obliging the law-maker to treat equals equally, and those who are not equal unequally, and to treat different subjects differently. However, the Constitutional Court remains cautious about such a 'simple' approach to equality, as it is often ineffective in practice. Equality in the case law of the Constitutional Court demonstrates a set of characteristic features: (1) the removal of unclear differentiations between the same subjects of law; (2) highlighting the equal aspects of persons; and (3) consideration of the relevant feature criterion. These will be discussed in turn.

First, the Constitutional Court removes unclear distinctions between the same subjects of law, as is discussed on the basis of several examples. For instance, teachers employed in kindergartens could not take advantage of the reduced fare tickets for public transportation available to all other teachers.[96] The Constitutional Court found that the exclusion of kindergarten teachers was not compatible with the constitutional principle of equality. As a consequence, it obliged the legislature to introduce provisions equalising the position of kindergarten teachers with other teachers. Another instance concerns participants of the freedom manifestations of December 1970 on the Baltic coast against the Communist authorities and an increase in food prices.[97] The Constitutional Court found a violation of the principle of equality, as those participants, who were shot at and injured, had to apply within a short timeframe for veteran status, which did not apply to any other veterans who received such a status *ex lege*.

A different example of violation of the equality principle concerned the case of officers of the former secret police during the Communist period.[98] A statute of 2009 introduced a new algorithm to calculate the amount of pensions and disability allowance of those officers.[99] This

Przegląd Sejmowy 167, 170 and 181; D Kała, 'Glosa do wyroku TK z dnia 30 września 2008 r., K 44/07' (2010) 55 *Palestra* 290, 296.

[95] Article 32(1) of the Constitution.

[96] Constitutional Court, judgment of 16 November 2010, K 2/10, OTK ZU 9A/2010, poz 102.

[97] Constitutional Court, judgment of 10 January 2012, P 19/10, OTK ZU 1A/2012, poz 2.

[98] Constitutional Court, judgment of 24 February 2010, K 6/09, OTK ZU 2A/2010, poz 15.

[99] The same principle was applicable to the members of the Military Council of National Salvation (*Wojskowa Rada Ocalenia Narodowego* (WRON)), a military junta during the period of martial law in Poland (1981–83).

algorithm lowered the benefits for the service of those officers before 1990 in comparison to other persons in uniformed services, as well as to those covered by the universal pension system. One of the main questions was whether that reduction in the benefits – concerning only the officers of the secret police – was in breach of the equality principle. This group maintained that the lowering of their benefits not only violated the equality principle, but also constituted a form of repression against them. However, the Constitutional Court found that the principle of equality was not infringed. It ruled that the benefits of the officers in question represented a form of 'unjustified privilege'. The pensions of that group were particularly advantageous; the amount of those benefits expressed a form of privilege awarded by the Communist authority to persons who particularly contributed to maintaining the totalitarian regime. Thus, according to the Court's judgment, equality before law was not violated and the law at hand was not repressive in character vis-a-vis the officers.

The second characteristic aspect of the application of the equality principle is that the Constitutional Court aims to highlight the equal aspects of persons. For example, this is evident in a case concerning the way in which the state adjusts the level of disability benefits and pensions.[100] The Court approved the statute's departure from a percentage-style adjustment for one year (2012) in favour of a quota adjustment (the disability benefit and the pension increased by an identical amount, regardless of their initial amount). The lump sum approach benefited those with lower benefits (who protected their value) relative to those with higher benefits. Such a differentiation in the situation of benefit recipients was constitutional according to the Court, as the legislature aimed to provide a certain minimal living standard for poor pensioners.[101] The relevant feature of all recipients was not 'merit', understood as saving enough money in the Social Security Fund, but the ability to make ends meet. From this perspective, in particular during a period of budget imbalance, all recipients were equal. On the one hand, this judgment violated the trust of some pensioners in law, as it set aside the 'merit' criterion. On the other hand, the principle of equality was balanced against other constitutional principles. In the case in question, the principle of social justice and the balanced budget principle prevailed over the principle of equality before the law.

[100] Constitutional Court, judgment of 19 February 2012, K 9/12, OTK ZU 11A/2012, poz 136. On this case, see P Roicka, 'Glosa do wyroku TK z dnia 19.12.2012 r. K 9/12 [Dot. Waloryzacji świadczeń emerytalno-rentowych]' (2015) *Ubezpieczenia Społeczne. Teoria i Praktyka* 52.

[101] Article 67 of the Constitution grants everyone a right to social security.

The third feature of the equality case law is the relevant feature criterion. Equality and inequality are not presented such that equality is always good and inequality is always bad and to be condemned. The principle of equality does not function in a way that the more equality, the better, or the less differences between people, the better. Equality at any price – at the cost of other principles and constitutional values – leads to the re-emergence of inequality. One possible example is the valorisation of pensions and disability benefits discussed earlier. The functioning of the principle of equality before the Constitutional Court is thus linked to accepting that there are differences between people. As a consequence, the Constitutional Court must always balance equality against the backdrop of a criterion referred to as relevant feature (common for a certain group of subjects under comparison). For instance, in the case concerning the valorisation of pensions, adoption of the criterion of 'making ends meet' as a relevant feature led to accepting the same increase in benefits for everyone.[102] Had the Constitutional Court applied 'merit' as the relevant feature, the valorisation of pensions would have probably been unconstitutional.

When the Constitutional Court agrees with a departure from the principle of equality, it requires that the legislature provides 'adequately convincing arguments'.[103] Such arguments should be relevant and proportional, and must be linked to other constitutional principles and values, justifying a different treatment of similar subjects. The principles of social justice play an important role in justifying different treatment of similar subjects.[104] In the jurisprudence of the Court, these principles adopt various forms, for example, 'to make the ends meet', 'everyone deserves dignified life' or 'everyone should get what they deserve', and they vary depending on the relevant aspects of social life. Thus, the Constitution does not contain one principle of social justice. Also, it does not contain an ideal of social justice.

The principle of equality before the law differs from the principles of social justice. Social justice is in its essence a dynamic concept, which aims at moving the limits between equality and inequality. The Constitution orders the 'implementation of social justice', but there is no 'commanding' of that principle.[105] From the Constitution, it follows that

[102] Constitutional Court, K 9/12.

[103] See, eg, Constitutional Court, judgment of 28 March 2000, K 27/99, OTK ZU 2/2000, poz 62 and many others.

[104] Article 2 of the Constitution.

[105] ibid.

the implementation of the principles of social justice can take place only within the limits of a state ruled by law. This is exemplified by a prominent case concerning the amount of income free of personal income tax. The Constitutional Court found that people should not live below certain minimal living conditions and at the same time be forced by law to pay income tax.[106] This situation forced poor taxpayers to rely on social benefits. The Court indicated that the state ruled by law has obligations vis-a-vis its citizens, in the form of valorisation of the tax-free amount. Failing to appropriately set the amount that was free of tax, the state pushed people to live on social benefits. According to the Court, in a state ruled by law, such a regulation infringed the principles of social justice and tax justice.

In the case law of the Constitutional Court, the principle of equality before the law is key to understanding the principles of social justice. If a request before the Constitutional Court indicates a violation of the principles of social justice, then the Constitutional Court conducts the review applying the principle of equality before the law. In most cases, the violation of the equality principle implies an infringement of the principles of social justice. The example of an unequal treatment of different types of groups of pensioners shows that the principles of social justice can be also independent of the principle of equality. In such a case, a violation of one of the principles does not imply a violation of the other principle. It is thus possible to depart from the principle of equality in favour of social justice principles. The Constitutional Court underlined that unequal treatment of different groups of pensioners is compatible with the principles of social justice and is embedded in other principles and constitutional values, such as the protection of citizens' trust in the state and its laws, and the protection of acquired rights.

In addition to equality and social justice, the Constitution's preamble also contains the pure principle of justice, which is understood traditionally and derived from Plato ('giving everyone his or her due').[107] The Constitution's preamble places the principle of justice as a foundation next to freedom, cooperation between the public powers, social dialogue and subsidiarity. It would be hard to imagine that the Constitution would not introduce such a principle. In the case law of the Constitutional Court, social justice is treated as a subcategory of classic justice. The

[106] See Constitutional Court, judgment of 28 October 2015, K 21/14, OTK ZU 9A/2015, poz 152.

[107] Platon, *Państwo, Księga I, 332 C, przełozyl Władysław Witwicki* (Kęty, Wydawnictwo Antyk, 2009) 19.

functioning of both principles remains controversial, especially when these principles diverge, as was in the case in the valorisation of social benefits and pensions at a time of financial crisis. According to the pure principle of justice, the increase should be differentiated (a percentage depending on the 'merits'), while according to the social justice principles – applied by the Constitutional Court in the case in question – everyone should receive an increase of an equal amount.

The Constitution establishes a general prohibition upon discrimination in political, social and economic life for any reason.[108] The Constitutional Court understands discrimination as a particular type of inequality that lacks a justification. Unjustified inequality is labelled by the Court as arbitrary and as a consequence means discrimination. The prohibition of discrimination is often described as the negative aspect of the principle of equality.

In its case law, the Constitutional Court found discriminatory provisions in a regulation which forced medical committees to declare any policeman who was HIV positive as unfit to work.[109] Under the regulation, the policeman had to be released from service in every case, regardless of the stage of the illness. The automatic character of this provision did not allow for a proper (flexible) assessment of the policeman by the medical committee and also prevented continued work outside of patrol duty in an area, where being HIV positive would not make much difference (eg, administration, education, analytics). The Court has also dealt with cases concerning the retirement age (eg, the early retirement of women) or the retirement of people of certain professions (eg, shipyard workers) from the perspective of possible discrimination.[110]

The prohibition of discrimination is also safeguarded in the ECHR. As such, the relevant provision of the Convention – Article 14 – cannot be used as a self-standing benchmark of review.[111] Protocol No 12 to the ECHR – which has not been ratified by Poland – contains an independent non-discriminatory clause and widens the scope of the prohibition of discrimination.[112] Thus, in practice, the Constitutional Court has

[108] Article 31(2) of the Constitution.

[109] Constitutional Court, judgment of 23 September 2009, P 61/08, OTK ZU 10A/2009, poz 150; and judgment of 10 December 2013, U 5/13, OTK ZU 9A/2013, poz 136.

[110] Constitutional Court, judgment of 29 July 2010, K 63/07, OTK ZU 6A/2010, poz 60; and judgment of 5 July 2011, P 14/10, OTK ZU 6A/2011, poz 49.

[111] See J Gerards, 'The Discrimination Grounds of Article 14 of the European Convention on Human Rights' (2013) 13 *Human Rights Law Review* 99.

[112] See https://www.coe.int/en/web/conventions/full-list/-/conventions/treaty/177/signatures?p_auth=Ro96HAGe.

relied on the non-discrimination clause only in connection with another right, such as the right to education.[113] Another limitation is that constitutional complaints must concern violations of freedoms and rights expressed in the 1997 Constitution,[114] thus excluding the ECHR rights as a relevant benchmark.[115]

An important case of the Strasbourg Court regarding the prohibition of discrimination is *Bączkowski v Poland*.[116] In this case, the organisers of the Warsaw Equality Parade sought permission from the Warsaw authorities to march through the city to alert the public about the problem of discrimination against minority groups (including homosexuals) and women. In an interview the mayor criticised the 'homosexual propaganda' of the march, and shortly thereafter the city authorities refused permission, citing road traffic regulations. Despite the ban, the march took place. Afterwards, the decision of the city authorities was quashed on appeal, only after the planned date of the march. The ECtHR found Poland to be in violation of the prohibition of discrimination, among other provisions. It indicated that although there was no overt discrimination behind the ban, it was reasonable to think that the mayor's views could have affected the decision-making process, thereby infringing the freedom of assembly of the applicants in a discriminatory manner. The judgment of the Strasbourg Court, and that delivered by the Constitutional Court in the meantime declaring parts of the national legislation to be unconstitutional,[117] led to legislative changes that allowed a refusal to be quashed in time.[118] In practice, the new law enabled timely appeals in similar cases.[119]

Against this background, a statutory provision that penalises refusal to provide a service without a valid reason offers the broadest protection

[113] Constitutional Court, judgment of 2 July 2002, U 7/01, OTK ZU 4A/2002, poz 48.

[114] See ch 6.

[115] See, eg, Constitutional Court, judgment of 7 May 2002, SK 20/00, OTK ZU 3A/2002, poz 29.

[116] ECtHR, *Bączkowski and Others v Poland* (Application No 1543/06). See also S Van den Bogaert, 'ECHR Rules on Illegal Ban of Warsaw Equality Parade: The Case of *Bączkowski and Others v Poland*' (2007) 8 *German Law Journal* 889.

[117] Constitutional Court, judgment of 18 January 2006, K 21/05, OTK ZU 1A/2006, poz 4.

[118] Law of 24 July 2015, Law on Assemblies. See Ombudsman, *Raport Rzecznika Praw Obywatelskich, Wolność zgromadzeń w latach 2016–2018* (Warsaw, Biuro Rzecznika Praw Obywatelskich, 2018) 43.

[119] 'Sąd w Lublinie uchylił zakaz organizacji Marszu Równości i kontrmanifestacji środowisk narodowych' *Rzeczpospolita* (12 October 2018).

against discrimination in comparison to the ECHR, EU law[120] and the Polish Constitution.[121] This can be seen in several cases decided before the ordinary courts. Some of these cases included a situation in which the owner of a shoe shop declined to help a disabled client in a wheelchair, the owner of a clothing store who did not allow a customer with a stroller to enter, and a trainer who declined to provide self-defence training in an organisation that works against sexual discrimination.[122] In 2017, an ordinary court issued a final guilty judgment (though without imposing a fine) regarding an employee of a printing company who – citing personal convictions – refused to make a roll-up for an LGBT foundation. The case in its facts is reminiscent of the *Masterpiece Cakeshop* decision of the US Supreme Court concerning the refusal of a baker to make a wedding cake for a gay couple and his claim to freedom of religion.[123] The Polish Supreme Court upheld the decision of the lower instance court, finding that freedom of conscience and religion may constitute a justified refusal to provide a service, but conflicts of values need to be assessed each time in the context of the case.[124] If religious beliefs are clearly in contrast with the features and character of a certain service, that service can be refused even if this is in conflict with the prohibition of discrimination. In turn, an individual feature of the client – his or her confession or sexual preferences – cannot justify a refusal. In the case in question, the printer's refusal could not be supported as the requested service was reproductive and technical in character, and did not promote behaviour contrary to his Catholic faith. Finally, the Constitutional Court declared the relevant provision of the Code of Offenses as disproportional interference in the freedom of the person providing services, thereby violating the constitutional principle of the democratic state ruled by law.[125]

[120] Poland implemented a number of EU equality directives in the Law of 3 December 2010 on the implementation of some of the provisions of the European Union concerning equal treatment, JL 2016 Pos 1219. On practical problems arising in the application of this law before courts, see P Śmiałek, 'Powództwo przeciw dyskryminacji w Ustawie z dnia 3 grudnia 2010r. o wdrożeniu niektórych przepisów Unii Europejskiej w zakresie równego traktowania' (2017) 20 *Studia Prawa Publicznego* 165, 176.

[121] Article 138 of Law of 20 May 1971, Code of Offenses, JL 2018 Pos 618, 911, 2077.

[122] District court in Tarnobrzeg, judgment of 8 March 2013, II W 13/13; district court in Warszawa-Wola, judgment of 5 December 2016, V W 4937/16; district court in Poznań-Nowe Miasto i Wilda, judgment of 20 March 2018, VI W 1441/17 (nieprawomcny).

[123] US Supreme Court, Masterpiece Cakeshop v Colorado Civil Rights Commission, 584 US__(2018).

[124] Polish Supreme Court, decision of 14 June 2018, II KK 333/17.

[125] Constitutional Court, judgment of 26 June 2019, K 16/17 (not yet published). See also ch 2.

In sum, the principle of equality before the law is the second most common benchmark of constitutional review before the Constitutional Court, after the democratic state ruled by law principle.[126] In its jurisprudence, the Court deals with equality and inequality by indicating the relevant feature and balancing the principle of equality against other principles. Fortunately, the Court does not attempt to forcefully equalise people or 'design' equality or inequality. Instead, it takes into account that people are equal in some aspects and unequal in other aspects. The case law seems to confirm that equality is a 'particularly controversial' principle of law.[127]

IV. THE LIMITED SCOPE OF INDIVIDUAL OBLIGATIONS

The Constitution does not delve too deeply into either the obligations of (Polish) citizens or those of all persons. Those obligations that are treated conclude the Constitution's chapter on freedoms and rights,[128] but some can also be found at other points. For instance, within the section on the rights of children, the Constitution foresees the obligation of parents to 'consider and, insofar as possible, give priority to the views of the child'.[129]

There are a number of reasons why the Constitution de-emphasises obligations. First, and most prominently, the Constitution of 1997 adopts a liberal approach to the regulation of human rights, putting an individual and his or her rights before the interests of the state. This approach is typical of similar constitutions in other democratic countries. For instance, in the German Basic Law, the only provision on obligations concerns military service,[130] while in France, the Declaration of the Rights of Man and of the Citizen of 1789 and the preamble of the 1946 Constitution remain silent with regard to obligations.[131] Second, the drafters of the 1997 Constitution possibly tried to avoid associations with the historical notion of 'unity of citizens' rights and obliga-

[126] See, eg, Constitutional Court, *Informacja o istotnych problemach wynikających z działalności i orzecznictwa Trybunału Konstytucyjnego* w 2015 roku (Warsaw, 2016) 128; and *Informacja o istotnych problemach wynikających z działalności i orzecznictwa Trybunału Konstytucyjnego* w 2016 roku (Warsaw, 2017) 93.

[127] R Alexy, *A Theory of Constitutional Rights* (Oxford, Oxford University Press, 2010).

[128] Articles 82–86 of the Constitution.

[129] ibid art 72(3).

[130] Article 12a of the Grundgesetz für die Bundesrepublik Deutschland vom 23. Mai 1949 (BGBl. S. 1), zuletzt geändert durch Artikel 1 des Gesetzes vom 13. Juli 2017 (BGBl. I S. 2347) ('German Basic Law').

[131] Déclaration des droits de l'homme et du citoyen de 1789; préambule de la constitution du 27 octobre 1946.

tions', which implied that the exercise of rights was conditional upon the fulfilment of obligations. This idea was present in the Polish constitutionalism of the interbellum period, as well as – under completely different conditions – during the Communist period after the Second World War. During each of these periods, the reasons behind the notion of unity of citizens' rights and obligations were different. In the first, it expressed the support for the state, while in the second, the Polish People's Republic, a 'universalist concept' of the relationship between the state and the citizens was in place. According to this doctrine, the state gave effect to aims that were superior to the aims of people – an individual was only a means or a tool of the state. Rights and obligations of citizens were not supposed to remain constant, but instead depended on the conditions of the social and economic state system.[132] Under these circumstances, the exercise of rights by the citizens could be conditioned on their fulfilment of obligations.

The Constitution of 1997 incorporates only a small number of individual obligations towards the state. Some of them are addressed to all legal subjects, thus including foreigners, while others concern only Polish citizens. The obligations addressed to all legal subjects include observing the law of the country, complying with public duties (including taxes) and care for the environment.[133] The Constitutional Court specified what constitutes a tax, as well as other issues of tax law in its extensive case law. Some of the key issues of that case law include the 'considerable freedom' of the legislature to design tax law. This concerns both the matters subject to taxation as well as its scope. For instance, the legislature is free to indicate the subjects exempted from tax.[134] Moreover, the tax obligation does not constitute a 'limitation' under the Constitution's proportionality test.[135] However, the decision-making freedom of the legislature cannot violate the 'essence' of constitutional rights, leading to the bankruptcy of the taxpayer.[136]

A key principle of the Constitution of 1997 concerning the obligations of an individual is the direct application of its provisions. According to this principle, the provisions of the Constitution should be invoked and applied whenever it is possible in legal transactions. Such an application

[132] See A Burda, *Polskie prawo państwowe* (Warsaw, PWN, 1976) 370–71.

[133] Articles 83, 84 and 86 of the Constitution.

[134] See Constitutional Court, judgment of 28 October 2015, K 21/14, OTK ZU 9A/2015, poz 152.

[135] ibid.

[136] See Constitutional Court, judgment of 25 June 2002, K 45/01, OTK ZU 4A/2002, poz 46.

of the Constitution contributes to, on the one hand, treating the Constitution as an act of supreme legal power and, on the other hand, as a law which has a real meaning for the people. However, an exemption from the direct application of the Constitution applies vis-a-vis the provisions on citizens' obligations. These provisions cannot be applied directly, to the extent that imposing obligations on an individual – eg, to pay taxes or to serve in the military – is possible only on the basis of a statute. Only the obligation to observe the law could possibly be directly applied.[137]

V. THE MECHANISMS OF PROTECTION OF FUNDAMENTAL RIGHTS

The Constitution of 1997 concludes the catalogue of freedoms and rights with a set of mechanisms for their protection. This approach indicates the willingness of the Constitution's drafters to create favourable conditions for the protection of human rights. Constitutional freedoms and rights are protected both by legal institutions and specific state organs established for that purpose. The former includes the right to compensation for harm caused by any action of an organ of public authority contrary to law, the right of access to court, the prohibition of barring the recourse by any person to the courts in pursuit of claims alleging infringement of freedoms or rights, and the right of constitutional complaint.[138] The state organs protecting human rights include the Ombudsman and the Commissioner for Children's Rights, as well as other organs not present in the Constitution, such as the Government's Representative for Equal Treatment, the Financial Ombudsman (*Rzecznik Finansowy*) and various consumer ombudsmen established in the units of local self-government, for instance, in cities. The Constitution does not exhaustively regulate all possible tools of fundamental rights protection. Some of these are present in procedural regulations, such as the possibility to challenge an administrative decision before administrative courts.[139] Finally, a complaint to the Strasbourg Court has been perceived as the last resort in cases of human rights violations.

[137] Article 83 of the Constitution. See L Garlicki, *Polskie prawo konstytucyjne. Zarys wykładu* (Warsaw, Wolters Kluwer, 2017) 139; and K Działocha et al (eds), *Konstytucja Rzeczypospolitej Polskiej. Komentarz*, vol III (Warsaw, Wydawnictwo Sejmowe, 2003).

[138] Articles 77(1), 45, 77(2) and 79(1) of the Constitution, respectively. The constitutional complaint is discussed in ch 6.

[139] See ch 5.

Against this background, this section deals with three mechanisms of human rights protection encompassed by the Constitution: (a) state liability; (b) right to access to the court; (c) the Ombudsman. These instruments play the most important role in safeguarding the freedoms and rights of the individual in Poland.

A. State Liability and its Problematic Enforcement

The March Constitution of 1921 already provided the right of the citizens to claim compensation for damage done by organs of the state as a consequence of an action of an official that was contrary to law. Nowadays, this early regulation is perceived as 'significantly exceeding its times, objective circumstances and tradition of legal thinking'.[140] The Constitution of 1997 grants individuals a right to compensation for any harm done to them by an unlawful action of an organ of public authority.[141] This constitutional right not only offers guarantees to an individual in cases of violations of law by an organ of public power,[142] but also forces that power to respect the legality principle.[143]

The specific conditions for state liability were developed by the Constitutional Court.[144] First, damage to an individual includes both material and immaterial loss, and its understanding follows civil law regulations. Second, the notion of public power organs includes the institutions of legislative, executive and judicial power, as well as the organs of self-government. Moreover, state liability extends over institutions exercising public power as conferred upon them by organs of public power or self-government. The crucial question is whether the organ at stake acted to exercise its prerogatives. In contrast, the formal character of the relationship between the immediate perpetrator and the public authority is less important. Third, the action of the relevant state organ encompasses all of the actions falling within its competence. It can take the form of an action, such as issuing an administrative decision, or a regulation. It is debatable as to whether such an action can take the form

[140] M Safjan, *Odpowiedzialność odszkodowawcza władzy publicznej* (Warsaw, LexisNexis, 2004) 15.

[141] Article 77(1) of the Constitution.

[142] Constitutional Court, judgment of 4 December 2001, SK 18/00, OTK ZU 8/2001, poz 256.

[143] Constitutional Court, judgment of 20 January 2004, SK 26/03, OTK ZU 1A/2004, poz 3.

[144] Constitutional Court, SK 18/00.

of the legislature failing to act (abstention from adopting a legislative act).[145] In sum, the Constitutional Court eliminated, as unconstitutional, the requirement to prove the culpability of the liable actor in a criminal court judgment or in disciplinary proceedings.[146] Thereby, it disposed of the culpability requirement, which was a crucial obstacle in liability proceedings. Still, a court is required to confirm the unlawfulness of the action of a state organ. Such a court judgment then provides the basis for compensation.

In practice, the basis for state liability claims before courts remains the Civil Code and not the Constitution.[147] The Civil Code expresses the general principle of state liability for delicts – the state is liable for any damage caused by an illegal action or omission on the part of a state organ exercising its public powers. There are no immunities for the state in terms of liability; for instance, the state can be sued if the fire brigade arrives late to extinguish a fire. However, such cases are usually dismissed by courts, as it is difficult to assess what constitutes appropriate behaviour on the part of the police or the fire brigade. In addition, the Civil Code also foresees contractual liability for state organs that fail to fulfil a contract.[148] In cases of state liability, the State Treasury is responsible for the state and legally represented by the General Counsel (*Prokuratoria Generalna*) before the courts.

A tragic example of the application of state liability concerns the catastrophic construction disaster in Katowice in the winter of 2006. A snow-covered roof collapsed, killing 65 attendees of an international carrier pigeon fair. In 2018, the regional court in Warsaw found a link between the catastrophe and abnormalities in the supervision of the building by state organs.[149] The court indicated that negligence in supervision led to the tragedy. This judgment allowed the relatives of the victims to sue the state for compensation. The case, which took five years until the judgment was issued, shows that despite the long tradition of state liability in the Polish legal order, in its enforcement, individuals may encounter other problems of the judicial system, such as lengthy court proceedings.

[145] See ch 6.

[146] Constitutional Court, SK 18/00.

[147] Article 417 and 417' of the Law of 23 April 1964, Civil Code, JL 2018 Pos 1025, 1104, 1629, 2073. See P Sobolewski, 'Komentarz do art. 417 Kodeksu cywilnego (odpowiedzialność Skarbu Państwa)' in K Osajda, *Kodeks cywilny. Komentarz* (Warsaw, CH Beck, 2018).

[148] Article 471 of the Civil Code.

[149] Regional Court in Warsaw, judgment of 23 April 2018, II C 172/15.

B. The Right to Access to the Court: The Fundamental Constitutional Right

The Constitution provides the right of access to the court in order to enable an individual to obtain protection of his or her freedoms and rights. It indicates that everyone has the right to a fair and public hearing of his or her case, without undue delay, before a competent, impartial and independent court.[150] This concerns all types of rights and not only those provided by the Constitution. At the same time, the Constitution prohibits closing access to the court: a statute cannot bar anyone from recourse to the court to pursue infringement of freedoms or rights expressed in the Constitution.[151] Thus, access to the court cannot be refused based on a statute; only the Constitution could in principle do so, but this would be absurd. In general, the right of access to the court is the basic, most practical and most accessible means of protection of human rights.

The Constitutional Court had an important impact on the development of the right to access to court by delineating its content and scope.[152] According to the case law, the right encompasses three aspects. First, it implies a right to launch proceedings before courts. No individual case can be excluded from the courts' jurisdiction. Second, judicial proceedings should comply with the requirements of justice and transparency. The aim is to offer a real possibility to pursue one's rights. Third, the right to access to the court involves obtaining a court judgment – in other words, a binding conclusion of the case. Beyond these three criteria, the Constitutional Court found the right to access to the court to encompass the right to an appropriate design of the court system.[153] This meant that so-called assessors – judges who were appointed by and dependent upon the Justice Minister – should not decide court cases. Finally, the right to access to the court encompasses two tiers of proceedings. Thus, it does not guarantee a 'third instance' appeal to the Supreme Court. However, where a statute makes such a procedure available, it should comply with the standard of a fair trial.[154]

[150] Article 45(1) of the Constitution.

[151] ibid art 77(2).

[152] Constitutional Court, judgment of 24 October 2007, SK 7/06, OTK ZU 9A/2007, poz 108.

[153] ibid.

[154] Constitutional Court, judgment of 30 May 2007, SK 68/06, OTK ZU 6A/20076, poz 53.

The right of access to the court is available to everyone, but not in every case. Under the Constitution, the notion of a 'case' implies the administration of justice or, in other words, deciding on the rights of a person. Taking into account such a broad understanding of the right to access to the court under the Constitution of 1997, it is easier to exclude issues where this right does not apply. For instance, in the light of the Constitutional Court's case law, the question of whether a student cheated in a high school final exam (*matura*) does not constitute a case.[155] In the dispute in question, the Central Examination Committee declared the final exams in chemistry to be invalid due to cheating. The law did not offer the affected students an opportunity to refer their case to court. Thus, when they brought a complaint before the administrative courts, both judicial instances declared themselves incompetent, as the decision concerning the invalidity of their exams did not represent an administrative decision. The students then lodged constitutional complaints claiming violations of their constitutional right to access the court. However, the Constitutional Court decided that an assessment of whether the students undertook the exam independently implied an assessment of the merits of the exam. As a consequence, it declared that the issue at stake was not a 'case' per the definition applicable in the Constitution. The statutory provisions concerning the conduct of final exams were declared constitutional. The students then brought an application before the ECtHR, which was accepted and is still pending.[156]

Another issue concerns the pace at which the Constitutional Court decides cases. Until 2015, the Court worked to reduce delays in the adjudication of cases, with benefits for individual rights. In 2014, the average time for deciding a case in which a judgment was issued was 18 months, a month shorter than in the preceding year.[157] It is worth highlighting that the Court did not see the shortening of its decision-making process as a value in itself. In other words, what was most important was a comprehensive analysis of a case. Since 2015, when the constitutional crisis surrounding the Court erupted, the issue of the length of proceedings lost its importance.

[155] Constitutional Court, judgment of 22 June 2015, SK 29/13, OTK ZU 6A/2015, poz 83.

[156] ECtHR, Request no 783/16, *Bartosz Sypioła against Poland and 17 Other Requests*, case communicated on 16 February 2018.

[157] Constitutional Court, *Informacja o istotnych problemach wynikających z działalności i orzecznictwa Trybunału Konstytucyjnego w 2014 roku* (Warsaw, 2015) 94.

C. The Independent Ombudsman

The Constitution foresees specialised organs safeguarding fundamental rights. Amongst these, the most important is the Ombudsman.[158] The establishment of the Ombudsman presented a certain paradox. According to the 1987 law, the Ombudsman was established to strengthen the Socialist rule of law.[159] However, after 1989, the Ombudsman has seamlessly transitioned into the role of the key institution fighting for human rights in Poland. The constitutional provisions of 1989 vested the Ombudsman with competences to safeguard the freedoms and rights of citizens. Moreover, the office of the Ombudsman was one of the tools that enabled the transition to democracy and became a symbol that the Communist system was crumbling. The appointment of the Polish Ombudsman preceded similar appointments across other European post-Communist countries.[160]

The Polish Ombudsman presents characteristics typical of a hybrid model of ombudsman. It marries the classic Scandinavian version of that office – which focuses on good administrative practice – with the 'human rights model', which places the protection of freedoms and rights at the centre of its activities.[161] One of the characteristic features of this Polish institution is that the competences of the Ombudsman are expressed in a general way, and the practice often forces the Ombudsman to deal with any type of case. Accordingly, the Ombudsman monitors observance of the Constitution, but his or her special tasks include safeguarding equality and the prohibition of torture. Moreover, the personality and ambitions of the Ombudsman himself or herself have an impact on the scope of their tasks.

The Constitution guarantees everyone the access to the Ombudsman.[162] Beyond the Warsaw office, three other representative offices of the Ombudsman are located in Gdańsk, Katowice and Wrocław. The employees of the Ombudsman's office also visit smaller cities to meet with those who wish to make a complaint to the Ombudsman. In addition, the Ombudsman often calls on detention centres or prisons,

[158] Article 80 of the Constitution.

[159] Preamble of the Law of 15 July 1987 on the Ombudsman, JL 2018 Pos 2179.

[160] N Abedin, 'Conceptual and Functional Diversity of the Ombudsman Institution: A Classification' (2011) 43 *Administration & Society* 896, 901.

[161] WJ Hopkins, 'Ombudsman' in *Max Planck Encyclopedia of Comparative Constitutional Law* (Oxford, Oxford University Press, 2016) 2.

[162] Article 80 of the Constitution.

hospitals, social welfare homes and refugee centres to review compliance with human rights standards.

The Chamber of Deputies, acting by an absolute majority of votes, with the consent of the Senate, elects the Ombudsman for a five-year term.[163] The Ombudsman is independent in terms of his or her activities and acts independently from state organs.[164] He or she is accountable only before the Chamber of Deputies. The Constitution guarantees the formal immunity and personal inviolability of the Ombudsman, thereby ensuring the role's independence.[165]

The role of the Polish Ombudsman is to defend the freedoms and rights of persons and citizens expressed in the Constitution and other normative acts.[166] The Ombudsman acts as human rights watchdog through non-imperative tools and does not issue judgments or decisions. In his or her activities, the Ombudsman fulfils the role of both the 'firewatcher' and 'firefighter', as indicated below. As a firewatcher – acting preventively – the Ombudsman is the crucial organ bringing cases on fundamental rights violations before the Constitutional Court. This role of the Ombudsman before the Constitutional Court has found a significant degree of appreciation. The Ombudsman, as an applicant with general standing, which is granted to the crucial state organs such as the President or the Prime Minister, can request a review of the constitutionality of laws.[167] For years, the Ombudsman has been an active initiator of constitutional review. For instance, in 2016, the Ombudsman lodged 24 requests for constitutional review of the total 42 requests made by applicants with general standing.[168] In general, many crucial human rights cases were launched by the Ombudsman, such as the case concerning the valorisation of pensions and disability benefits discussed earlier. Finally, the Ombudsman may also participate in all proceedings before the Constitutional Court, except for those involving preventive control. In 2017, the Ombudsman joined 10 new proceedings before the Constitutional Court.[169]

In his or her capacity as firefighter, the Ombudsman acts on his or her own initiative or on the initiative of the citizens, their organisations,

[163] ibid art 209(1).
[164] ibid art 210.
[165] ibid art 211.
[166] ibid art 208.
[167] See ch 6.
[168] Constitutional Court, *Informacja o istotnych problemach* (n 126). See ch 6.
[169] Ombudsman, *Informacja o stanie przestrzegania wolności i praw człowieka i obywatela w 2017 r.*

organs of local self-government or the Commissioner for Children's Rights. The Ombudsman acts in individual cases, as well in cases of importance for the general public. Individual complaints to the Ombudsman are free in form and do not require the payment of a fee. Each year, the Ombudsman receives more than 20,000 new complaints.[170] If he or she takes on the case, he or she can independently investigate the case or request investigation by a competent organ. The Ombudsman has access to files in judicial proceedings and can participate in them. He or she can also lodge any appeal measure foreseen in judicial proceedings. Appropriately, in 2017, the Ombudsman submitted 61 cassations to the Supreme Court and 10 cassation complaints to the Supreme Administrative Court.[171] Additionally, he or she can partake in cases concerning constitutional complaints before the Constitutional Court. In 2017, the Ombudsman joined 10 such proceedings.[172]

As has already been mentioned, the hybrid design of the Polish Ombudsman includes the investigation of maladministration. Involvement in this area was established in practice rather than as a consequence of competences provided for in the relevant laws. For instance, when the Ombudsman enquires into administrative proceedings, he or she also looks at the implementation of general principles governing that procedure: access to relevant organs or the length of proceedings before them, or the organ's workplace culture. It is worth noting that in cases of maladministration on the part of EU institutions, bodies and agencies, the EU Charter foresees a complaint to the European Ombudsman.[173]

The Ombudsman also completes several tasks concerning equal treatment. For instance, as a consequence of the implementation of EU equal treatment legislation, the Ombudsman was vested with the function of being the independent organ for equal treatment.[174] In this capacity, he or she deals with complaints on unequal treatment, monitors and supports equality, and provides independent analysis on discrimination issues. Moreover, he or she acts as an independent authority charged with supporting and protecting people with disabilities under the UN

oraz o działalności Rzecznika Praw Obywatelskich (Warsaw, Biuro Rzecznika Praw Obywatelskich, 2018) 528.

[170] ibid 527.

[171] ibid 528.

[172] ibid.

[173] Article 43 of the EU Charter of Fundamental Rights.

[174] M Wróblewski, 'Niezależność i kompetencje krajowego organu do spraw równego traktowania w Unii Europejskiej – prolegomena', in P Mikuli et al (eds), *Ustroje, tradycje i porównania* (Warsaw, Wydawnictwo Sejmowe, 2015) 383.

Convention on the Rights of Persons with Disabilities, which was ratified in 2012.

In sum, the office of the Ombudsman has been a successful institution, with significant achievements for the protection of human rights.

VI. CONCLUSION

After 1989, the new legal position of an individual has been shaped by three factors. The first of is the catalogue of freedoms and rights – typical of a liberal democratic state – enshrined in the 1997 Constitution. Polish courts apply personal and political freedoms and rights in a similar manner to courts in other democratic states. The issues arising in their application are comparable to those present in well-established democracies. For instance, the questions of the limits on practising religion, or freedom of expression in art, or freedom of the press to criticise the government are typical of other democratic systems. Second, the catalogue of freedoms and rights and its implementation was enriched by European and international sources of human rights protection. Third, in practice, a crucial role in ensuring fundamental rights in Poland has been played by the Constitutional Court and the Ombudsman.

Since 2015, due to its marginalisation by the governing majority, the role of the Constitutional Court as a human rights defender has been limited. In this situation, the position of the Ombudsman has naturally grown in importance. The problems of fundamental rights protection are also reflected in the EU Commission's launch of the 'Article 7(1) procedure' vis-a-vis Poland. Concerns about the independence of courts and judges in Poland are even more pertinent because, as has been shown in this chapter, the right of access to the courts and, in particular, the right to a fair trial represent the basic tools of human rights protection. The changes in the court system and in its functioning clearly weaken the effectiveness of the judicial protection of individuals. For instance, in the period in question, the length of proceedings before national courts has increased.[175] This in turn leads to the increased importance of European instruments of fundamental rights protection, as illustrated by the preliminary reference of the Irish High Court to the CJEU on the EAW. The problems in safeguarding the rule of law have led some of the European courts to halt the execution of the EAW vis-a-vis Poland.

[175] See ch 5.

Unfortunately, these developments highlight the deterioration of human rights protection achieved post-1989.

FURTHER READING

Bodnar, A, *Wykonywanie orzeczeń Europejskiego Trybunału Praw Człowieka w Polsce. Wymiar instytucjonalny* (Warsaw, Wolters Kluwer, 2018).

Florczak-Wątor, M *Horyzontalny wymiar praw konstytucyjnych* (Kraków, Wydawnictwo Uniwersytetu Jagiellońskiego, 2014).

Garlicki, L, 'Przesłanki ograniczenia konstytucyjnych praw i wolności' (2001) *Państwo i Prawo* 5–24.

Niżnik-Mucha, A, *Zakaz naruszania istoty konstytucyjnych wolności i praw w Konstytucji RP* (Warsaw, Wydawnictwo Sejmowe, 2014).

Nußberger, A 'Poland: The Constitutional Tribunal on the Implementation of the European Arrest Warrant' (2008) 6 *International Journal of Constitutional Law* 162–70.

Safjan, M, 'Odpowiedzialność państwa na podstawie art. 77 Konstytucji RP' (1999) *Państwo i Prawo* 3–18.

Tuleja, P, *Normatywna treść praw jednostki w ustawach konstytucyjnych RP* (Warsaw, Wydawnictwo Sejmowe, 1997).

Wojtyczek, K, 'Horyzontalny wymiar praw człowieka zagwarantowanych w Konstytucji' (1999) *Kwartalnik Prawa Prywatnego* 405–14.

Wróblewski, M, 'Karta Praw Podstawowych Unii Europejskiej w polskim sądownictwie – problemy i wyzwania' (2015) *Kwartalnik Krajowa Rada Sądownictwa* 17–23.

——. 'The Legal Value and Implementation of the Charter of Fundamental Rights in Poland' in G. Palmisano (ed), *Making the Charter of Fundamental Rights a Living Instrument* (Brill, Nijhoff, 2015) 314–42.

9

Facing the Future

Constitutional Amendment – Constitutional Identity – Rule of Law – Judiciary – Socio-economic Rights – Executive – Bicameralism – Constitutional Values – Referendum

I. INTRODUCTION

THE CONSTITUTION OF 1997 has been in force for over 20 years. It is certainly not perfectly crafted. Nonetheless, it has 'passed the test' of fitness for purpose over that period. The Constitution has encouraged stable governments: changes of Prime Minister or government outside of elections are the exception. Moreover, the Constitution has enabled Poland's accession to the EU. Furthermore, it has provided extensive freedoms and rights for the citizens. However, as it has transpired, the true test for the Constitution began in the autumn of 2015, when the Law and Justice party took over power. As was pointed out earlier, especially in Chapters 5 and 6, many of the legal reforms introduced by this government were questionable from a constitutional perspective, and some violated the Constitution.

Polish constitutional law after 2015 found itself in a unique position, in that the 1997 Constitution did not undergo any formal amendments. On the one hand, the Constitution thus remains the supreme law, despite, as it turned out, being powerless in the face of the attacks of the governing majority. On the other hand, many citizens have started engaging with the Constitution and the notion of Constitution became a battle cry. As such, the Constitution has moved beyond being a specific, formal legal act and has become an important symbol in the ongoing struggle.

II. THE CONSTITUTION IN ACTION

The principal issue for the Constitution today is the ongoing attack on the independence of the judiciary. The Constitution created a judicial system with strong guarantees of independence of courts and judges. These legal concepts were new to Poland at the time and expressed opposition to the Communist system, which did not tolerate an independent judiciary. According to the Constitution, the principle of separation and balance of power is crucial for the independence of the judiciary. This is why the Constitution introduced this principle in its widest sense. In particular, it explicitly stated that the system of government should be based on the separation of and balance between the legislative, executive and judicial powers.[1] Many scholars regard the principle of separation and balance of power not as a mere instrument of, but rather as the backbone of the system of government.[2] In practice, the Constitution established a robust judiciary including the Constitutional Court and the Supreme Court, as well as the ordinary and administrative courts. Since 2015, this independence has been put to the test: the governing majority has subjected the judiciary to allegations of a 'judicial state' in order to appeal to their political supporters, forgetting that strong and independent courts were among the major demands of the Solidarity movement in the 1980s. The new laws reforming the judiciary affected the independence of courts in several ways, including forcing experienced judges into retirement, and unconstitutional changes to the functioning of the Supreme Court and National Council of the Judiciary. The changes introduced by the governing majority have raised concerns among Poland's citizens, who took to the streets of Warsaw and other cities to protest against the changes.[3] Moreover, the EU – committed to maintaining the rule of law – remains alarmed about the situation in the Polish judiciary. This is evident in the triggering of the 'Article 7(1) TEU procedure' against Poland, as well as in the pending proceedings before the CJEU that are discussed in section III below.

What has become clear over time is that despite all of its advantages, the 1997 Constitution is not able to defend itself. The experience of the rule of law crisis demands a rethinking of the judicial independence guarantees in place for the judicial power, that Chapter 5 at face value assessed as sufficient. There are two directions for such reforms. The first includes strengthening existing institutions, for instance, amending constitutional accountability to make it better enforceable in practice,

[1] Article 10 of the Constitution. See further ch 2.

[2] See, eg, G Kuca, *Zasada podziału władzy w Konstytucji RP z 1997 roku* (Warsaw, Wydawnictwo Sejmowe, 2014) 31–46.

[3] 'Poland Purges Supreme Court, and Protesters Take to Streets' *New York Times* (3 July 2018).

the election of judges to the Constitutional Court by a two-thirds parliamentary majority, or extending the competences of the Ombudsman. The second direction concerns rethinking political culture in Poland.

In the context of defending the Constitution, of particular interest remains the possibility of decentralised constitutional review.[4] Within such a review, the courts would apply both the Constitution and the statutes when deciding a case and would confirm the compliance of a provision of a statute with the Constitution, currently an exclusive competence of the Constitutional Court. The effects of such a judgment would be limited to the case in question, as there is no principle of stare decisis in Polish law. Due to the marginalisation of the Constitutional Court, the role of the decentralised constitutional review exercised by ordinary courts should increase.

The second issue for the Constitution concerns socio-economic rights. The regulation of such rights is quite typical for European post-Communist states which underwent a transformation from authoritarian to democratic systems and faced new social challenges such as unemployment or homelessness.[5] In Poland, during the drafting of the Constitution, some politicians and legal scholars put forward the case that socio-economic rights should not be widely regulated in the Constitution, as society would attempt to claim those rights before courts.[6] In the end, the constitution-makers provided a rather broad regulation of socio-economic rights, yet in many cases subjected claiming these rights to limitations specified in a statute.[7] The Constitution contains so-called programme provisions, for instance, the right to the protection of one's own health or the right to social security.[8] These provisions oblige the state to undertake steps to implement socio-economic rights. Yet the Constitution does not compel the state to provide a specific outcome such as a pension, disability benefit or a place in a public school or public hospital.[9] In turn, the Constitutional Court's case law underlines the important role of the legislature that issues laws that implement such socio-economic rights. In practice, the implementation of the

[4] L Garlicki, 'Niekonstytucyjność: formy, skutki, procedury' (2016) *Państwo i Prawo* 3.

[5] See W Sadurski, *Rights before Courts* (Dordrecht, Springer, 2005) 171 ff.

[6] Chamber of Deputies, 'Wypowiedzi na posiedzeniach Sejmu – archiwum, Zgromadzenie Narodowe w Dniu 23.09.1994', available at: www.sejm.gov.pl/Sejm7.nsf/wypowiedz.xsp?posiedzenie=zn0&dzien=3&wyp=056&kad=2.

[7] See art 81 of the Constitution.

[8] ibid arts 68(1) and 67(1).

[9] See, eg, ibid arts 67, 68 and 72.

programme provisions has been difficult for the governments in power. However, since 2015, an important turn has taken place towards their realisation, especially in the fight against poverty and social exclusion through programmes such as the so-called '500+ child benefit' of 500 PLN (around €116), a one-off financial support for school expenses at the beginning of the school year, and other forms of support for retired persons. It remains to be seen whether in the long run the implementation of such programmes will not unduly strain the public finances.

The third issue concerns the unclear definition of the executive power, and especially the position of a popularly elected President. Without a doubt, the competences of the President do not reflect the strong democratic legitimacy of the office. In fact, given that the President's nomination stems from universal and direct elections, the office might be vested with increased powers and competences, and perhaps recognised as the head of the executive. The public perceives the popular elections of the President as positive, something that is reflected in the high turnout in comparison to all other types of election in Poland.[10] It is thus hard to imagine that the nation would be deprived that possibility in favour of indirect election of the President by the parliament. It has been argued that despite certain political dangers entailed by separate, universal parliamentary and presidential elections, such a design has become a permanent characteristic of Polish constitutionalism.[11] In sum, further debate on the shape of the presidency is required to resolve these issues.

A further problem concerns parliament and, in particular, the bicameral structure which typifies the Polish system. Both chambers tend to have very similar political configurations, which may be a consequence of the electoral system. A characteristic feature of the Polish bicameralism is that the Chamber of Deputies remains the 'higher' chamber and the Senate the 'lower' chamber.[12] Lack of any reform of the Senate is linked to two factors: the attachment to the Senate as a symbol of independence and the absence of any clear vision for its transformation. The simplest and least controversial direction of reform towards strengthening Polish bicameralism is the differentiation of the terms of the chambers – which currently always run in parallel – so that they do not start and end at the same time. Still, such a change would demand a (narrow) constitutional amendment.

[10] Compare at http://pkw.gov.pl/313_Wybory_Prezydenta_Rzeczypospolitej_Polskiej.
[11] See ch 4.
[12] See ch 3.

A characteristic element of the 1997 Constitution is the set of values adopted by its drafters. These values reflect that it was created at the intersection of two eras: that of the Communist regime and that of the democratic state. As a consequence, the Constitution's framers sought to reconcile values that often seemed contradictory. The main point at which these values are expressed is the preamble of the Constitution: 'we, the Polish Nation – all citizens of the Republic, both those who believe in God as the source of truth, justice, good and beauty, as well as those not sharing such faith but respecting those universal values as arising from other sources'. At the moment of adoption of the Constitution, this preamble raised controversies; however, nowadays, the definition of the law-making authority no longer seems to be in question. It appropriately reflects the pluralistic character of Polish society. A similar approach of merging values is evident in the reference to culture in the Constitution's preamble – 'culture rooted in the Christian heritage of the Nation and in universal human values'. Twenty years after the Constitution of 1997 was adopted, the tensions surrounding these issues have faded into the background. After the fall of Communism, *Invocatio Dei* was frequently postulated; nowadays, this is no longer the case. Despite all the problems regarding the expression of competing values in the Constitution, it also articulates fundamental values such as human dignity, freedom of the person and equality, values that are generally accepted as the foundations of liberal democratic order. This rich set of values plays an important role in the interpretation of the Constitution by the Constitutional Court. In its case law, the Court strongly defends constitutional values. For instance, it has attached a central role to human dignity and has interpreted constitutional freedoms and rights in its light.

The anchoring of the Constitution in these values has enabled it to function without major amendments for over 20 years. The fundamental values discussed above are particularly precious and, in general, until 2015 were not questioned by any of the major political forces. However, since then, some of these values – in particular the rule of law – have been weakened following the attack of the governing majority on the independence of the judiciary. In turn, the undermining of the rule of law also threatens individual freedoms and rights, expressed for example in the right to a fair trial or avoiding excessively long court proceedings.[13]

Experience since 1997 has shown that the Constitution can, to a large extent, evolve through the Constitutional Court's jurisprudence. For instance, the Constitution, in contrast to the French or German

[13] See ch 8.

Constitutions, does not contain provisions on Poland's membership of the EU.[14] Nonetheless, thanks to the constitutional interpretation, it was possible for the Constitutional Court to reconcile Poland's membership of the EU with the principle of state sovereignty.[15] However, as noted repeatedly, since 2015, the crucial role of the Constitutional Court in interpreting the Constitution has been attacked and labelled as judicial activism by politicians and even some legal scholars.[16]

In sum, several issues – as highlighted in this book – have arisen during the application of the Constitution. Today, the ongoing constitutional crisis surrounding the judiciary clearly remains the most crucial problem when it comes to the functioning of the Constitution. Questions – such as the double-headed executive, weak bicameralism, the manner in which social rights are expressed by the Constitution or the lack of coherence in the system of values – are important, yet against the backdrop of a major constitutional crisis, they are rendered secondary.

III. THE EU'S RESPONSE TO THE JUDICIAL CRISIS

A new thread in Polish constitutionalism concerns the reaction of the EU to the judicial crisis. This reaction highlights how deeply EU law has taken root in Polish constitutional law.

The EU has closely followed the ongoing changes occurring in Poland. In 2016, the EU Commission started a dialogue with Poland under the 'Rule of Law Framework', attempting to counter the controversial reforms at an early stage.[17] The first two recommendations of the Commission focused on the national processes damaging the independence

[14] See arts 88-1 to 88-7 of Constitution de la République française du 4 octobre 1958 and art 23 of Grundgesetz für die Bundesrepublik Deutschland vom 23. Mai 1949 (BGBl. S. 1), zuletzt geändert durch Artikel 1 des Gesetzes vom 13. Juli 2017 (BGBl. I S. 2347). The most serious attempt to introduce an 'European Chapter' to the Constitution failed for political reasons. See Chamber of Deputies, Print No 4450, 11 August 2011. See also A Kustra, '"Euronowelizacja" w projektach ustaw o zmianie Konstytucji RP. Próba oceny' (2011) 104 *Przegląd Sejmowy* 31.

[15] Constitutional Court, judgment of 11 May 2005, K 18/04, OTK ZU 5A/2005, poz 49; and judgment of 24 November 2010, K 32/09, OTK ZU 9A/2010, poz 108. See ch 2.

[16] See, eg, L Morawski, 'The Polish Constitutional Crisis and Institutional Self-Defence' (Symposium contribution, 09 May 2017, Trinity College, University of Oxford), available at: http://trybunal.gov.pl/fileadmin/content/uroczystosci_spotkania_wizyty/2017/2017_05_09_Oxford/Wystapienie_prof._L.Morawskiego_w_Oxfordzie.pdf. See further chs 6 and 8.

[17] European Commission, Communication from the Commission to the European Parliament and the Council, A New Framework to Strengthen the Rule of Law, COM(2014) 158.

and legitimacy of the Constitutional Court.[18] The Commission called for the three judges who were lawfully nominated in October 2015 by the legislature of the 7th term to take up their functions in the Constitutional Court and recommended that the Polish authorities publish the judgments of the Constitutional Court.[19] However, the systemic threat to the rule of law further deteriorated with new laws relating to the National Council of the Judiciary, ordinary courts and the Supreme Court, raising concerns about the principle of judicial independence and the separation of powers.[20] In the Commission's assessment, the situation merited the initiation, for the first time ever, of the 'Article 7(1) TEU procedure'.[21] Under this procedure, the Council, acting with a four-fifths majority of its members and the consent of the European Parliament, may establish the presence of a 'clear risk of a serious breach' of EU values. This preventive arm of Article 7 TEU aims at averting a possible breach through dialogue between the Member State and EU institutions, and does not lead to sanctions.[22] Any sanctions against Poland demand a separate Council vote.[23] However, the sanctioning mechanism becomes available only in cases of 'serious and persistent breach' of EU values, confirmed unanimously by the European Council with the consent of the European Parliament.[24]

There has been little development under the 'Article 7(1) TEU procedure'.[25] During the General Affairs Council meetings, Poland stood by its position.[26] However, in contrast to the political process, the EU legal actions seemed to bring about more tangible effects. Specifically, the Commission launched three treaty infringement procedures against

[18] See ch 6.

[19] ibid.

[20] European Commission, Commission Recommendations of 26 July 2017 and of 20 December 2017 regarding the rule of law in Poland.

[21] European Commission, Proposal for a Council decision on the determination of a clear risk of a serious breach by the Republic of Poland of the rule of law, 20 December 2017, COM(2017) 835. See D Kochenov, L Pech and K Lane Scheppele, 'The European Commission's Activation of Article 7: Better Late than Never?' *Verfassungsblog* (23 December 2017), https://verfassungsblog.de/the-european-commissions-activation-of-article-7-better-late-than-never.

[22] D Kochenov, 'Busting the Myths Nuclear: A Commentary on Article 7 TEU', EUI Working Paper 2017/10, 7–8.

[23] Article 7(3) TEU.

[24] ibid art 7(2).

[25] See L Pech and P Wachowiec, '1095 Days Later: From Bad to Worse Regarding the Rule of Law in Poland (Part I)' *Verfassungsblog* (13 January 2019), https://verfassungsblog.de/1095-days-later-from-bad-to-worse-regarding-the-rule-of-law-in-poland-part-i.

[26] See, eg, European Commission, 'Rule of Law: European Commission Refers Poland to the European Court of Justice to Protect the Independence of the Polish Supreme Court', press release, 24 September 2018.

Poland.[27] First, in December 2017, the Commission referred the Law on the Ordinary Courts' Organisation to the CJEU.[28] The Commission argued that the different retirement age for male and female judges infringed the EU principle of gender equality in employment, while the discretion of the Justice Minister to prolong the mandate of judges who reached the retirement age endangered judicial independence.[29] In the following months, Poland amended the relevant law, introducing a retirement age of 65 years for both genders.[30] This represents a positive development. However, it is likely to have little impact on the outcome of the case, as it is the settled case law of the Luxembourg Court to consider the actions of the Member State only before the case reaches its docket.[31] In his opinion of 20 June 2019, the Advocate General Tanchev argued that the 2017 Law does not comply with the guarantee of irremovability of judges and their independence protected by Article 19(1) TEU second subparagraph, which manifests the respect for the rule of law in the EU. Among other concerns, the Advocate General Tanchev indicated that the safeguards offered in the Polish law are insufficient to counteract the de facto removal of judges, especially when it occurs as part of a comprehensive reform of the judiciary. Thus, the opinion concluded that Poland was in breach of its obligations under the Treaty.

The second referral under the treaty infringement procedure, in September 2018, concerned the 2017 Law on the Supreme Court, which lowered the retirement age of Supreme Court judges.[32] In the view of the Commission, the new rules undermined the principle of judicial independence, which includes the irremovability of judges. At the request of the Commission, the Luxembourg Court, in a revolutionary move, ordered interim measures suspending, with retroactive effect, the application of the provisions lowering the retirement age of the Supreme Court judges.[33] Poland was to immediately ensure that the judges concerned

[27] Article 258 TFEU.

[28] CJEU, Case C-192/18, *Commission v Poland*, pending; Opinion of Advocate General Tanchev, EU:C:2019:529, para 103–115.

[29] European Commission, 'Rule of Law: European Commission Acts to Defend Judicial Independence in Poland', press release, 20 December 2017.

[30] See ch 5.

[31] CJEU, Case C-286/12, *Commission v Hungary*, EU:C:2012:687, para 41.

[32] Press release of 24 September 2018 (n 26), CJEU, Case C-619/18, *Commission v Poland (Independence of the Supreme Court)*, EU:C:2019:531.

[33] CJEU, Order of 19 October 2018 of the Vice-President of the Court in Case C-619/18 R, EU:C:2018:852, confirmed by the Order of 16 November 2018 of the President of the Court in Case C-619/18 R, EU:C:2018:910. See D Sarmiento, 'Interim Revolutions: The CJEU Gives its First Interim Measures Ruling on the Rule of Law in Poland' *EU Law Analysis Blog* (22 October 2018), http://eulawanalysis.blogspot.com/2018/10/interim-revolutions-cjeu-gives-its.html.

continued to perform their duties and enjoyed the same rights and status as was the case before the controversial law entered into force. No new measures concerning the replacement of the 'old' Supreme Court judges or concerning the appointment of a new First President of the Supreme Court were to be taken. As a consequence, the First President of the Supreme Court called on 22 of the affected judges to return to their duties, and indeed they all reported back to the court.[34]

A point of discussion remained whether the order of the CJEU is self-enforcing (as argued by the Supreme Court) or whether it demands amending national law to give it full effectiveness (as claimed by the governing majority).[35] In the end, the amendment of 21 November 2018 was adopted, reinstating the affected judges in their offices, and their terms are perceived to have been uninterrupted. The amendment sets the retirement age at 65 years (without the possibility to prolong the term) for all judges of the Supreme Court appointed after 1 January 2019. In the light of the introduced changes, the Law and Justice government expected the Commission to withdraw its action. By ordering the interim measures and the expedited procedure, the CJEU effected a timely reaction to the problematic changes in the Supreme Court.

On 24 June 2019 the CJEU decided that Poland's new retirement age regime in the Supreme Court and the President's discretion to extend the term of Supreme Court judges beyond their retirement age infringed the second subparagraph of Article 19(1) TEU, which obligates Member States to ensure effective judicial protection of individuals in the fields covered by EU law. The CJEU found the Polish reforms inconsistent with the principles of irremovability of judges and of judicial independence, both of which are protected under EU law. First, the CJEU indicated that although the organisation of justice in the Member States falls within the national competence as argued by Poland, yet when exercising that competence, the Member States must comply with their obligations deriving from EU law. One such obligation is to provide remedies sufficient to ensure effective legal protection in the fields covered by EU law. Second, courts – such as the Supreme Court which may decide questions of application or interpretation of EU law – need to meet the requirements of effective judicial protection, which in its essence demands that such courts

[34] Supreme Court, First President's summon of Supreme Court judges of 22 October 2018; First President's information to the European Commission of 6 November 2018, both available at: www.sn.pl/aktualnosci/SitePages/Wydarzenia.aspx.

[35] 'Warchoł: Wykonanie postanowienia TSUE o SN wymaga stworzenia podstawy prawnej' *Dziennik Gazeta Prawna* (24 October 2018); 'Sędzia Rączka: Postanowienie TSUE jest "samorealizujące" się,' *Dziennik Gazeta Prawna* (31 October 2018).

maintain their independence. Third, the irremovability of judges – central to their independence – requires that they remain in their post until they reach retirement age or the end of their (fixed term) mandate. The CJEU expressed doubts about the real aims of the Polish reform, and found that the measures in question undermined the principle of the irremovability of judges and judicial independence.

The third treaty infringement procedure – concerning the new disciplinary regime for judges – was launched in April 2019.[36] The EU Commission argued that Poland undermined the independence of judges by not shielding them from political control, because they are now subject to disciplinary investigations, procedures and sanctions on the basis of the content of their judgments. Also at stake is the independence and impartiality of the Disciplinary Chamber of the Supreme Court that reviews disciplinary decisions.[37] Depending on the response of the Polish government to the EU Commission's reasoned opinion expressing its legal concerns, the case may be brought before the CJEU.[38]

Tools such as the Article 7 TEU procedure and the infringement proceedings launched by the Commission face significant challenges, procedural hurdles and evasion techniques.[39] For this reason, the involvement of the national courts, including the courts of other Member States, offers another avenue, complementary to the actions of EU institutions, through which the rule of law in the Member States might be safeguarded.[40] Specifically, preliminary references from Polish courts offered the CJEU another opportunity, in addition to the treaty infringement proceedings, to step in. Indeed, the Luxembourg Court does appear to be interested in intervening in this area, recently concluding that EU primary law includes an obligation on the Member States to uphold judicial independence.[41] Taking into account the serious concerns of the Supreme Court, especially relating to judicial independence and judicial cooperation in the EU, the CJEU is also keen to decide the cases within a short

[36] European Commission, 'Rule of Law: European Commission Launches Infringement Procedure to Protect Judges from Political Control', press release, 3 April 2019.

[37] See ch 2.

[38] European Commission, 'Rule of Law: European Commission Takes New Step to Protect Judges in Poland against Political Control', press release, 17 July 2019.

[39] M Schmidt and P Bogdanowicz, 'The Infringement Procedure in the EU Rule of Law Crisis: How to Make Effective Use of Article 258 TFEU?' (2018) 55 *Common Market Law Review* 1061.

[40] On the preliminary references concerning the judicial crisis, see ch 5; for the crucial reference from the Irish High Court with regard to rule of law violations in Poland, see ch 8.

[41] M Bonelli and M Claes, 'Judicial Serendipity: How Portuguese Judges Came to the Rescue of the Polish Judiciary' (2018) 14 *European Constitutional Law Review* 622, 634.

timeframe pursuant to the expedited procedure, significantly shortening the judicial process.[42] In general, it allows for the expedited procedure and the interim measures discussed earlier in the treaty infringement proceedings in a very low number cases per year.[43] This highlights the willingness of the CJEU to afford legal certainty in a particularly important matter and to avoid irreversible changes.

Figure 9.1 The ongoing EU proceedings vis-a-vis Poland

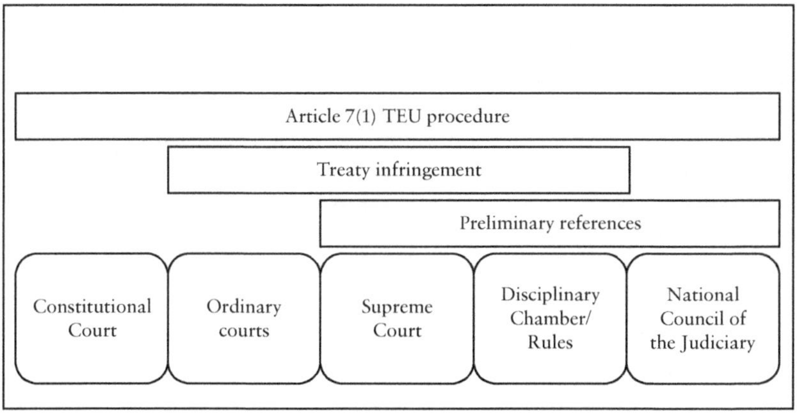

Figure 9.1 summarises the procedures currently launched by the EU against Poland. Clearly, the 'Article 7 procedure' is the broadest in scope, encompassing the changes with regard to the Constitutional Court, the ordinary courts and the Supreme Court, including its new disciplinary chamber, changes to the disciplinary regime vis-a-vis judges, and issues relating to the National Council of the Judiciary. In turn, the three treaty infringement procedures are narrower in scope as they focus on the new retirement regime in the ordinary courts, the Supreme Court and the disciplinary regime for judges. Finally, 12 preliminary references from Polish courts – discussed in Chapter 5 – concerning the Law on the Supreme Court (retirement age, disciplinary chamber), the amendments

[42] See CJEU, Orders of the President of the Court of 26 September 2018, EU:C:2018:786 (concerning Case C-522/18); of 26 November 2018, EU:C:2018:977 (concerning Cases C-585/18, C-624/18 and C-625/18); and of 11 December 2018 EU:C:2018:1003 (concerning Case C-668/18). The CJEU did not grant the request on the expedited procedure in Cases C-558/18 and C-563/18; see Order of the President of the Court of 1 October 2018, EU:C:2018:923.

[43] CJEU, Annual Report 2017, 117–18.

to disciplinary rules and the validity of the composition of the Council complete the picture. So far, addressing some of the Supreme Court's references, the Advocate General Tanchev stated that the Disciplinary Chamber, composed exclusively of judges selected by the National Council of the Judiciary – due to its membership and operation itself dependent on the legislative and executive branches – does not satisfy the EU requirements of judicial independence.[44] In July 2019, at the time of writing, the relevant judgments of the CJEU, with the exception of the second treaty infringement case, are still pending. The judgment of the CJEU concerning the retirement regime in the Supreme Court and the opinions of the Advocate General in the separate cases affecting other parts of the judiciary in Poland – that will probably be followed by the CJEU – highlight that the foundations of the Law and Justice government reforms pose problems as to their compliance with EU law and violate the rule of law principle. Regrettably, the changes concerning the Constitutional Court has thus far not been brought before the CJEU.

The question remains whether the EU will move beyond 'naming and shaming' Poland and towards using the 'Article 7 TEU procedure' for the first time to impose sanctions on a Member State. Conditional upon establishing that the situation in Poland has developed into a serious and persistent breach of the rule of law, further proceedings at the EU level could see Poland facing sanctions, such as the suspension of voting rights in the Council or, possibly, cutting access to EU funds.[45] Moreover, the EU has proposed new legislation protecting the EU budget in cases of rule of law deficiencies, such as endangering the independence of judiciary, in the Member States.[46] The envisaged sanctions include suspension of payments and of commitments, a reduction of funding under existing commitments, and a prohibition to conclude new commitments with the offending Member State.

Finally, it is also worth highlighting that the Venice Commission was alarmed about the ongoing changes in Polish judiciary. The Commission underlined that the paralysis of the Constitutional Court would challenge the three basic principles of the Council of Europe: democracy, human

[44] CJEU, Joined Cases C-585/18, C-624/18 and C-625/18, Opinion of Advocate General Tanchev, EU:C:2019:551.

[45] See G Halmai, 'The Possibility and Desirability of Economic Sanction: Rule of Law Conditionality Requirements against Illiberal EU Member States', EUI Working Paper 2018/06, 18.

[46] European Commission, Proposal for a Regulation of the European Parliament and of the Council on the protection of the Union's budget in case of generalised deficiencies as regards the rule of law in the Member States, COM(2018) 324.

rights and the rule of law.[47] It also found many of the judicial reforms to be ill-advised and concerning, to the extent that they enable the legislative and executive powers to 'interfere in a severe and extensive manner in the administration of justice, and thereby pose a grave threat to the judicial independence as a key element of the rule of law'.[48] Crucially, the Venice Commission indicated that the possibility to reopen final proceedings with an extraordinary complaint bore similarities to the former Soviet legal system, while the possibility to apply the extraordinary review for future judgments was labelled as 'even *worse* than its Soviet predecessor'. The Venice Commission's recommendations indicated, inter alia, that the representatives of the judiciary in the National Council of the Judiciary should remain elected by their peers and that lay members should not participate in proceedings before the Supreme Court.[49]

IV. CONSTITUTIONAL AMENDMENT PROPOSALS UNDER DISCUSSION

The Constitution of 1997 belongs to a group of rigid constitutions, meaning that it is not easy to amend. Naturally, the terms 'rigid' and 'flexible' denoting a constitution are relative.[50] Since its enactment in 1997, the Constitution has been amended only twice, and these changes are of limited significance.[51]

Despite its drawbacks, an immediate replacement or major amendment of the Constitution of 1997 seems neither necessary nor possible. The failure of the President's initiative to hold a referendum seems to confirm this. In 2017, the President surprised the political establishment, including his own governing majority, and also the electorate, by announcing plans for a national referendum.[52] It was supposed to take place on 10 and 11 November 2018, the 100-year anniversary of Poland's independence. This referendum was to have a consultative character. This meant that it would not have any legal effect, but the

[47] Venice Commission, Opinion No 833/2015 on Amendments to the Act of 25 June 2015 on the Constitutional Tribunal of Poland, 11 March 2016, para 138.

[48] Venice Commission, Opinion No 904/2017.

[49] ibid.

[50] See A Harding and P Leyland, 'Comparative Law in Constitutional Contexts' in E Örücü and D Nelken (eds), *Comparative Law: A Handbook* (Oxford, Hart Publishing, 2007) 321.

[51] L Garlicki, *Polskie Prawo Konstytucyjne. Zarys Wykładu* (Warsaw, Wolters Kluwer, 2017) 47. See ch 2.

[52] Article 125(2) of the Constitution.

outcome of the referendum could have been taken into consideration by the parliament if it decided to amend the Constitution. In July 2018, the President put forward 10 questions for the referendum.[53] They ranged from more general issues, such as whether the Constitution should be amended at all, to specific questions on the introduction of a reference to Poland's Christian heritage in the preamble of the Constitution. One of the questions concerned the choices between different models of government: a presidential system, a cabinet system or maintaining the current system of the executive. The nation was also to decide whether Poland's membership of the EU and NATO should be regulated in the Constitution. However, the Senate – the role of which has paradoxically been assessed in this book as generally limited – blocked the referendum, which as a consequence never took place.[54] It thus seems that the Senate's decision strengthens the position of the 1997 Constitution as an instrument that thus far has not undergone any major amendments.

As of July 2019, there have been no formal proposals for a constitutional amendment under the procedure of Article 235 of the Constitution.[55] Nonetheless, politicians, as is often the case, have entered into discussions concerning certain propositions; however, these do not seem realistic. For instance, a deputy Prime Minister proposed that in parliamentary elections, parents should be granted additional votes based on the number of children in their family.[56]

There is strong public support for the Constitution in its present form. In part, this is confirmed by social research that shows that only 30 per cent of respondents think that the Constitution should be changed.[57] Possible changes must maintain the most important aspects of identity of the 1997 Constitution, for instance, that the Constitution resulted from a political compromise. The Constitution expresses values that are especially valuable for the majority of the Polish people. Values such as sovereignty of the state and, simultaneously, membership of the EU, care for human dignity or socio-economic rights remain valid. Without assessing whether a constitutional amendment in this regard

[53] See www.prezydent.pl/gfx/prezydent/userfiles3/files/2018_referendum/projekt_postanowienia.pdf.

[54] Senate, vote of 25 July 2018 on granting consent to ordering a national referendum by the President, available at: https://www.senat.gov.pl/prace/senat/posiedzenia/glosowanie-drukuj,7758.html.

[55] ibid.

[56] 'Gowin: Niech rodzice głosują za dzieci' *Rzeczpospolita* (15 April 2018).

[57] CBOS, Komunikat z Badań Nr 37/2017, 6. See https://www.cbos.pl/SPISKOM.POL/2017/K_037.

is currently feasible, it is difficult to imagine that such values would be removed from the Constitution. They constitute part of the identity of the current Constitution.

An interesting discussion that has taken place in Poland for many years concerns the introduction of single-member constituencies for elections to the Chamber of Deputies. Although no new proposal has been put forward, the politicians constantly highlight this question. In 2015, single-member constituencies as an election slogan was so popular that it enabled its main supporter, the Kukiz'15 party, to enter the Chamber of Deputies for the first time. In addition, such an electoral reform has been supported by some of the Presidents. Nonetheless, the introduction of single-member constituencies was the subject of an unsuccessful referendum of 2015 ordered by President Bronisław Komorowski. The turnout in that referendum was 7.8 per cent (2.4 million voters), clearly below the constitutionally required levels (a referendum is only binding if more than half of the number of those having the right to vote have participated in it, which was around 30.6 million in the 2015 referendum and 30.1 million as of 2018).[58]

Many proposals put forward during the 6th and 7th term of the Chamber of Deputies were part of the ongoing political conflict and debate, and failed as the basis for valid constitutional amendment. One such example was a proposal of the agrarian Polish People's Party to make state forests available to the people.[59] Fortunately, these types of proposals – which were rather half-baked or random – were not successful. Attempts at hasty changes indicate that a stable Constitution performs a valuable function.

V. THE ROLE OF CONSTITUTIONAL IDENTITY IN THE BATTLE FOR THE CONSTITUTION

Any possible constitutional amendments must be assessed from the perspective of maintaining the identity of the Constitution.[60] In Poland,

[58] Article 125(3) of the Constitution. See http://referendum2015.pkw.gov.pl/pliki/1441638022_Protokol%20o%20wyniku%20refeerendum.pdf. For 2018, see https://wybory2018.pkw.gov.pl.

[59] Chamber of Deputies of 7th term, Print No 2374, available at: http://orka.sejm.gov.pl/Druki7ka.nsf/0/E91A5986578B068BC1257CD60038BC36/%24File/2374.pdf.

[60] G Jacobsohn, 'Constitutional Identity' (2006) 68 *Review of Politics* 316; Y Roznai, *Unconstitutional Constitutional Amendments: The Limits of Amendment Powers* (Oxford, Oxford University Press, 2017).

this concept has been shaped by the Constitutional Court in its case law.[61] Constitutional identity served the Constitutional Court for the purposes of delimiting an impassable boundary in conferring the competences of Polish state bodies to the EU. According to the Constitutional Court, if that boundary were surpassed, Poland would lose its sovereignty. The idea of constitutional identity adopted by the Constitutional Court is arguably similar to the approach taken by the constitutional courts of France and Germany.[62]

In some respects, the Polish Constitution needs to remain constant, for instance with regard to human dignity, freedom of the person and in securing the independence of courts and judges. In other matters, the Constitution needs more flexibility, for instance, regarding the bicameral structure of parliament or the division of competences between the President and the government. Such an approach would allow amendments to the Constitution, as long as these do not pose a threat to the constitutional identity of the nation. The recognition of a concept of constitutional identity would require that an amendment would result from extensive consultation and debate, while also seeking to develop the main principles of the Constitution.

In the ongoing discussion surrounding the Constitution of 1997, it is alarming that the proposed changes are perceived merely as a formal procedure demanding the support of a few relevant majorities. In that sense, amending the Constitution becomes a question of procedure and political dexterity, meaning that politicians can adopt any type of amendment. From the perspective of the involved politicians, the question of constitutional identity disappears or becomes at least exotic. For instance, it can mean adding an *Invocatio Dei* to the preamble, or erasing the entire preamble. Under such circumstances, the question of constitutional identity is set aside.

Constitutional identity presents an extremely important concept, acting as a barrier that protects the Constitution from careless changes. For this reason, in the light of the constitutional crisis in Poland, the role of the constitutional identity is particularly important. A constitution that does not maintain its constitutional identity cannot fulfil the function of a basic law.

[61] Constitutional Court, K 18/04 and K 32/09.

[62] K Wójtowicz, *Sądy Konstytucyjne wobec prawa Unii Europejskiej* (Warsaw, Wydawnictwo Trybunał Konstytucyjny, 2012) 68, 81–84.

VI. CONCLUSION

The changes taking place in recent years highlight the preciousness of the Constitution as a legal act. Since 2015, interest in the Constitution has been growing, and it has become a topic of conversation for many Polish citizens from all classes and backgrounds. The Constitution, the judiciary and fundamental rights feature prominently on the internet, in newspapers and on television programmes, even though until very recently, these issues were discussed mostly by scholars. Polish citizens seem to be taking a fast-track course in constitutional law, something that has not been experienced since the beginning of the 1990s. The resonance of constitutional affairs in Polish society presents a source of optimism that the Constitution will regain its position as the supreme law of the state.

FURTHER READING

Closa, C and Kochenov, D (eds), *Reinforcing Rule of Law Oversight in the European Union* (Cambridge, Cambridge University Press, 2016).

Garlicki, L, 'Konstytucyjność zmiany konstytucji' in D Dudek (ed), *Zmieniać Konstytucję Rzeczypospolitej czy nie zmieniać?* (Lublin, Wydawnictwo KUL, 2017) 19–42.

Granat, M, 'Rozumienie zmiany Konstytucji RP a tożsamość konstytucyjna' in R Chruściak (ed), *Problemy zmiany konstytucji* (Warsaw, Wydawnictwo Sejmowe, 2017) 255–82.

Jakab, A and Kochenov, D (eds), *The Enforcement of EU Law and Values: Ensuring Member States' Compliance* (Oxford, Oxford University Press, 2017).

Ludwikowski, RR, *Prawo konstytucyjne porównawcze* (Toruń, TNOiK, 2000).

Śledzińska-Simon, A, 'Constitutional Identity in 3D: A Model of Individual, Relational, and Collective Self and its Application in Poland' (2015) 13 *International Journal of Constitutional Law* 124–55.

Wójtowicz, K, *Sądy Konstytucyjne wobec prawa Unii Europejskiej* (Warsaw, Wydawnictwo Trybunał Konstytucyjny, 2012).

Index